SOCIAL PURPOSE IN ARCHITECTURE

D1826952

978 0289700501

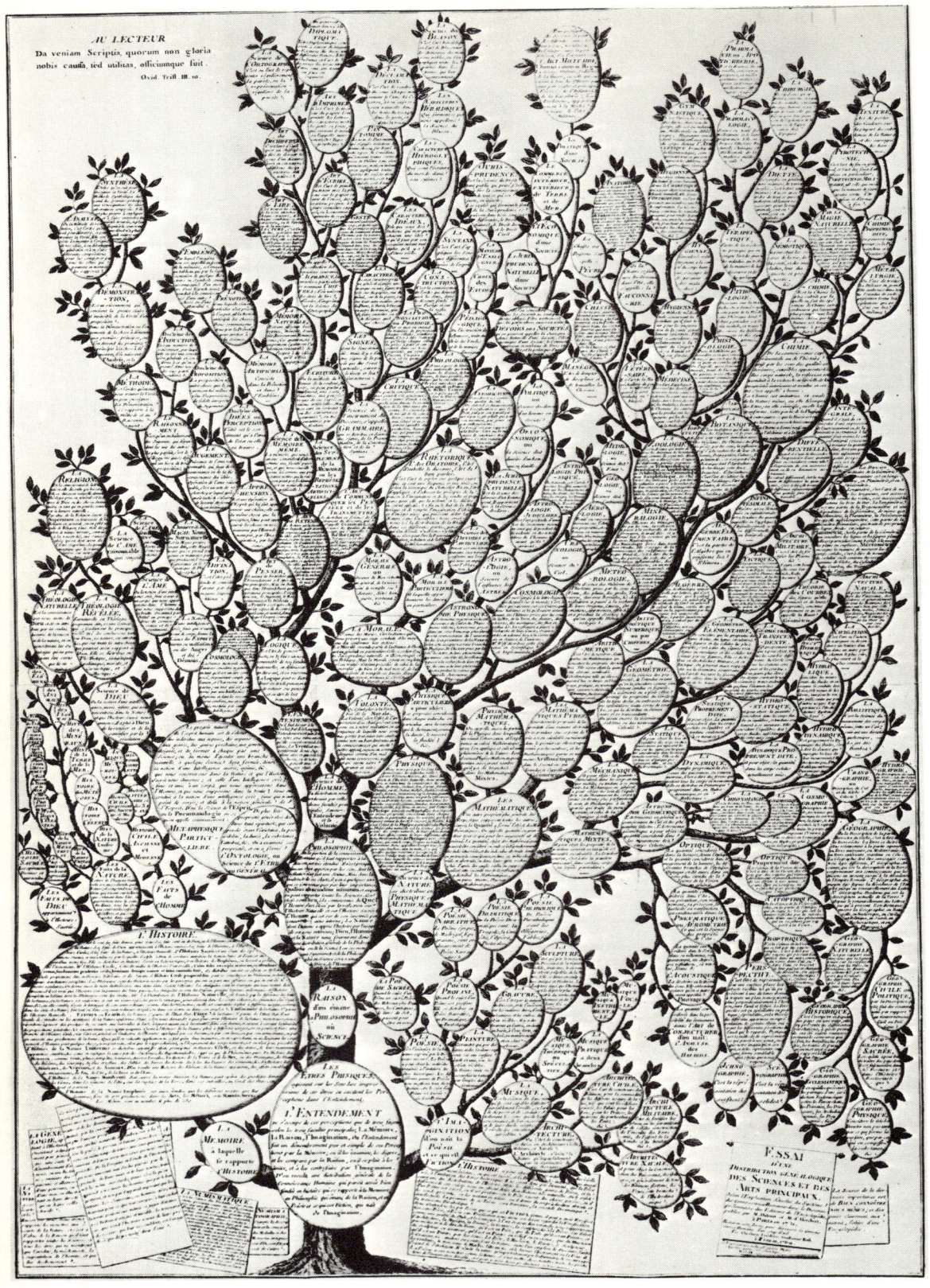

Tree of Knowledge; from the Encyclopédie.

SOCIAL PURPOSE IN ARCHITECTURE

Paris and London Compared, 1760 – 1800

HELEN ROSENAU

Studio Vista

Q720·94

BA 41283

Produced by November Books Limited,
23–9 Emerald Street, London, WC1N 3QL

Published by Studio Vista Limited, Blue Star
House, Highgate Hill, London, N19

Text set by Yendall & Company Limited,
Riscatype House, 22–5 Red Lion Court, Fleet
Street, London, EC4

Printed and bound by C. Tinling & Company
Limited, Prescot and London

© November Books Limited 1970

SBN 289.70050.7

Contents

Preface & Acknowledgements

'Architecture goes beyond utilitarian needs.'

LE CORBUSIER: *Towards a New Architecture*

The period of the late 18th century in Europe is worth study not only for its own sake, but also as a turning point in human history. It possesses a special fascination at the moment, for many of its problems are still topical. A comparison of Paris and London, the two capitals of the civilized world at that time, illuminates their architectural evolution, and shows their mutual influence.

Naturally, such a survey cannot pretend to be comprehensive, but an attempt is made to single out the most important trends in the development of architectural types serving a social purpose. Once these types are established it should be possible to study their adaptations and variations. Anglomania and Anglophobia, as well as Francophilia and Francophobia, characterized the late 18th century. These attitudes remain with us today, and may make objective assessments difficult. It is usually considered that the English approach is pragmatic, whereas the French are more inclined to rely on the light of reason. But these assumptions, partially true though they may be, underestimate the practical elements in French thought and the idealism found in England.

An enquiry into the history of the two capitals will lead to a discussion of their past rather than their present appearance. The socially significant buildings are, because of their emphasis on function, particularly liable to obsolescence and replacement, and many have been destroyed. Others, although planned, were not executed. In contrast, buildings which serve a religious or ceremonial purpose may gain in appreciation because of their age, and they have often survived.

The task presented by the study of architecture in its social context is not an easy one and the difficulty is aggravated by the multiplicity of aims which buildings such as hospitals, prisons and schools had then to fulfil. Furthermore the material available in Paris and London is formidable, and selection is thus a necessity. It is hoped that this will seem neither too arbitrary nor too subjective.

Change was precipitated in France by the advent of Napoleon and in England by the upsurge of Romanticism and the Gothic Revival, tendencies which challenged the Industrial Revolution. The Enlightenment had its precursors and lingered on, so it will not always be possible to confine this study to the years mentioned in the title. Nevertheless, the period 1760–1800 constitutes a clearly defined epoch, reaching out into the future. Interest in the subject seems to be increasing at present and the following pages are intended to contribute to its study.

It is quite impossible to name here all those who in one way and another have helped in the completion of this study. My greatest debt for facilities is to the Staffs of the British Museum, the Royal Institute of British Architects, the Sir John Soane's Museum, the Cabinet des Estampes of the Bibliothèque Nationale, the Musée Carnavalet and the Avery Library, New York. I wish especially to thank M. Adhémar, Sir Nikolaus Pevsner and Sir John Summerson for advice, Miss P. Alderidge for allowing the study of the Archives of the Bethlem Royal and Maudsley Hospitals, Miss E. D. Mercer, B.A., F.S.A., for facilitating my work at the Archives of the Greater London Council, and the Authorities of the Royal Naval Hospital, Plymouth, for valuable information. The History of Art Department of the University of Manchester provided photographs and the University kindly allowed me leave of absence to study abroad. The John Rylands Library and the Central Public Library, both of Manchester, gave valuable assistance.

On a more personal level, I wish to remember my late friend, Miss V. F. Forrest, who, up to her fatal illness, was greatly concerned with my work. Dr M. A. M. B. Carmi, in spite of many commitments, maintained his interest in the study's progress. My friends, Mrs Ilse Barasch and Mrs Jane Howard, helped in reading the proofs and I wish to express my gratitude: Mr R. J. Danik gave valuable information with regard to Russia, and Miss E. Hobley helped in collating the text.

Lastly I want to thank Mr Dennis Sharp for advice on publication and Mr Ian Cameron, Mr Tom Carter, Mr John Leath and Miss Elizabeth Kingsley-Rowe for the care and attention they have given to the progress of this work.

Abbreviations

L'Architecture:	C.-N. Ledoux:	*L'architecture considérée sous le rapport de l'art, des moeurs et de la législation,* Paris 1804–46.
Boullée:	E.-L. Boullée:	*Treatise on Architecture,* London 1953, edited by H. Rosenau.
Chaux I, II, III:		See *L'Architecture* above for stages of planning for Chaux.
Colvin:	H. M. Colvin:	*A Biographical Dictionary of English Architects, 1660–1840,* London 1954.
Encyclopédie:		*Encyclopédie ou Dictionnaire Raisonné des Sciences, des Arts, et des Métiers,* Paris 1772, etc.
Hautecoeur:	L. Hautecoeur:	*Histoire de l'architecture classique en France,* Paris 1943, etc.
Hillairet:	J. Hillairet:	*Dictionnaire historique des rues de Paris,* etc., 3rd ed., Paris 1966.
Journal of the R.I.B.A.:		Journal of the Royal Institute of British Architects.
Précis:	J.-N.-L. Durand:	*Précis des leçons d'architecture,* etc., Paris 1802-5.
Prix:		'The Engravings of the Grands Prix of the French Academy of Architecture', *Architectural History* III, 1960, p. 17ff.
Recueil:	J.-N.-L. Durand:	*Recueil et parallèle des édifices de tout genre, anciens et modernes,* Paris, year IX.
Rochegude:	F. de Rochegude and M. Dumolin:	*Guide Pratique à travers le vieux Paris,* numerous editions.
Summerson:	J. Summerson:	*Georgian London,* 1st ed. 1945, 2nd ed. Pelican Books, 1962 (used here).
The Ideal City:	H. Rosenau:	*The Ideal City,* London 1959.

1
The Intellectual
Background

In the late 18th century art was regarded as a means to an end, rather than an end in itself. This doctrine, proclaimed by the *Philosophes*, was not intended to deny the importance of the arts, but rather to increase their significance. They were seen as a vital factor in a civilization which aimed at the betterment of man, and believed in progress. The period between 1760 and 1800 formed a marked contrast to the preceding Rococo period and the ensuing neo-classicism of the Napoleonic and Georgian styles. In the former, art for art's sake was fully appreciated, in the latter art was seen as an expression of personal ambition and individual taste. The late 18th century, by contrast, saw an emphasis on communal and civic ideals, especially in France, but to a lesser degree also in England. The intellectual background of the arts was part of a conscious process, and made for unity and coherence, especially in the field of architecture.

The political and economic conditions of the period have been widely studied, and there cannot be much doubt as to the significant changes in class structure, which was antiquated in France, progressive in England. The Third Estate, to which the *Philosophes* belonged, was in the vanguard of social transformation, whilst in England the Industrial Revolution altered the established relations between rich and poor, town and country.[1] In both cases a new outlook emerged, which influenced the arts and especially architecture.

France

Architecture in France underwent a profound change in the late 18th century. Although this fact is generally accepted, the reasons for it have received little attention. Purely formal considerations fail to give an adequate explanation, as the change was both speedy and ubiquitous. It may have been based on a new emphasis on rational persuasion and on secular and 'benevolent' commissions. These in turn can be connected with the rise of a social group of outstanding intelligence who, in spite of their origin, possessed no definite class commitments.[2] This group, known as the *Philosophes*, played a dominant role in contemporary thought, and it is therefore worth investigating how far it influenced architecture. In order to do this, an enquiry into the thought of the period has to be attempted.

Social conditions in France called for radical change; the prevalent economic and political problems were widely discussed and theoretical solutions canvassed, but these factors proved abortive and failed to avert the Revolution. The thought of the period culminated in the political fight for human rights, and was crystallized in the Constitution of 1791, expressing lofty ideals of aid to the poor and establishing national, as opposed to communal or private, responsibility.

François Quesnay (1694–1774), founder of the school of Physiocrats, originally a physician by profession, had become one of the fathers of Political Economy, which he regarded as the study of a comprehensive 'science' of society.[3] The Physiocrats, in their conviction of the paramount importance of, and their overriding respect for, agriculture, saw here the only truly creative type of work: they distrusted the 'sterile' occupations of the nobility and the middle classes. Nevertheless, they allowed the artist a significant position, but only if and when the necessary wealth had been created, and the demands of agriculture had been fully satisfied.

Their influence was widespread and is clearly seen in the writing of French architects such as Pierre Patte (1723–1814) in his *Monumens érigés en France à la gloire de Louis XV*, first published in Paris in 1765. Here the author gives a survey of the cultural and scientific achievements of the French nation, and includes a major chapter on agriculture and the need for experiment and rapid change in this field. When the architects Etienne-Louis Boullée (1728–99), Claude-Nicolas Ledoux (1736–1806) and their contemporaries discussed the value of simplicity and rejected sterile ornament and superfluous decoration, they thus not only used the language, but expressed the thought of the Physiocrats. This view discouraged private architectural ostentation, and could, properly understood, lead to the fostering of public programmes aimed at benefiting all classes of society. It is clearly illustrated by the pedestal

Boullée, Opera. Cabinet des Estampes, Bibliothèque Nationale, Paris. The interior contains arches reminiscent of the Gothic style.

SALLE D'OPERA

of the statue of Louis XV in Rheims, executed by the famous sculptor Pigalle before 1765. This shows the Citizen, scantily clad, holding a bag of coins, and accompanied by a watch-dog. He appears poor rather than rich, dignified and honourable.

A related source of concepts, not without æsthetic implications, is the writing of Helvetius (1715–74), whose distrust of the unnecessary reinforced the Physiocrats' teaching, and gave it a more direct political slant. In Helvetius' own words: 'In the majority of kingdoms there are only two kinds of citizens: the one that lacks the necessities of life, the other which is crammed with the superfluous.' It is clear that Helvetius was equally opposed to great riches and great poverty, the ideal for him being the mean, represented by the middle classes.[4]

This attitude, with an admixture of admiration for primitive man based on Jean-Jacques Rousseau's philosophy, is apparent in an anonymous engraving in the *Architecture* of Ledoux illustrating *'L'Abri du Pauvre'*; it shows a man seated under a tree by the sea, whilst the gods are disporting themselves

Above
Pigalle, 'Citizen' on the pedestal of the statue of Louis XV at Rheims; from a pre-war photograph.

Left
Ledoux, The Abode of the Poor; from L'Architecture.

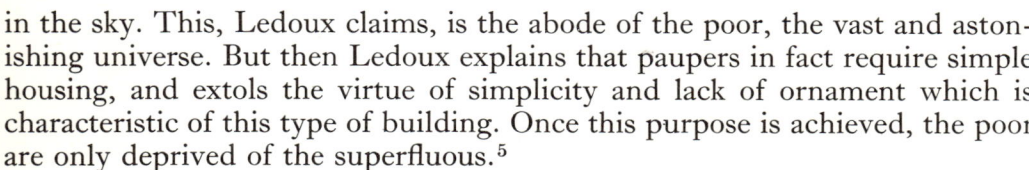

in the sky. This, Ledoux claims, is the abode of the poor, the vast and astonishing universe. But then Ledoux explains that paupers in fact require simple housing, and extols the virtue of simplicity and lack of ornament which is characteristic of this type of building. Once this purpose is achieved, the poor are only deprived of the superfluous.[5]

Other significant sources of æsthetic import are found in the *Encyclopédie*, the repository of knowledge of the age. Here basic concepts, equally applicable to the intellectual, the scientific and the visual spheres were expressed in one system, which was to include all branches of knowledge. A table inserted before the dedication in its first volume, printed in 1751 but not published until 1776, illustrates this fact. The scheme was further elaborated in a plate of the *Table analytique raisonnée* of the *Encyclopédie*, representing the 'Tree of All Knowledge'. This followed a medieval prototype, and was engraved in 1769 by Roth of Weimar, and published in 1780.

Two concepts relevant to art and architecture are of paramount importance to the *Encyclopédie*. The first is *caractère*. It is expressed in science as well as in the arts, and refers to nations as well as to individuals. The *caractère* of an author, and by association of an artist, is found in his own personal manner, *la manière qui lui est propre*.[6] The second significant concept is *fonction*, which is described as an action corresponding to the purpose of an organ. Figuratively, according to the *Encyclopédie*, *fonction* is a concept which can be applied to moral judgement, and, as the arts were regarded as a means of improving the quality of life, they also had to fulfil this *fonction*.[7] A similar thought is expressed by E.-L. Boullée, who devoted a whole chapter of his *Essai sur l'art* to *caractère*, and whose major architectural schemes are based on a direct expression of *fonction*.

In the past the view of the ordered cosmos had perhaps been best expressed by the Abbé Charles Batteux (1713–80) in *Les beaux arts réduits à un même principe*, first published in 1746. This book had a powerful influence throughout the 18th century, because it looked at the affinity of art with the laws of nature from a functional point of view. The work was translated into English in 1761. At almost the same time, Edmund Burke (1729–97) published the first edition of his influential book, *A Philosophical Enquiry into the Origin of our Ideas of the Sublime and Beautiful* (1757). This treatise, apart from its theoretical considerations and the suggested convergence of ethical and æsthetic concepts, also gives practical hints to the architect. It suggests that large scale dimension helps to generate the experience of the sublime, and that the effect of darkness, as opposed to light, enhances the sense of the sublime. Although Boullée failed to mention Burke in his *Essai*, there can be little doubt as to the latter's influence on him, either indirectly, or through Des François' French translation of 1765. For Boullée the most important element in art is the concept of nature, manifest in the moods engendered by the seasons and by light and shadow. Here the traditional teaching of Batteux is reinterpreted in an almost pantheistic spirit, and in this manner an original and personal note is struck.

The social message of the *Encyclopédie* reached, and had an impact on, architects and town planners. In the article '*Architecte*' in the *Supplément* of the *Encyclopédie* it is stated that the architect should build up sites as complete units.[8] Some architects should be state pensioners, *pensionnés du public*. (This article was written by the German philosopher Sulzer [1720–79] and amended in translation. In the original German text Sulzer had demanded scholarships for architectural students. In France this demand was unnecessary as such scholarships were numerous, and Academicians received a pension.) The arts

Tree of Knowledge (detail); from the Encyclopédie.

were to penetrate into the hut of the humblest citizen. The morally harmful was to be made to appear hideous, while the effect of the beautiful, harmonious and fitting would be to elevate the mind. In the latter passage the influence of Burke is apparent, although he is not specifically mentioned. A Ministry of Fine Arts is regarded with favour, as a means of disseminating the appreciation of art.[9]

Quatremère de Quincy (1755–1849), the leader of neo-classical æsthetics, retained and transformed these concepts. He restated and emphasized Abbé Laugier's ideas on an imitation of nature, based on law and harmony as manifested by the primitive hut. He expounded in particular the theory that architecture imitated itself, meaning that it imitated its own structural principles, a view specifically repudiated in the article '*Art*' in the *Encyclopédie*. To this he added a penetrating analysis of the moral value of the arts, stressing the significance of psychological associations. These he believed led to a more widespread appeal than that of a purely æsthetic approach. Art thus becomes a significant element in education, and should be appreciated in its natural environment. He therefore objected to collectors' museums, or '*cabinets*' as he still called them; and for this reason he also disapproved of Napoleon's raids on Italian art treasures, and demanded their return to their country of origin, so that they could be seen in their natural setting.[10]

Revolutionary and Utopian thought appear to have been intermingled, especially in France, perfection being confidently expected to follow political change. The 18th century *Philosophes*, including the writers Morelly and Mably who were both advocates of a communistic society, adapted the 'law of nature' as favouring community of possessions. Proudhon's well-known statement, that private property is theft, was indebted to their thought.[11] Morelly is especially outstanding because of his architectural interests. He based his theories on his understanding of the laws of nature, and published his *Code de la Nature* anonymously in 1755, a work which was first attributed to Diderot. According to him, cities almost equal in size were each to be centred on a large square, surrounded by regular quarters; the streets were to be identical – presumably a reminiscence of More's *Utopia*.[12] Houses also were to be indistinguishable from each other, but this raised difficulties, since no special provision was made for the requirements of large families. For the town as a whole, however, Morelly favoured conscious expansion, and the addition of new districts as and when required. Once a certain optimum size was reached – a size not clearly defined – a new town had to be founded.

The prospectus of a study, *L'Avant-Coureur du changement du monde entier*, probably by N. Collignon, is mentioned in the correspondence between Babeuf and Dubois de Fosseux in 1786–87. It gives a full blue-print for world betterment, demanding *inter alia* the disappearance of existing cities and the creation of new ones; free board and lodging for all citizens without imposing any taxes, the cost to be defrayed, astonishingly enough, by the King and the Republic of Poland.[13]

The approach of François-Noël Babeuf (1764–97), who adopted the name Caius Gracchus, was that of a Puritan and communist. In his view large cities lead to vice and the prevalence of artists, priests, procurors and thieves, an intriguing mixture of occupations, which, according to Babeuf, makes equality between citizens impossible. Consequently he wanted to go back to more primitive arrangements. In his own words as transmitted by F. M. Buonarroti: 'No more capitals, no more large cities. . . When there are no more palaces, there will be no more huts; the houses will be simple and the magnificence of architecture and the arts . . . will be reserved for public stores, for amphitheatres, for circuses, for aqueducts, for bridges, for canals, for public squares, for archives, for libraries, and above all for the places which are dedicated to the deliberations of magistrates and the exercise of the popular will.'[14]

Ledoux has been regarded by architectural historians as a revolutionary in architecture, because they failed to assess him within the context of his period. But the more one studies his work, especially his plans for Chaux, the more apparent it becomes that he was influenced by Babeuf, and was no innovator

Ledoux, Chaux III; from L'Architecture.

Vue perspective de la Ville de Chaux

but rather a propagator of progressive views. This influence is particularly pronounced in the rare *Prospectus* of Ledoux's *Architecture* which was published in 1802. Here he expresses egalitarian tendencies and a concern with the whole of the social order. This attitude came late in life for Ledoux, who had been a fashionable architect before the Revolution and was imprisoned as a Royalist in 1793. In contrast, Babeuf was executed in 1797 as too ardent a Revolutionary.[15]

It can now be seen how closely intellectual, economic and political changes were interlinked, and how difficult it is to accord priority, or to separate the various fields of change. However, one material factor could perhaps be singled out: the pressure of population. The peasants left the land, and a new proletariat grew up in Paris and other important cities. Sebastian Mercier in two anonymous works, *Tableau de Paris* and *L'An deux mille quatre-cent quarante*, gave a sarcastic but accurate description of the congestion of the streets and the misery of the unemployed. Robespierre's awareness of these growing numbers led him to demand a hall of assembly for ten thousand citizens, and he contrasted the speed at which a magnificent opera house could be erected with the lack of interest shown in a meeting-place for large-scale democratic gatherings.[16]

The destitution of the peasant and the slowly growing proletariat made no direct impact on French architects in official positions. They were working for royal or noble patronage as well as for the wealthy bourgeoisie and were established in the national and provincial capitals, Paris, Bordeaux, Nancy, Rennes and many other cities. Nevertheless, they felt involved in the libertarian aspirations of the period, rather more than in the purely political Revolution. Boullée remained a Royalist, Ledoux and Bélanger were imprisoned as reactionaries. Some weaker characters paid lip service to the Revolution, as Brogniart did in Bordeaux between 1793 and 1795. One notable exception to this attitude was Auguste Cheval de St Hubert, who, under the influence of his brother-in-law, the painter Jacques-Louis David, sympathized with the radicals and was involved with the organization of festivals, which formed a significant element in Revolutionary propaganda.[17]

England

The picture of English intellectual life represents a contrast to the French. Nothing equivalent to the Physiocrats and *Encyclopédistes* comes to mind. Intellectual groupings connected with literary and scientific pursuits, such as the Royal Society and the Royal Institution, were more coherent but less widely influential than the French intelligentsia (the earlier groups of Levellers and Quakers were committed to religious movements and their concern was not with the arts). One has therefore to turn to individual thinkers, and this makes the choice more difficult and necessarily more subjective.

It is remarkable that Adam Smith (1723–90), the propagator of free enterprise, advocated a certain amount of State intervention in his *Wealth of Nations*, first published in 1776. According to him defence and justice have to be subsidized. The duty of a sovereign or commonwealth consists in 'erecting or maintaining those public institutions and those public works which, though they may be in the highest degree advantageous to a great society, are, however, of such a nature that the profit could never repay the expense'. Furthermore, commerce requires publicly maintained roads, navigable cuts and canals. Although Smith doubted the value of universities, he advocated Government intervention in order to protect the labouring poor by extending their education, the masters to be partly but not wholly paid from the public purse.[18]

With regard to architecture, Adam Smith specifically objected to a window tax, since it particularly affected the poor with large families, and this offended his sense of justice. He also pointed out that the labourer in the country suffered many disadvantages compared with the town-dweller, while the land-owner enjoyed great privileges and amenities in the countryside.

Indeed, in England it was the country rather than the town which gave impetus to planning. To quote just one author, the surveyor Robert Morris discussed building within its setting in his *Rural Architecture* of 1750 and *The Architectural Remembrancer* of 1751. He favours simplicity: 'If you will be lavish in Ornament, your Structure will look rather like a Fop.' This accent on restraint is characteristically English, especially when coupled with the sense of humour apparent in the latter work. His Advertisement there states: 'There is now in the Press . . . A Treatise on Country Five Barr'd Gates . . . elegant Pig-styes . . . according to the Turkish and Persian Manner. . . Some designs . . . in the Muscovite and Arabian Architecture . . . all adapted to the Latitude and Genius of England . . . under the immediate inspection of Don Gulielmus de Demi Je ne sçai quoi.'[19]

This attitude represented a challenge to the advocacy of Chinese art by Sir William Chambers, found in his *Design for Chinese Buildings* of 1757, a work which appeared in French translation in the same year, and enjoyed great popularity in both capitals.

A special place should be allotted to J. C. Loudon (1783–1843) in this context. In his numerous publications his aim was to combine the *utile* with the *dulce*, in other words the functional and the beautiful. This is made clear not only in his writings, but also in his many illustrations, which reveal the charm of the countryside, enhanced rather than diminished by farms and adjacent buildings.[20]

The situation was summed up in the words of Thomas Hardwick, a pupil

Loudon, Tew Lodge Farm; from Designs for Laying out Farms and Farm Buildings.

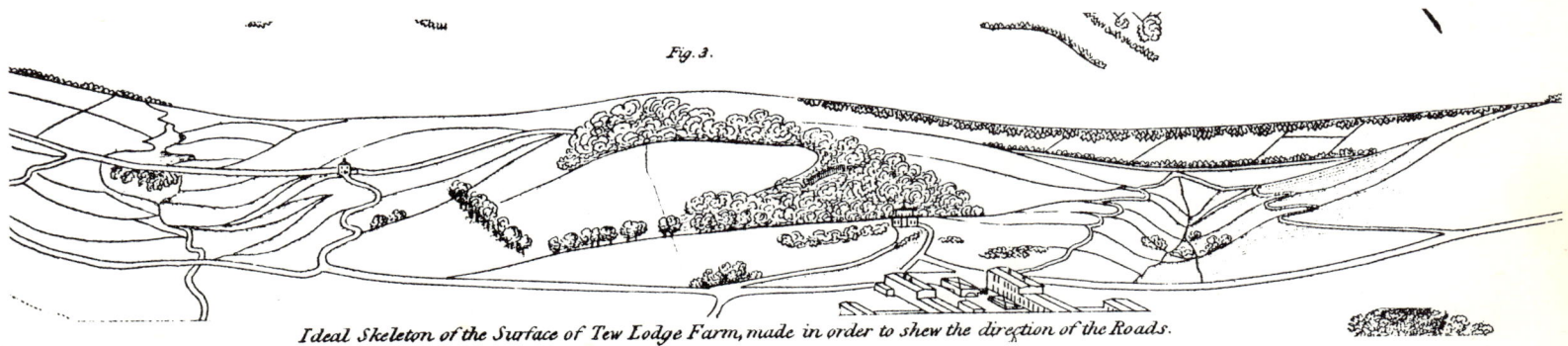

Ideal Skeleton of the Surface of Tew Lodge Farm, made in order to shew the direction of the Roads.

of Sir William Chambers, in his *Memoir* to his master of 1825. Here he desired that 'Architecture may again flourish uncontaminated by the baseness of ignorant pretenders, uninfluenced by the caprice of power or the erroneous notions of originality'. His main concern was for balance, and he therefore envisaged a threefold approach, against the lack of academic knowledge, the whims of *je ne sçai quoi*, already criticized by Robert Morris, and the danger of unbridled subjectivity and individualism. This was similar to the French attitude: in France the academic tradition remained paramount, and the collective rather than the personal element was emphasized, thus ensuring that the individual was firmly kept in his place.

It is interesting to note how revolutionary the politically uncommitted appear when carried away by their subject. Robert and James Adam in the Preface to Book I of their *Works in Architecture*, published from 1776 onwards and including a French translation, voiced a concern similar to Robespierre's regarding the lack of public commissions: 'Yet we must not expect that the fine arts will ever meet with their most ample reward, or attain their utmost degree of perfection, deprived as they are of that emulation which is excited by public works, and by the honourable applause of a refined and discerning Public.' On the other hand, such concern is lacking in the writings of Sir William Chambers, who had been given a public commission for the erection of Somerset House in 1775. Indeed, Chambers appears throughout to have been more of a traditionalist and individualist than his famous rivals.

The sociological insight of the architect John Wood the Younger (1728–81) is remarkably original. In his book *A Series of Plans for Cottages, Habitations*

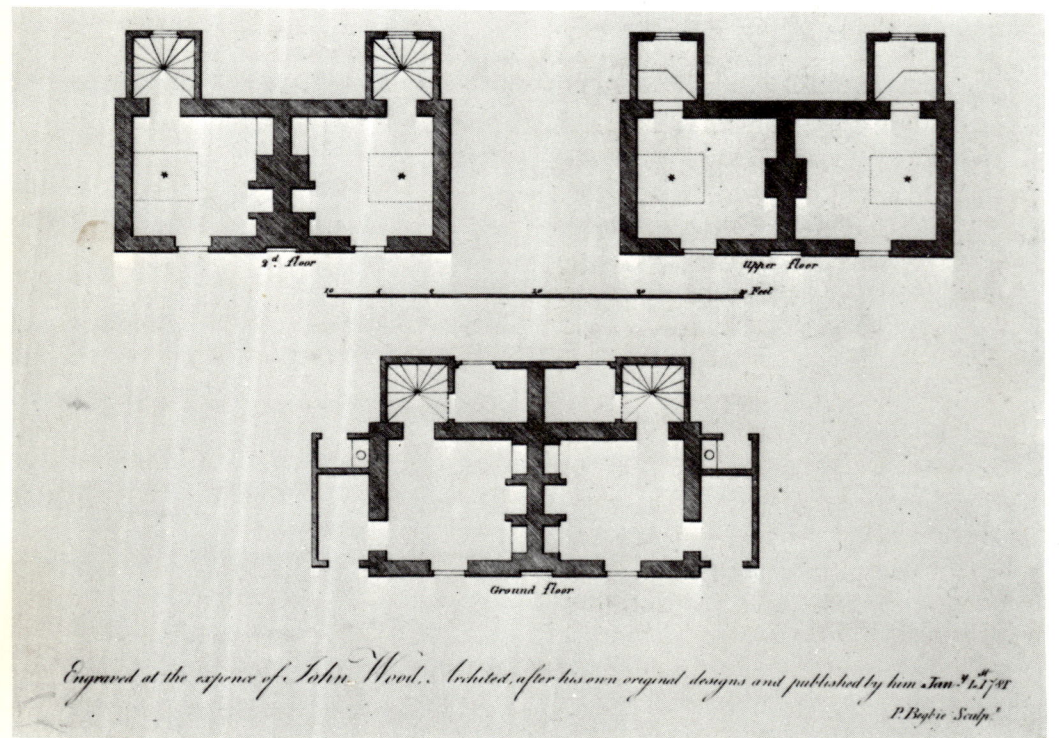

John Wood the Younger, Cottages with three rooms; from A Series of Plans, *etc.*

of the Labourer, Adapted as well to Towns as to the Country, planned in 1781, he states: 'In order to make myself master of the subject, it was necessary for me to feel as the cottager himself . . . no architect can form a convenient plan unless he ideally places himself in the situation of the person for whom he designs.' He demands active participation by the architect in problems of re-housing, for town and country alike. He advocates ideal planning, embracing not only the rich, but also the poorer classes, a concept which was later to bear fruit.[21]

John Plaw is more typical of his time, subservient to the English resident landowner who dominated the countryside. In his book *Sketches for Country Houses, Villas and Rural Dwellings* of 1800 he states explicitly on page ten, 'a Farmhouse intended for a Gentleman . . . should be designed as an object to be seen from his mansion', and, one may add, not primarily for the benefit of its inhabitants. Nevertheless, the average resident landowner had some personal knowledge of, and concern for, his labourers, and was therefore more desirable from the tenants' point of view than his French absentee counterpart.

English supremacy, especially in philosophy, was widely acknowledged. In an age passionately interested in ethics, the emphasis on moral values and harmonious balance so vividly described by Anthony Ashley Cooper, 3rd Earl of Shaftesbury (1671–1713), in his *An Inquiry Concerning Virtue* of 1699, may be singled out. It inspired a view of the arts as a means for human betterment, a view shared by the *Encyclopédistes*. Edmund Burke (1729–97) has already been mentioned in the discussion on Boullée. In his treatise on the Sublime, he not only profoundly influenced French thought, but also revolutionized Kant's view of such ideas. Indeed, through Kant's *Critique of Understanding* of 1790, available in numerous translations all over Europe, this concept achieved perhaps not only its most penetrating formulation, but added to Burke's reputation as a philosopher.

Kant's æsthetic concepts were influenced by F. Hutcheson, who, in his *An Inquiry into the Original of our Ideas of Beauty and Virtue* of 1725, had differentiated between absolute and relative beauty. Kant was also indebted to Henry Home, Lord Kames, who continued Hutcheson's thought, and published his *Elements of Criticism* in 1762. Here he separated intrinsic from relative beauty. The two treatises were translated into German, and therefore easily accessible to Kant, the former in 1762, the latter between 1763 and 1766. From these premises much of modern æsthetic theory developed, and the 'difficult' art, sensitively analysed by Bosanquet, can readily be understood.

It is in the idea of the sublime that æsthetic and moral considerations combine, and, when applied to architecture, they are meant to lead to elevated thought, expressed in monumental form. Hence the emphasis on simplicity and largeness of scale, as well as on a noble purpose. It is astonishing that this theory, first developed in England, had comparatively little influence on neo-classical architecture there in the 18th century, while, due to a revolutionary climate of opinion, it became decisively established in France.

Converging Tendencies

The emphasis on social thought shifted from France to England during the late 18th and early 19th centuries, with radicalism, pragmatism and co-operation creating new possibilities for the development of architecture. John Howard's (1726–90) combination of practical and theoretical remedies in the treatment of prisoners is an instance of social concern reflected in architectural planning. His influence, on a European scale, will be studied in more detail below.

A few characteristic architectural projects merit special consideration, because of their theoretical relevance and intellectual distinction. Jeremy and Samuel Bentham's 'invention' of the Panopticon must be mentioned. This was a centrally planned structure,[22] divided into wings with individual cells, adaptable to all manner of purposes – prisons, hospitals, or schools. Robert

Left
S. Bentham, Panopticon; from Panopticon.

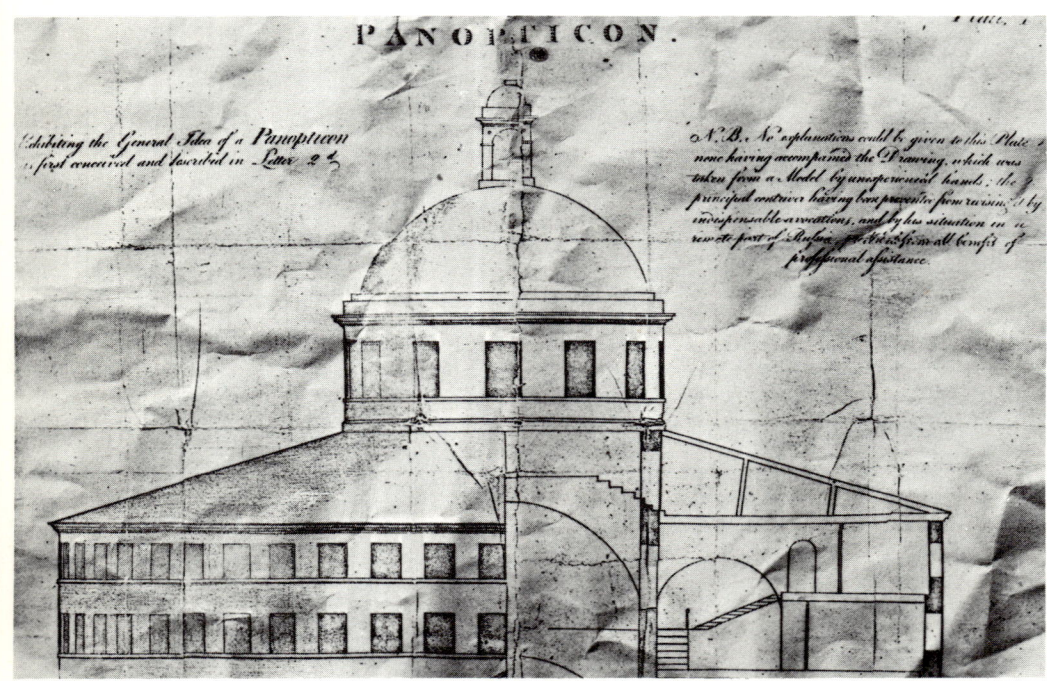

Left
S. Bentham, Panopticon; from Panopticon.

Fourier, plan of Phalanstère; from Le nouveau monde.

Owen (1771–1858) in his *New Harmony*, gave a blue-print for 'villages of co-operation'. Industrial, agricultural and educational activities were thus potentially combined and the influence exerted by these attempts at comprehensive planning had a powerful impact. Owen was a determinist, convinced that the right environment would automatically produce beneficial results. But in spite of the money poured into them by their founder, especially in the United States, the Owenite communities proved a disappointment because of lack of selection regarding settlers and the emergence of a growing capitalist economy.[23]

By contrast, the Fourierite system was more philosophical in its approach, extolling the passions, and their value for human relationships. Fourier's blue-print for communal settlements, the *Phalanstères*, was not without practical application, however, especially in the *Familistère*, founded by the socialist J. B. A. Godin in conjunction with his castings manufactory at Guise.[24] There is little doubt that François-Marie-Charles Fourier (1772–1837) was influenced by, and perhaps for this reason appeared jealous of, Owen, especially as the latter's more pragmatic and paternalistic approach could produce quicker results. Owen was wealthy and could afford to implement his own plans for communist settlements. His ideas were egalitarian and tended towards atheism, while Fourier was of a profoundly religious nature and believed in gradual evolution.

Fourier's *Phalanstères* were conceived as units of co-operative and associative living between unequal partners. As a minor employee, he waited in vain

Owen, view of an Establishment for 1,200 inhabitants; from his Report to a Committee of the House of Commons, *1817.*

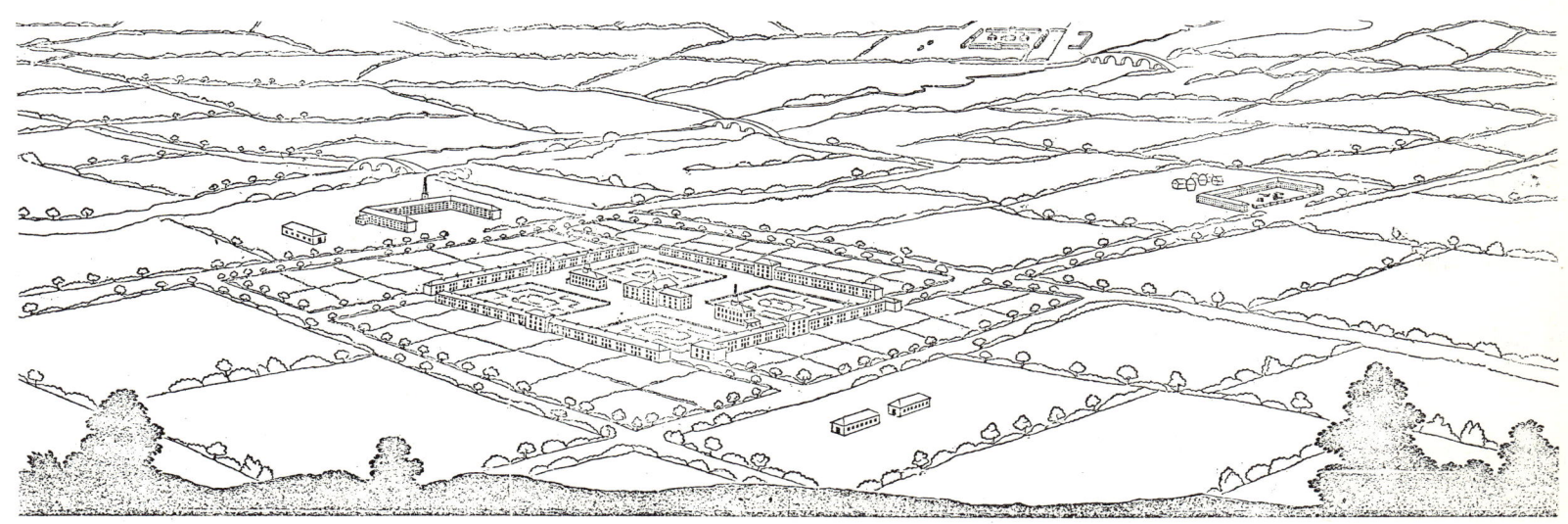

The above Plan exhibits, in the Foreground, an Establishment, with its Appendages and appropriate Quantity of Land ; and at due distances, other Villages of a similar description.

Extracted from Mr. Owen's Report, presented to the Committee of the House of Commons on the Poor Laws, in the Session of 1817.

SQUARES of buildings are here represented sufficient to accommodate about 1200 persons each; and surrounded by a quantity of land, from 1000 to 1500 acres. Within the squares are public buildings, which divide them into parallelograms. The central building contains a public kitchen, mess-rooms, and all the accommodation necessary to economical and comfortable cooking and eating. To the right of this is a building, of which the ground-floor will form the infant school, and the other a lecture-room and place of worship.

The building to the left contains a school for the elder children, and a committee-room on the ground floor; above, a library, and a room for adults. In the vacant space within the squares, are enclosed grounds for exercise and recreation: these enclosures are supposed to have trees planted in them. It is intended that three sides of each square shall be lodging-houses, chiefly for the married, consisting of four rooms in each; each room to be sufficiently large to accommodate a man, his wife, and two children. The fourth side is designed for dormitories for all the children exceeding two in a family, or above three years of age. In the centre of this side of the squares are apartments for those who superintend the dormitories: at one extremity of it the infirmary; and at the other a building for the accommodation of strangers who may come from a distance to see their friends and relatives. In the centres of two sides of the squares are apartments for general superintendants, clergyman, schoolmasters, surgeon, &c.; and in the third are store-rooms for all the articles required for the use of the establishment.

On the outside, and at the back of the houses around the squares, are gardens, bounded by roads.

Immediately beyond these, on one side, are buildings for mechanical and manufacturing purposes. The slaughter-house, stabling, &c. to be separated from the establishment by plantations.

At the other side are offices for washing, bleaching, &c.; and at a still greater distance from the squares are some of the farming establishments, with conveniences for malting, brewing, and corn-mills, &c.: around these are cultivated enclosures, pasture-land, &c. the hedge-rows of which are planted with fruit-trees.

Each lodging-room within the squares is to accommodate a man, his wife, and two children under three years of age; and to be such as will permit them to have much more comforts than the dwellings of the poor usually afford. It is intended that the children above three years of age should attend the school, eat in the mess-room, and sleep in the dormitories; the parents being of course permitted to see and converse with them at meals, and all other proper times: that before they leave school they shall be well instructed in all necessary and useful knowledge; that every possible means should be adopted to prevent the acquirement of bad habits from their parents or otherwise; that no pains shall be spared to impress upon them such habits and dispositions as may be most conducive to their happiness through life, as well as render them useful and valuable members of the community to which they belong.

It is proposed that the women should be employed, in the first place, in the care of their infants, and in keeping their dwellings in the best order. 2dly, In cultivating the gardens to raise vegetables for the supply of the public kitchen. 3dly, In attending to such of the branches of the various manufactures as women can well undertake; but not to be employed in them more than four or five hours in the day. 4thly, In making up clothing for the inmates of the establishment. 5thly, In attending occasionally, and in rotation, in the public kitchen, mess-rooms, and dormitories; and, when properly instructed, in superintending some parts of the education of the children in the schools.

It is proposed that the elder children should be trained to assist in gardening and manufacturing, for a portion of the day, according to their strength; and that the men should be employed, all of them, in agriculture, and also in manufactures, or some other occupation for the benefit of the establishment.

SCHEDULE of EXPENSES *for forming an Establishment for* TWELVE HUNDRED MEN, WOMEN, AND CHILDREN.

If the land be purchased,

1200 acres of land, at 30l. per acre	£36,000
Lodging apartments for 1200 persons	17,000
Three public buildings within the square . . .	11,000
Manufactory, slaughter-house, and washing-house	8,000
Furnishing 300 lodging-rooms, at 8l. each	2,400
Furnishing kitchen, schools, and dormitories	3,000
Two farming establishments, with corn-mill, malting, and brewing appendages	5,000
Making the interior of the square and the roads	3,000
Stock for the farm under spade cultivation	4,000
Contingencies and extras	6,000
	£96,000

which, being divided by 1200, gives a capital to be advanced of 80l. per head ; or, at 5 per cent. per ann. 4l. each per year.

Thus, at so small an expense as a rental of 4l. per head, may the unemployed poor be put in a condition to maintain themselves; may be easily conceived, quickly to repay the capital advanced, if thought necessary.

But, if the land be rented, only 66,000l. capital would be required.

for a wealthy patron. It is not surprising that he objected to Owen's work, attacking the plan of *New Harmony* far more violently than the architectural facts seemed to warrant. According to Fourier, Owen's square lay-out, traditional to English colleges, was subject to noise and disturbance by manual work, whilst the palatial unit he advocated facilitated provision for living in communities. In particular, the location of manual jobs in the wings ensured their isolation and made for undisturbed tranquillity. An opera house and a church were to be added as separate units, expressing Fourier's love for the arts and his religious convictions. He based co-operation on psychological contrasts; he abhorred competition, and thus endeavoured to use human passions for constructive purposes. It is regrettable that his numerous repetitive and frequently abstruse books and essays have discouraged many potential readers, as his creative approach is always challenging and frequently of an almost prophetic nature.

The visionary, artist and thinker, John Martin (1789–1854), should also be remembered in this context. Not unknown in France, where he was appreciated by the critic Sainte-Beuve, as pointed out by Seznec,[25] he showed in his illustrations the impact of French architectural inspiration, especially that of designs by Boullée's followers, accessible as engravings. (Boullée's own work was by then largely forgotten, his drawings remaining unpublished in the Bibliothèque Nationale.) John Martin also published numerous treatises on technical matters, among them 'A Plan for abundantly supplying the Metropolis with pure water from the River Coln' (1834); the fusion of practical philanthropic and visionary elements which characterized his approach may be regarded as intrinsically English.

An interesting contrast thus appears between French and English developments. In France the main contribution was made by intellectuals and men of letters; in England by economists, architects, farmers and philanthropists. The emphasis in England was therefore not so much on theoretical thinking, but on the contribution made by practitioners in their respective fields. This point is clarified by the main trends of criticism of the period; in Paris it was mainly directed against noise and traffic congestion, in London against air pollution. In France it was thus the improvement of the city which was regarded as paramount, whilst in England there existed a hankering for the countryside and its amenities. The Industrial Revolution seemed still distant; although its impact began to make itself felt, it was not yet recognized as a major change.[26]

Finally the question arises as to whether it was the intellectual background rather than economic necessity which led to a change in social consciousness – a change which found expression in architectural purpose and form. There cannot be much doubt that the two elements were simultaneously at work, influencing and reflecting each other. This fact was recognized even by Engels, the co-protagonist of historical materialism, when he wrote to Starkenburg in 1894: 'It is not that the economic position is the *cause and alone active*, while everything else only has a passive effect.' It was the 'superstructure' which influenced art in general, and architecture, the most functional of the arts, in particular. The intellectual climate of this period is thus shown to be intrinsically more autonomous than derivative.

1. cf. *Summerson*, who deals succinctly with sociological problems, pp. 98 ff. and *passim*. E. J. Hobsbawn: *The Age of Revolution, Europe 1789–1848*, London 1962, gives a brilliant exposition of the problems involved.

2. K. Mannheim: *Ideology and Utopia*, numerous editions. Also E. Cassirer: *The Philosophy of the Enlightenment*, Princeton U.P. 1951.

3. Especially *Tableau économique*, Paris 1758, and the articles '*Fermier*' and '*Grains*' in the *Encyclopédie*, 1756 and 1757 respectively. cf. R. L. Meek: *The Economics of Physiocracy*, London 1962.

4. Helvetius: *De l'homme*, London 1773, II, Chapter III, p. 169. It is worth noting that this book, like many others with political implications, was published abroad.

5. *L'Architecture* I, pp. 104 ff. and pl. 33.

6. *Encyclopédie*, II, pp. 646 ff., especially p. 668, article by Mallet. cf. also the interesting remarks by Grunwald on character in medicine, *Supplement* II, pp. 229 ff.

7. *Encyclopédie*, VII, col. 51a, by d'Aumont. Function as applied to morals, *Supplement* III, col. 83. cf. among modern authors, J. A. Leith: *The Idea of Art as Propaganda in France, 1750–1799*, University of Toronto Press 1965; this gives a blatant over-simplification of the complex subject matter, and fails in dealing with the relevant problems of content and form.

8. *Encyclopédie Supplement*, Amsterdam 1776, p. 537, col. a: 'Il doit savoir bâtir des places entières, des villes mêmes.' *Encyclopédie*, as above, article '*Art*', p. 591, col. a: 'Il est . . . nécessaire qu'ils [les arts] pénètrent jusqu'à l'humble cabane du moindre des citoyens.' It is right to 'donner à tout ce qui est nuisible une figure hideuse', p. 588, col. b. On the more general theme, p. 588, col. a: 'C'est donc aux beaux-arts à revêtir d'agrémens divers nos habitations . . . principalement afin que les douces impressions de ce qui est beau, harmonieux et convenable, donnent une tournure plus noble, un caractère plus relevé à notre esprit et à notre coeur.'

9. cf. J. G. Sulzer: *Allgemeine Theorie der Schönen Künste*, etc., Leipzig 1771.

10. A. Q. A. C. Quatremère de Quincy: *Lettres sur le préjudice qu'occasioneroient aux Arts et à la Science, le déplacement des monumens de l'art de l'Italie*, etc., Paris 1796. Also *Considérations morales sur la destination des ouvrages de l'Art*, etc., Paris 1815.

11. In *Qu'est-ce que la propriété*, first published in Paris in 1840, 2nd ed. 1848, first *Mémoire*, p. 1 ff. It is of course not suggested here that this slogan fully represents Proudhon's thought, although his disdain for property is characteristic. cf. ibid., p. 101, a critical review of Saint-Simon's and Fourier's theories. cf. also *Système des contradictions économiques ou philosophie de la misère*, Paris 1846, to quote only one other of Proudhon's many publications.

12. Morelly, pp. 197 ff.

13. It speaks for the fame of Stanislaw Poniatowski and the reputation of freedom possessed by the Polish Republic – combining ideologically a republic with an elective monarchy – that *L'Avant-Coureur* expected the Polish nation to meet expenses, and this from a country poor and disorganized, suffering from the after-effects of the first partition in 1772. cf. J. Fabre: *Stanislas-Auguste Poniatowski et l'Europe des lumières*, Strasbourg 1952.

14. 'Quand il n'y aurait plus de palais, il n'y aurait plus de masures; les maisons seraient simples, et la magnificence de l'architecture et des arts . . . serait réservée aux magasins publics, aux amphithéâtres, aux cirques, aux aqueducs, aux ponts, aux canaux, aux places, aux archives, aux bibliothèques, et surtout aux lieux consacrés aux délibérations des magistrats et à l'exercice de la souveraineté populaire.' Ph. Buonarotti: *Histoire de la conspiration pour l'égalite dite de Babeuf*, Paris 1850, pp. 146 ff. This statement seems to be equivalent to a catalogue of *Prix de Rome* designs. cf. *Prix*, *passim*. V. Advielle: *Histoire de Gracchus Babeuf et du Babouvisme*, Paris 1884, 2nd part, vol. II, pp. 32 f. and *passim*.

15. cf. H. Rosenau in *Gazette des Beaux Arts*, March 1964, pp. 173 ff.

16. *Lettres de Maximilien Robespierre à ses Commettans: Le Défenseur de la Constitution*, Paris 1793, No. 9, pp. 390 f.

17. *Prix*, p. 25, pls. 25–27. D. L. Dowd: *Pageant-Master of the Republic, J.-L. David and the French Revolution*, University of Nebraska Studies, 1948. cf. A. C. Hubert's *Rapport* on the 25th Floréal, An II, on the building of a National Palace. cf. also on Brogniart's politics, F. G. Pariset: *Bulletin et Mémoires de la Société Archéologique de Bordeaux*, LXII, 1965, pp. 20 ff.

18. *An Inquiry into the Nature and Causes of the Wealth of Nations*, ed. E. Cannan, II, 6th edition, 1950, p. 214.

19. R. Morris: *Rural Architecture*, etc., London 1750, Preface, p. 1. *The Architectural Remembrancer*, etc., London 1751, p. XV f. On the general background, cf. Chr. Hussey: *The Picturesque*, London 1927; F. D. Klingender: *Art and the Industrial Revolution*, London 1964; and J. Burke: *Hogarth and Reynolds*, London 1943.

20. cf. especially: *Designs for Laying Out Farms and Farm-Buildings in the Scotch Style*, etc., London 1811.

21. *The Ideal City*, pp. 97 ff. Also L. Benevolo: *The Origins of Modern Town-Planning*, London 1967.

22. cf. *The Works of J. Bentham*, ed. by J. Bowring, VIII, Edinburgh 1843, pp. 372 f. cf. J. Bentham: *Panopticon; or The Inspection House*, London 1791, translated in an abridged version into French in the same year, under the title *Panoptique*, and published in Paris.

23. R. Owen: *A New View of Society*, London 1813, and his other numerous writings. G. D. H. Cole: *The Life of Robert Owen*, 2nd ed., London 1930, *passim*.

24. cf. Fr. Ch. M. Fourier, especially his book *Le nouveau monde industriel et sociétaire*, Paris 1829, a title reminiscent of Owen's work mentioned above. Also M. Friedberg: *L'influence de Charles Fourier sur le mouvement social contemporain en France*, Paris 1926.

25. J. Seznec: *John Martin en France*, London 1964. T. Balston: *John Martin*, 1st ed., London 1934. *The Ideal City*, pp. 127 f.

26. K. Marx and F. Engels: *Correspondence, 1840–95*, London 1934, p. 517. A. B. C. Cobban: *The Myth of the French Revolution*, London 1955, and *The Social Interpretation of the French Revolution*, Cambridge 1964. cf. also R. Sampson: *Progress in the Age of Reason*, London 1956. For a broad outline on the intellectual background in England, cf. R. Williams: *Culture and Society, 1780–1950*, London 1958, numerous editions, *passim*. On economics, the still unsurpassed study of Ch. Gide and Ch. Rist: *A History of Economic Doctrines*, originally published in French in 1909, numerous editions, and translated several times into English. E. J. Hobsbawm: *The Age of Revolution*, London 1962, and for a more complex view, J. E. C. Hill: *Reformation to Industrial Revolution, A Social and Economic History of Britain, 1530–1780*, London 1967. A negative interpretation of the period concerned is found in H. Sedlmayr: *Verlust der Mitte*, Salzburg 1951, translated into English under the title *Art in Crisis*, London 1958.

2
The Growing Capitals

During the 18th century the population in Europe increased, while the architectural dominance of palace and church diminished. Markets grew in importance and their sites were increased; housing for the lower and less privileged strata of society was considered, and it is here that the basic difference between London and Paris, the rival capitals, can perhaps be most clearly appreciated. The emphasis on the social element in housing in Europe had grown with the centuries. Workers' houses were included in Filarete's *Trattato d'Architettura* in the middle of the 15th century. The famous banking family of Fugger built a settlement in Augsburg in the early 16th century, the so-called Fuggerei, and isolated instances of such planning are found from time to time, including the cottages adjacent to the Gobelins factory in Paris in the 17th century.[1]

However, no conscious social theory can be discerned behind these isolated efforts, and it was left to the late 18th century to formulate a theory, which in turn profoundly influenced planning. It led to the development of communal design, as opposed to the commissions of private patrons to individual architects. In France it also led to the *immeubles de rapport*, houses for letting which were conceived as investments.[2] They were mainly the homes of the middle classes and varied in comfort and quality. The Hosten estate by Ledoux, built for a rich speculator just before the Revolution, represents an outstanding achievement, combining units of design with a sub-division into separate flats, and in this way providing a contrast to the terraced London houses. Even more important are Ledoux's designs for compact dwellings including four houses in a large unit, such as the one intended for a father

Ledoux, House for four members of one family; from L'Architecture.

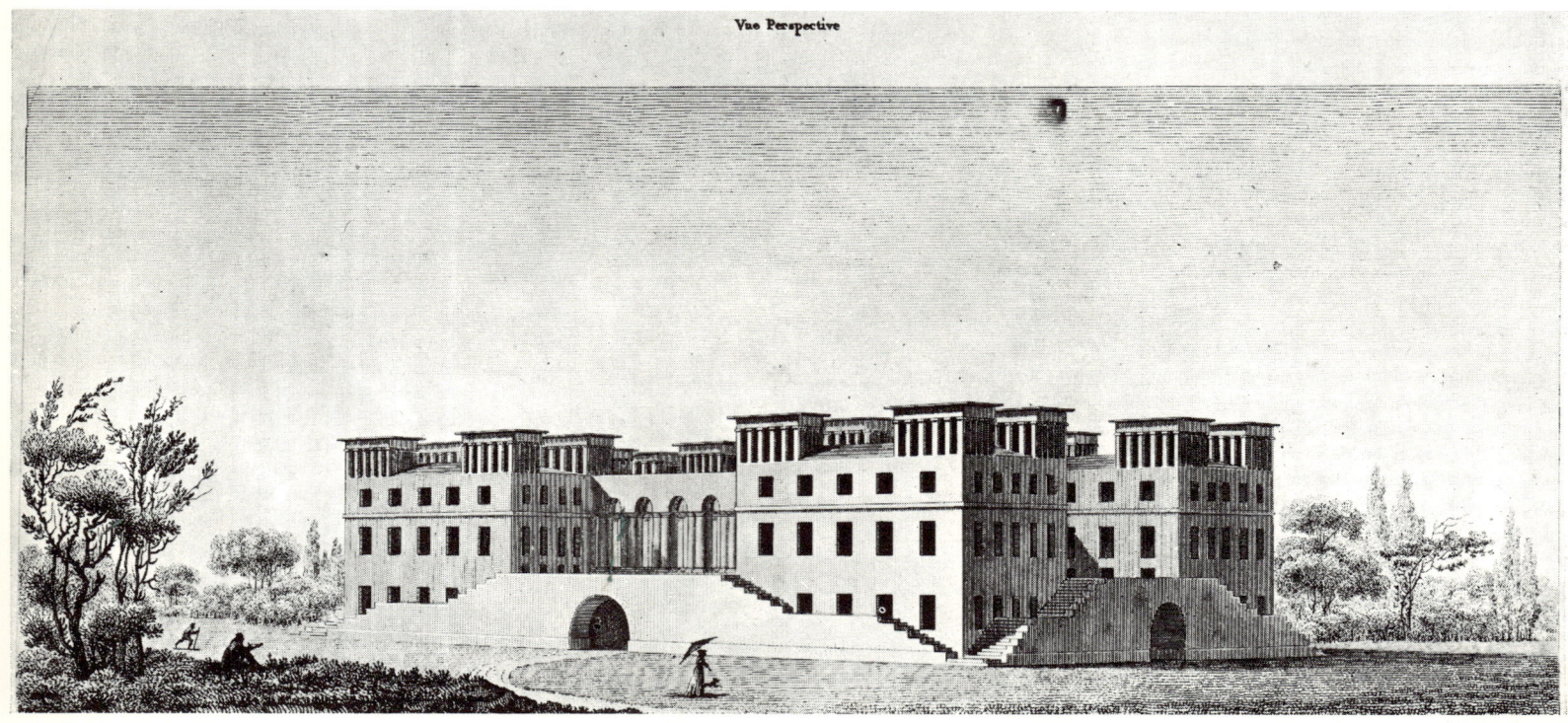

Vue Perspective

with his three adult children. This system combined easy communication with independence. Lower in the social scale were the Portiques du Temple, a group of arcaded buildings surrounding an oval. These small houses contained flats on the first floor, with shops on the ground floor.

Social concern was to spread even to the capitalist and entrepreneur classes. Thus Sobry stated in his *De l'architecture* of 1776 that special care should be bestowed on amenities for the dwellers in lodging houses.[3] The seedy aspect of decaying large houses in multi-occupation, so vividly described by Balzac, belongs to a later date.

In London the counterpart of housing in flats was the development of chambers for the professional classes, of which The Albany, built by Alexander Copland in 1803, was characteristic.[4] Here the English tradition of college life has to be remembered, not in the academic sense, but in the meaning associated with John Bellers' *Proposals for Raising a Colledge of Industry*, published in 1695, and republished by Owen in his *New View of Society* in 1818. The early 19th century housing schemes, such as J. C. Loudon's College for Working Men, projected in 1818, derive from such precedents.[5]

Private housing for the wealthier classes was the mainstay of an architect's career. In England, especially, sumptuous country seats set in vast gardens and grounds, inspired by the paintings of Claude Lorrain, provided a coveted outlet; while in France the centralizing tendency of the French Court attracted the nobility to Paris and thus accelerated the decline of the countryside.

Town houses, in Paris and London, catered for the higher and middle income groups, but the needs of the poorer sections of the population were largely, though not entirely, ignored. In England, John Wood the Younger remembered the needs of the agricultural workers, and resident landowners were willing to improve their conditions. On the other hand, in France the absentee aristocrats cared little about the situation in the country, where the standard of living for peasants was low. This fact is confirmed by numerous references in the *Moniteur*, the official government organ, especially in 1794, when demands were made for the improvement of accommodation for rural workers. In England in 1797, F. M. Eden advocated an investigation into the best type of dwelling for the labouring classes.[6]

Paris at the time was still strongly imbued with the classical tradition, and was regarded as a prototype of architectural quality throughout Europe. The capital was a prosperous and expanding city, which crystallized and accentuated the prevailing tendencies of French planning. Indeed, whether one studies Nancy or Bordeaux, the basic principles applied remain the same, and although the provinces may on occasion have achieved priority, the full fruition of planning was centred in Paris and its environs.[7] A telling example is seen in the relationship between the Place de la Concorde of 1754 and the siting of the first church of the Madeleine, begun in 1764. Here the emphasis was on multifocal planning, sequences of several *places* serving a variety of utilitarian and ceremonial purposes. A new type of open square or circus emerged, distinct from the self-contained and homogeneous unit of the Renaissance past, opening into wide avenues, and differing from the Baroque type of plan in avoiding the focus on one dominating building.

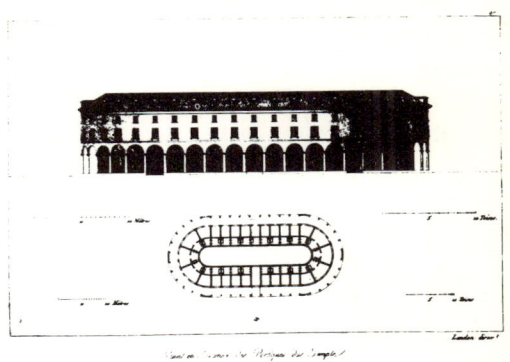

The Portiques du Temple, from Landon.

Naturally, the older type of planning was not entirely superseded, and the Baroque antecedents especially made themselves felt. Thus the commanding position of the Ecole Militaire, begun in 1757 by Jacques-Ange Gabriel on virgin ground, still followed a Baroque prototype; it will be more fully discussed in a subsequent chapter.[8] On the other hand, Gondoin's Ecole de Chirurgie of 1769–86, set on a cramped site in the centre of the university quarter, had to be accommodated within the precincts of the monastery of the Cordeliers, to the regret of the architect, who published his ideal plan in

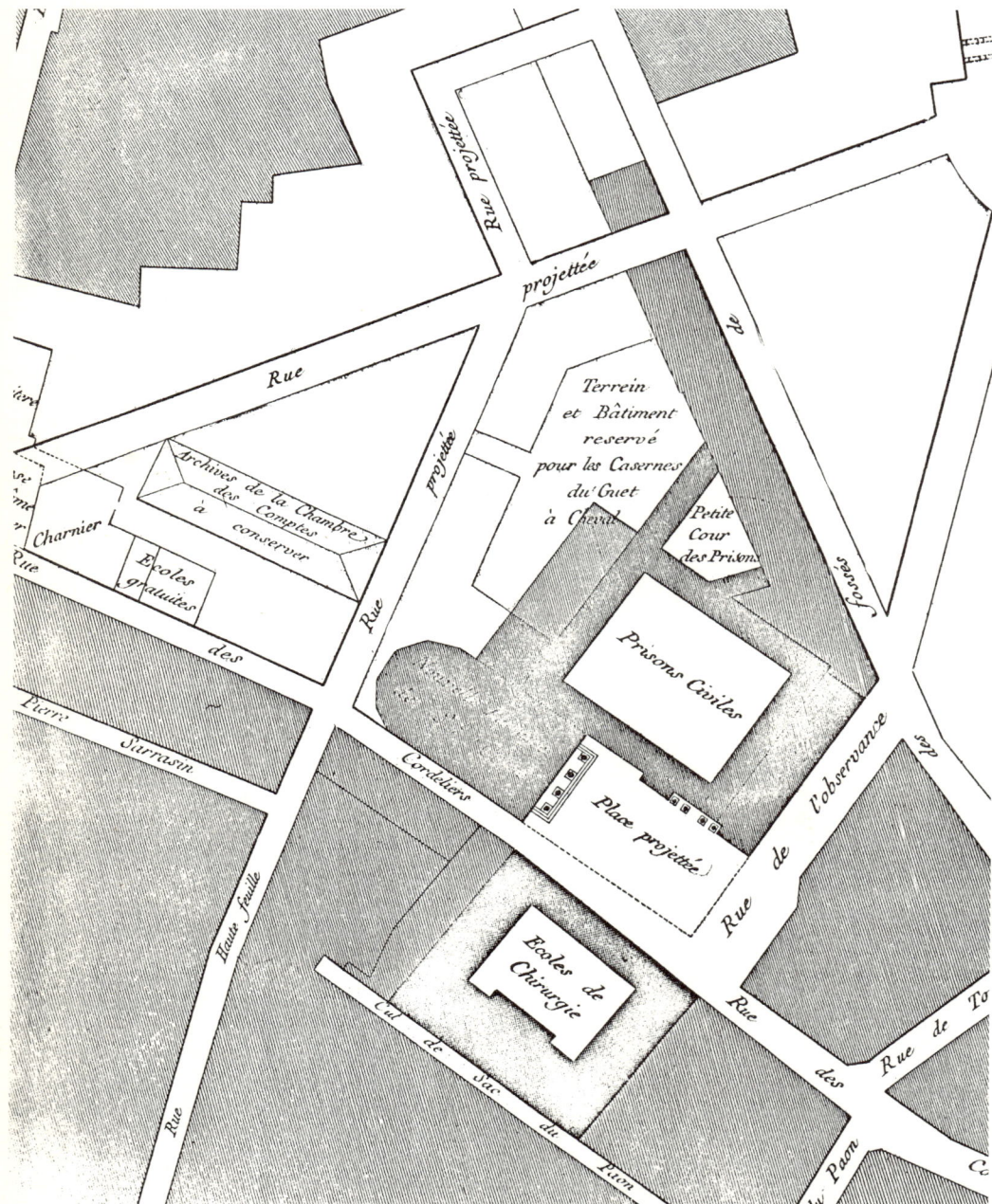

Gondoin, plan for the development connected with the Ecole de Chirurgie (detail); from Description des Ecoles de Chirurgie.

1780.[9] Even so, this plan presented a multifocal tendency, with a *place* opening in front of the school itself, replacing the nave of the church, and a columned portico added to the chancel as an entrance.

The theoretical base for this type of planning was Père Marc-Antoine Laugier's *Essai sur l'architecture*, first published in 1753, and translated into English as early as 1755. There is a marked contrast between this work and Jacques-François Blondel's famous *Cours d'architecture*, published between 1771 and 1777, and completed by Patte, the aims of the latter being more practical and utilitarian. Laugier's approach, although not entirely original, marked the ascendancy of the intellectual over the practitioner. His tenets on *bienséance* – on the appearance of architecture as conditioned by the social status of the inhabitants – went back to Alberti, and ultimately to Vitruvius. However, some of his ideas were more original, and heralded a new age. Laugier emphasized the *place* including its approaches as a regularizing principle. He advocated straight, wide avenues, ending in triumphal arches, and based his concept on the forest, with its wide *percées* for hunting. In fact this attitude to the forest was anything but romantic. He saw it as a planned environment, characterized by large thoroughfares. The streets of the city are for him identical with avenues in forests. '*Les rues de celle-là* (the city) *sont les routes de celle-ci* (the forest).[10] A good example of what he had in mind appeared in the tome by Germain Boffrand, *De Architectura Liber*, published in Paris both in Latin and French in 1745. In it were shown the radiating avenues surrounding the Château of Bouchefort, near Brussels, which seem to foreshadow Laugier's theory.

It was Pierre Patte, however, who formulated the new programme most

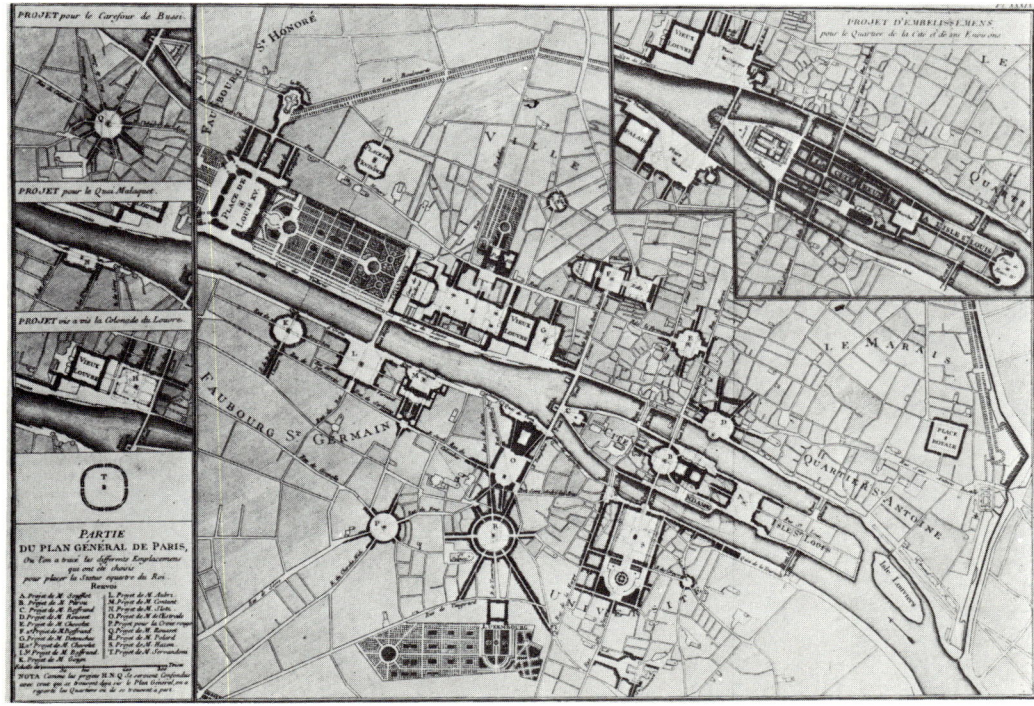

Patte, plan of Paris; from Monumens.

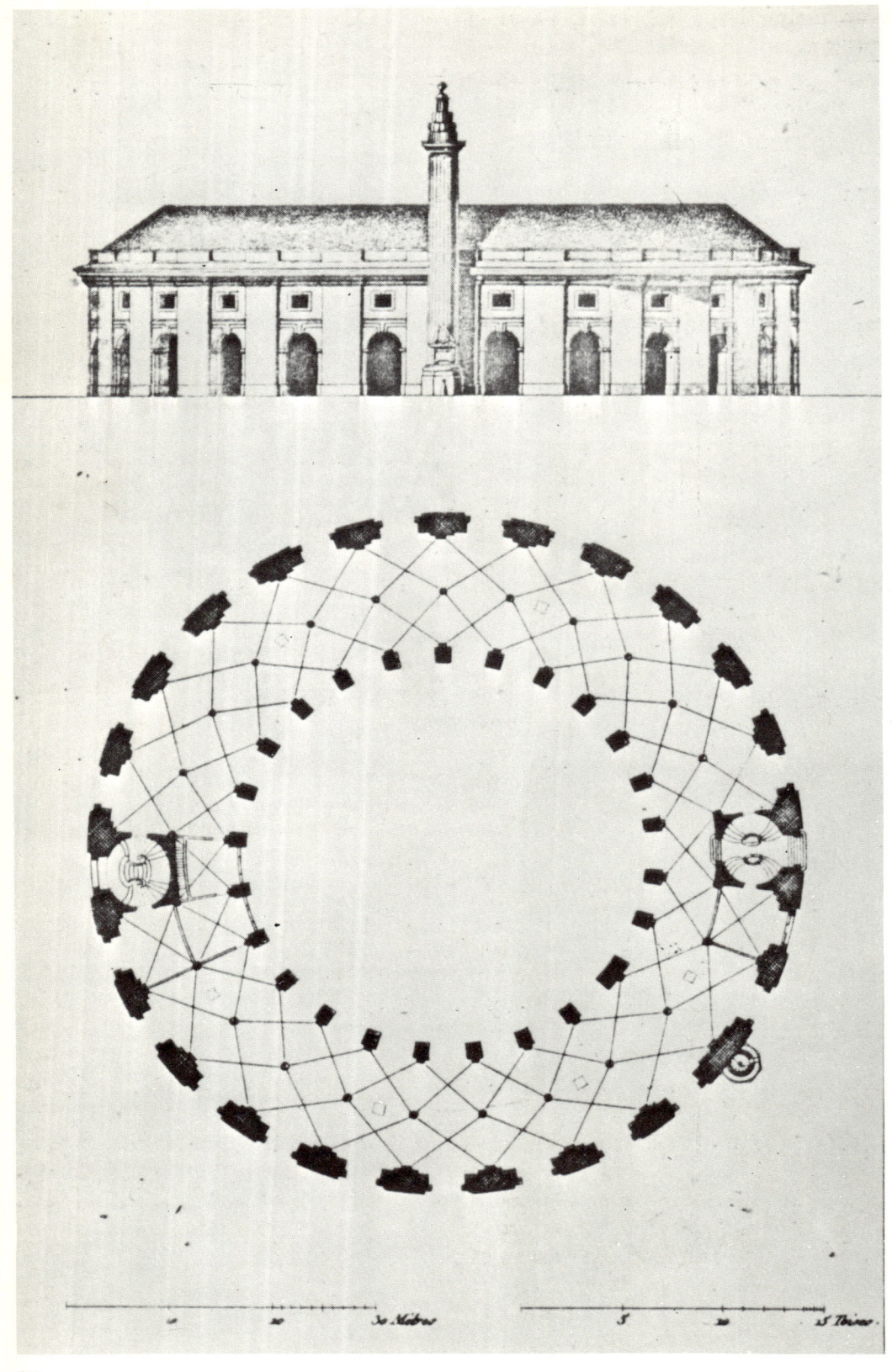

Plan and elevation of the Halle aux Blés; from Landon.

precisely. In his work on the monuments planned for the glorification of Louis XV, he dealt with his subject in a prophetic manner by incorporating a number of interconnected *places* in his ideal plan for Paris, thus ensuring a multifocal arrangement.[11] His *Monumens* was first published in Paris in 1765, and the influence of this work cannot be exaggerated, either in France or abroad.

Among the detailed plans represented here, those of Boffrand were outstanding. His importance tends to be overlooked, but in attempting a synthesis between the æsthetically satisfying and the utilitarian, Boffrand deserves a special place. In one of his designs a sequence of three piazzas contained fish and vegetable markets, a square for the statue of King Louis XV and a grain market, culminating in an exedra. These piazzas were to serve a dual purpose; they were not only to be used as markets, but were to include shops and flats. Sculpture was to represent architectural function by including vegetable and flower motifs. The triumphal arches, favoured by Laugier, which were to enclose the precinct, added a further touch of grandeur. The scheme was not implemented, but replaced by a single building, the Halle aux Blés, erected by Camus de Mézières between 1763 and 1767, and completed by Bélanger; a more modest scheme, but nevertheless of outstanding architectural significance.[12]

Another important design, reproduced by Patte, is the one by Hazon for the Right Bank of the Seine in Paris, then an underprivileged area. The intention was to demolish the ancient prison, the Petit Châtelet, and replace it with a rectangular *place* and a semi-circle, adorned by a rock surmounted by the statue of the King guided by Victory. The plans published by Patte also included his own design for a duplication of the Louvre on the Left Bank, and it is from this that some of the later experiments for a Place Louis XVI are derived. Among these, the numerous attempts to connect the palaces of the Louvre and the Tuileries were outstanding, especially Bélanger's scheme of 1787. This project was finally developed in the 19th century under Napoleon I and Napoleon III.

Pierre-Louis Moreau, usually called Moreau-Desproux, executed plans for the development of Paris in 1768; they were presented to, and approved by Louis XV in 1769. They reflected Patte's influence, being based on linear developments along the Seine, simpler than those found in Patte's *Monumens*, but nearer to day-to-day 18th century primary requirements. Moreau concentrated on the improvement of the quays, and the reclamation of older parts of Paris; for instance, he suggested a new piazza in front of the church of Ste Eustache. But his most important achievement was perhaps the design for a new town hall for Paris, including a central court, thus making an attempt at tidying up the older quarters of the city in a symmetrical manner.[13]

The development of river-frontages and harbours played a significant part in a period in which trade had improved and the beauties of nature were more and more appreciated. In this way, utilitarian and æsthetic factors reinforced each other. The influence of Ledoux was apparent in such diverse places as the Admiralty of St Petersburg and the quays of Marseilles, but perhaps of even greater importance were the plans for the borders of the Garonne in Bordeaux, starting with the Place de la Bourse by Jacques Gabriel, a member

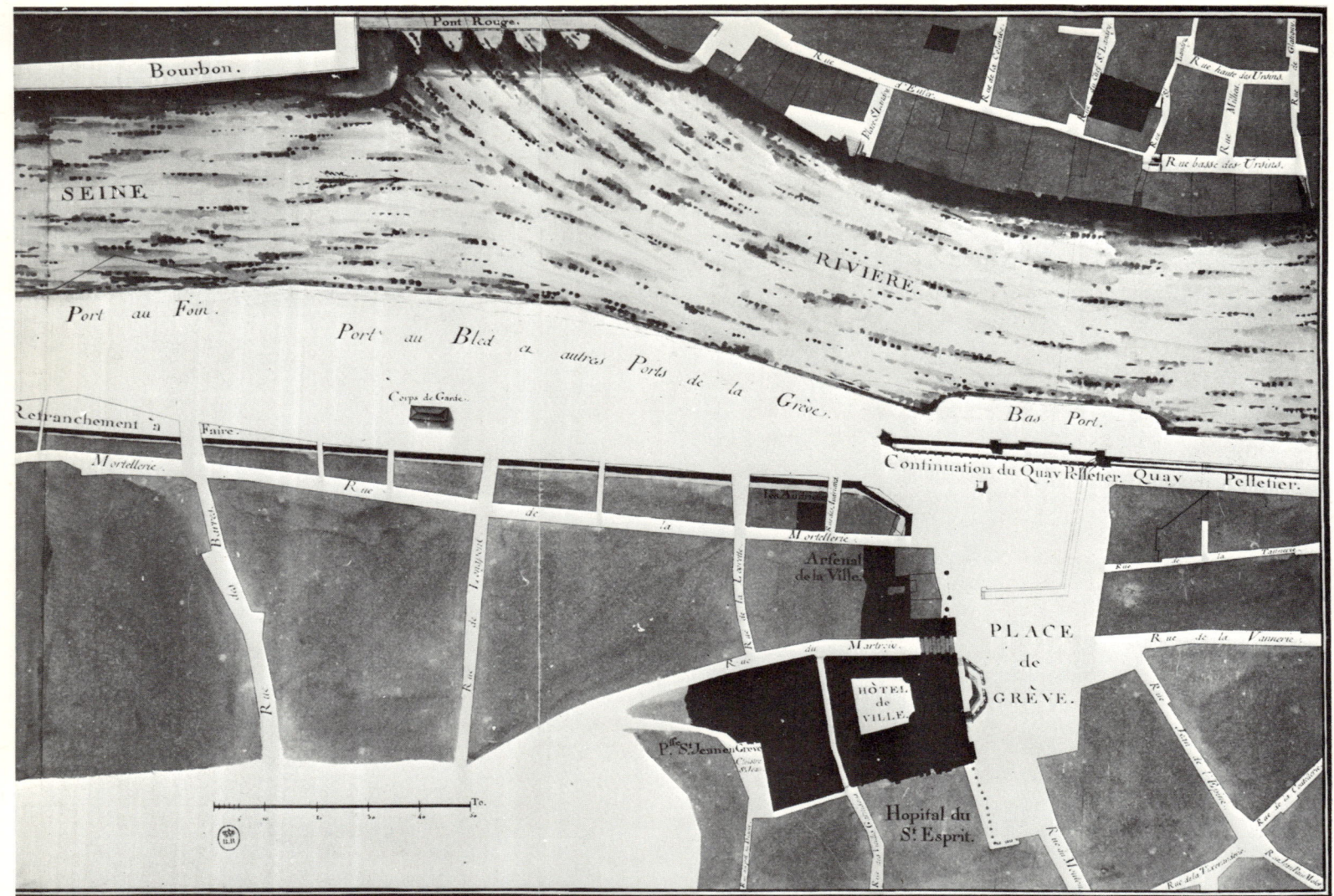

of the famous family of architects.

At a slightly later period the architect Combes designed monumental plans for the development of the harbour of Bordeaux, designs which were reproduced by the Brothers Varin in 1785. Here again the combination of utility and vision is characteristic and impressive.[14]

An important engraving, a plan of Paris of 1788, included numerous embellishments, and that only just before the outbreak of the Revolution. It was not the work of an architect or town planner, but of the famous *Géographe du Roi*, Brion de la Tour. It shows the walls, although incomplete, as projected by the *fermiers-généraux*, to facilitate the collection of tolls at certain check points. Their outline is marked by avenues of trees, which are found in profusion on this plan. Some of the monumental toll houses, 'Propylæa', as Ledoux liked to call them, are included, as well as a plan for Versailles and the theatres of the new Comédie Italienne and Comédie Française.

Above
Plan for the site of the Hôtel de Ville, Paris. Cabinet des Estampes, Bibliothèque Nationale, Paris.

See illustration on page 34, above

Right
P.-L. Moreau, plans for the site of Ste Eustache, Paris. Cabinet des Estampes, Bibliothèque Nationale, Paris.

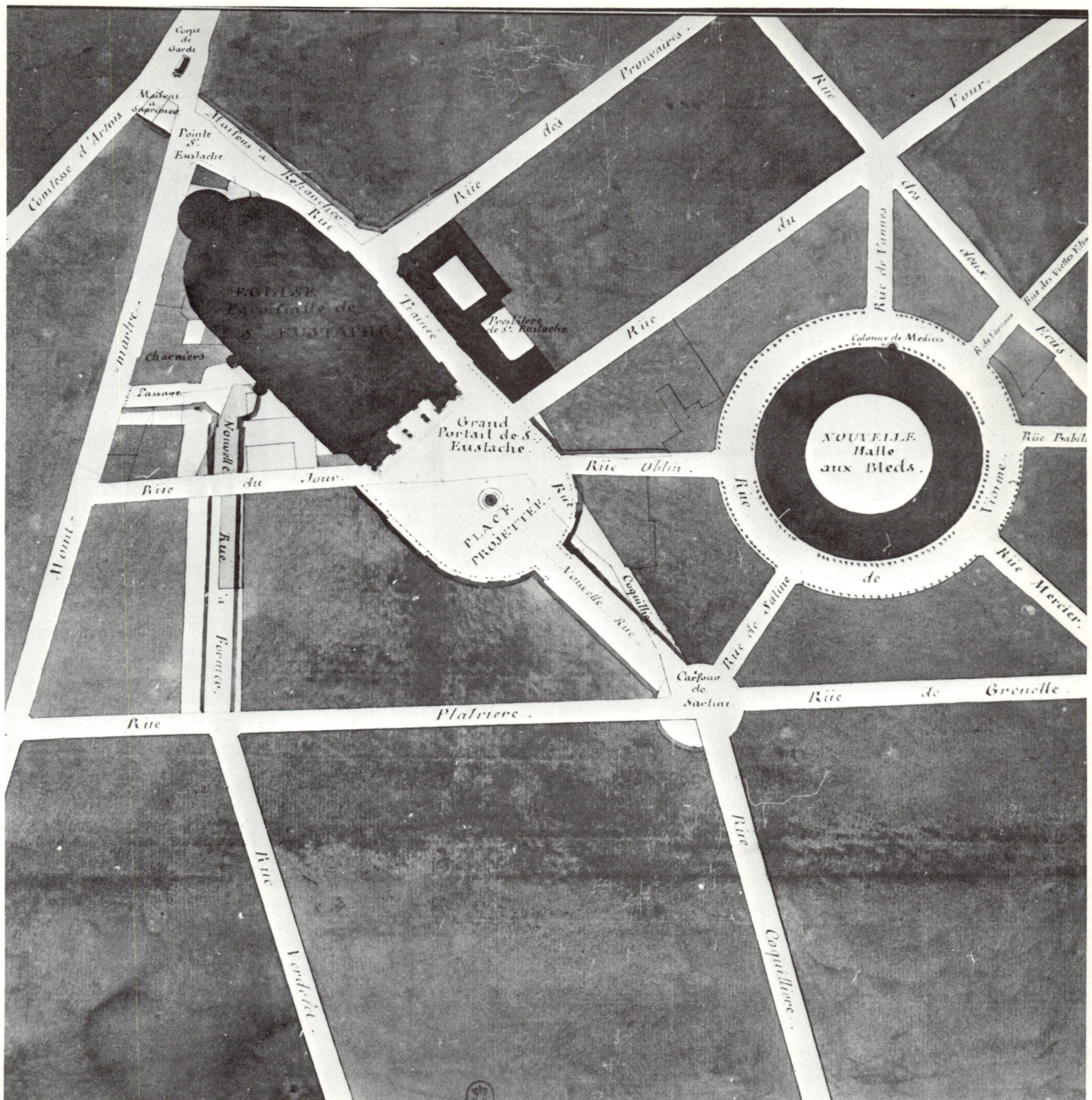

c

Combes, Bordeaux Harbour; Municipal Archives, Bordeaux. By kind permission of M. Lavisseau, Archiviste Municipal.

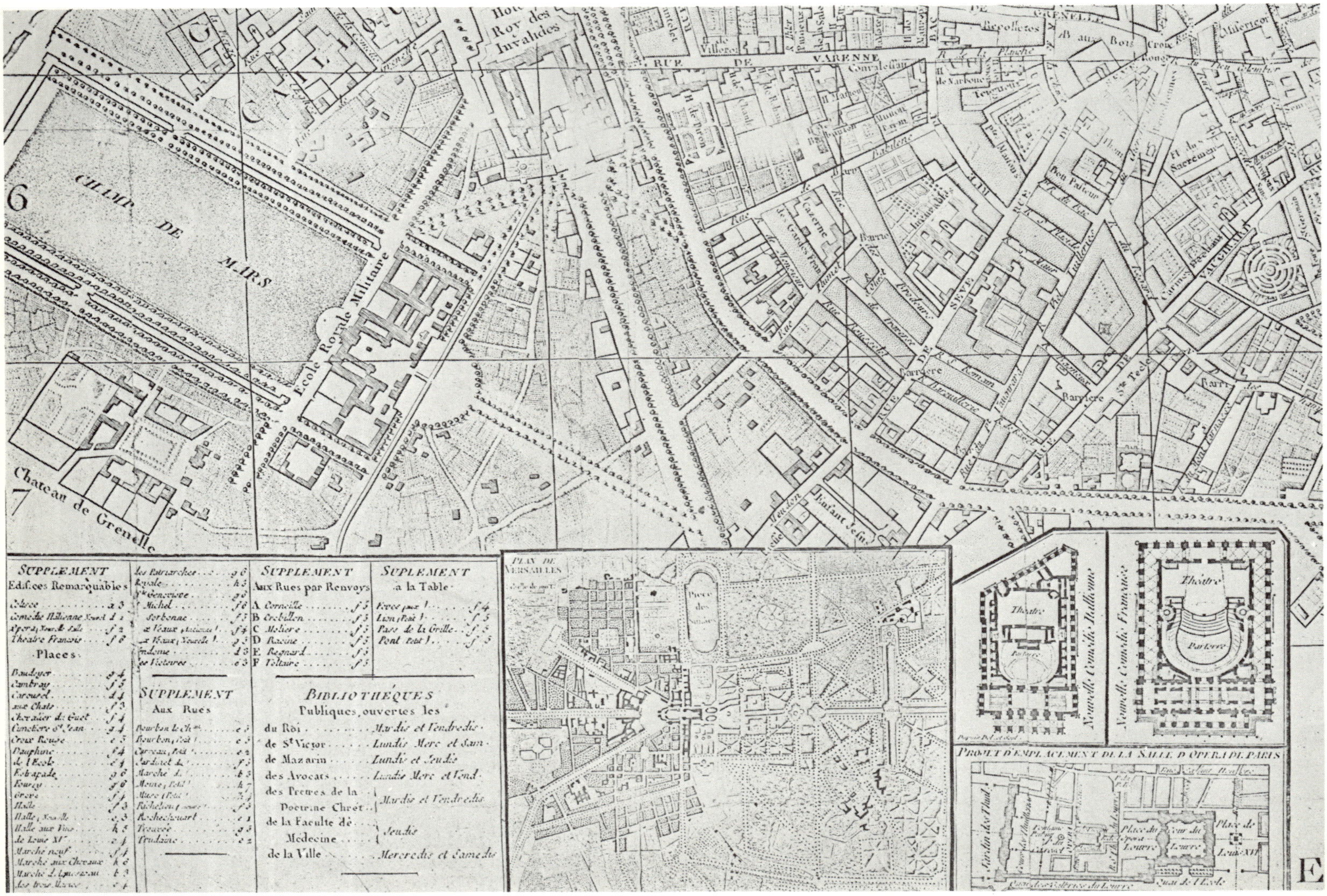

Brion de la Tour, plan of Paris. Map Room, British Museum, London.

The *plan des artistes*, compiled during the Revolution, continued this tradition,[15] and even in the Napoleonic era the late 18th century lay-out persisted. A palace for the King of Rome, Napoleon's small son, was drawn up by Percier and Fontaine for the Mount of Chaillot, a plan which included an additional town development to accommodate the service quarters. This plan was partly indebted to Baroque inspiration, more so than the suggested designs for uniting the palaces of the Louvre and the Tuileries. These went back to schemes for a Place Louis XVI, and culminated in a project by Baltard, which included a circular 'Odeum'. In this field, as in so many others, the Empire in its glorification of the Emperor, represents the negation as well as the fulfilment of the Age of Enlightenment.[16]

In this context a remarkable set of drawings for a 'Cité Napoléon' by Huvé should be mentioned. These drawings of about 1800 – previously kept in the Kunstgewerbe Museum in Berlin, but now unfortunately lost – were initially

 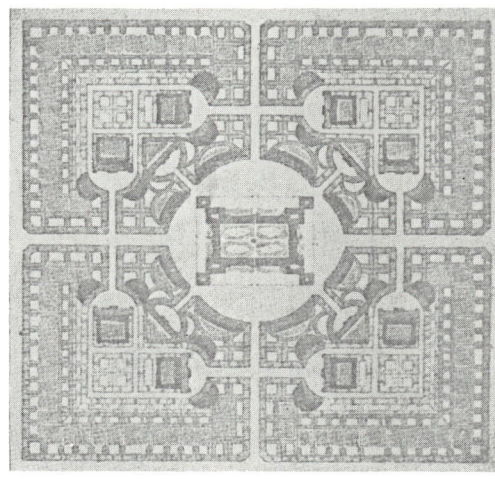

Huvé, plan of Paris; from Brinckmann's Stadtbaukunst.

discussed by A. E. Brinckmann.[17] They represented a sequence of squares, similar to Morelly's intentions in lay-out, and were, like his, intended to promote comfort, happiness and equality throughout the whole nation, according to the accompanying text. The work of E.-L. Boullée should also be briefly considered here. It is usual to reproach him for being a visionary, a mere designer of Utopian and unrealistic schemes. Like Beethoven, who continued composing after he had become deaf, Boullée learned to be satisfied with drawings rather than buildings. At any rate his seminal influence on disciples and pupils would presumably have been less had he concentrated more on pleasing patrons and erecting conventional buildings. His significance far transcends his interest in stereometric forms. He was careful to relate his projects to existing buildings, when required, and frequently used the measurements of these structures for his designs (*s'assujettir*, as he called it, which he regarded as a necessity).[18] He was equally careful in the siting of his projects, showing the Pointe Ste Eustache in Paris with its church in the background as a foil to his austere fountain, or the circular opera house set

against the Tuileries, thus contrasting the tall chimneys of the earlier building with his classical structure. Boullée's concern for *caractère* led him to an appreciation of historical continuity. He was also far-sighted in favouring regional planning, as is made clear in his *Essai* on the subject of the relationship between the capital and provincial cities, which in his opinion should be one of mutual assistance. He appreciated the structural qualities of the Gothic style and the pointed arch, as seen in his opera house, and understood the compactness of medieval structure as shown in his Fort and City Walls.

See illustration on page 11

36

Boullée, Fort. Cabinet des Estampes, Bibliothèque Nationale, Paris.

Boullée, City walls. Cabinet des Estampes, Bibliothèque Nationale, Paris.

INTÉRIEUR DE VILLE

It should not be forgotten that Paris was traditionally regarded as an enclosed city. The medieval walled enclosure had been maintained by François Blondel's fortifications and gates, and it also formed part of the improvement plan of 1676 by his pupil, Bullet. Indeed, the tradition of fortification led to the 6th *enceinte*, the wall facilitating the collection of tolls, started by Ledoux in 1785 and completed by Antoine just before the Revolution.[19] The enclosure was largely demolished at that time, in order to implement the temporary abolition of local tolls. How widely accepted the city boundary in the form of a wall had become, is reflected in the words of the writer on architecture, Sobry, who stated in 1776 that 'a town without a wall is not a town'.[20]

By contrast, the evolution of modern London as an open city developed through natural rather than through man-made causes. The Great Fire of

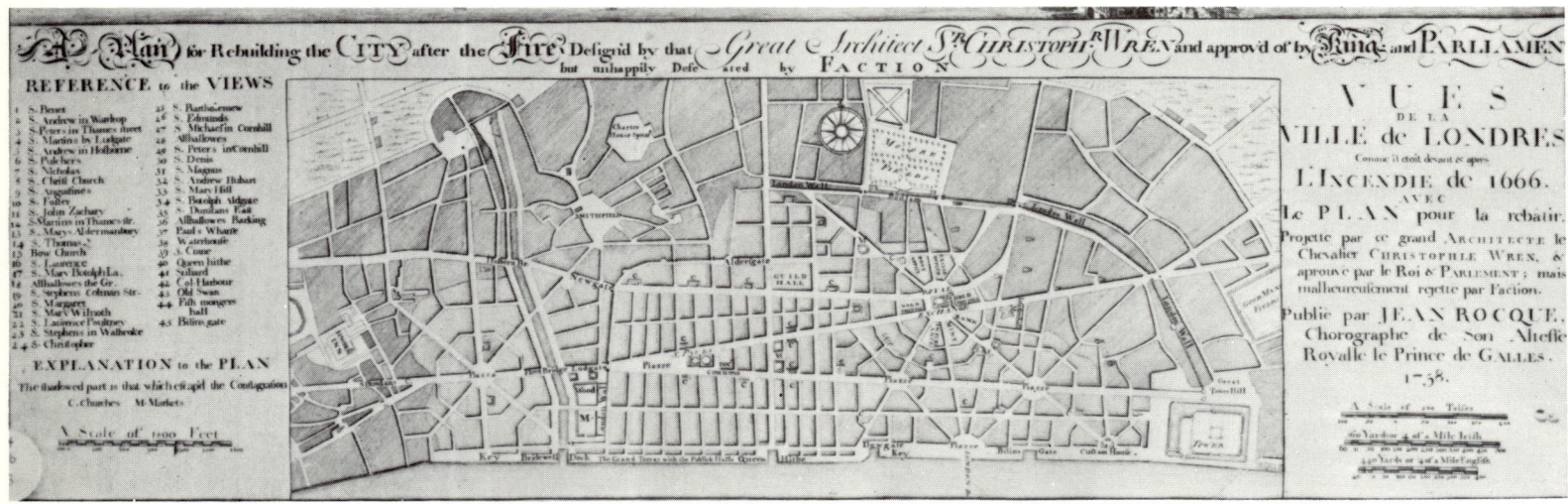

1666 led to the conception of Sir Christopher Wren's ambitious plan.[21] His vision of the city as a whole, based on a synthesis of French and Italian ideas, was rejected and thus failed to leave a lasting mark. John Evelyn, the writer, also produced a plan for the rebuilding of London. He had toyed with ideas of city design some years previously, especially in his *Fumifugium* of 1661, and also his assessment of Paris in *The State of France* of 1651. In the latter he contrasts the two cities, and his pithy description cannot be bettered: 'Paris is a city in a ring', its streets are as 'in some Italian opera'. Meanwhile, he deplores the 'exorbitant increase in tenements' in London. These were not luxurious apartment houses, but according to Evelyn, 'poor nasty cottages'.[22] He was concerned with the paving of the streets, at that time almost unknown in France, as is clear from Patte's *Monumens* and Mercier's *Tableau*, as well as a reference of 1781 to the pavements of the Rue de l'Odéon in Paris. Earlier pavements had existed on the Pont-Neuf, but they remained the exception. Social concern, practically expressed, is thus obviously an important element in Evelyn's work.

Two basic elements, clearly seen in Evelyn's plan, characterize the develop-

Sir Christopher Wren, plan for rebuilding the City of London after the Great Fire; published by Jean Rocque in 1738 (note French captions).

See illustration on page 29

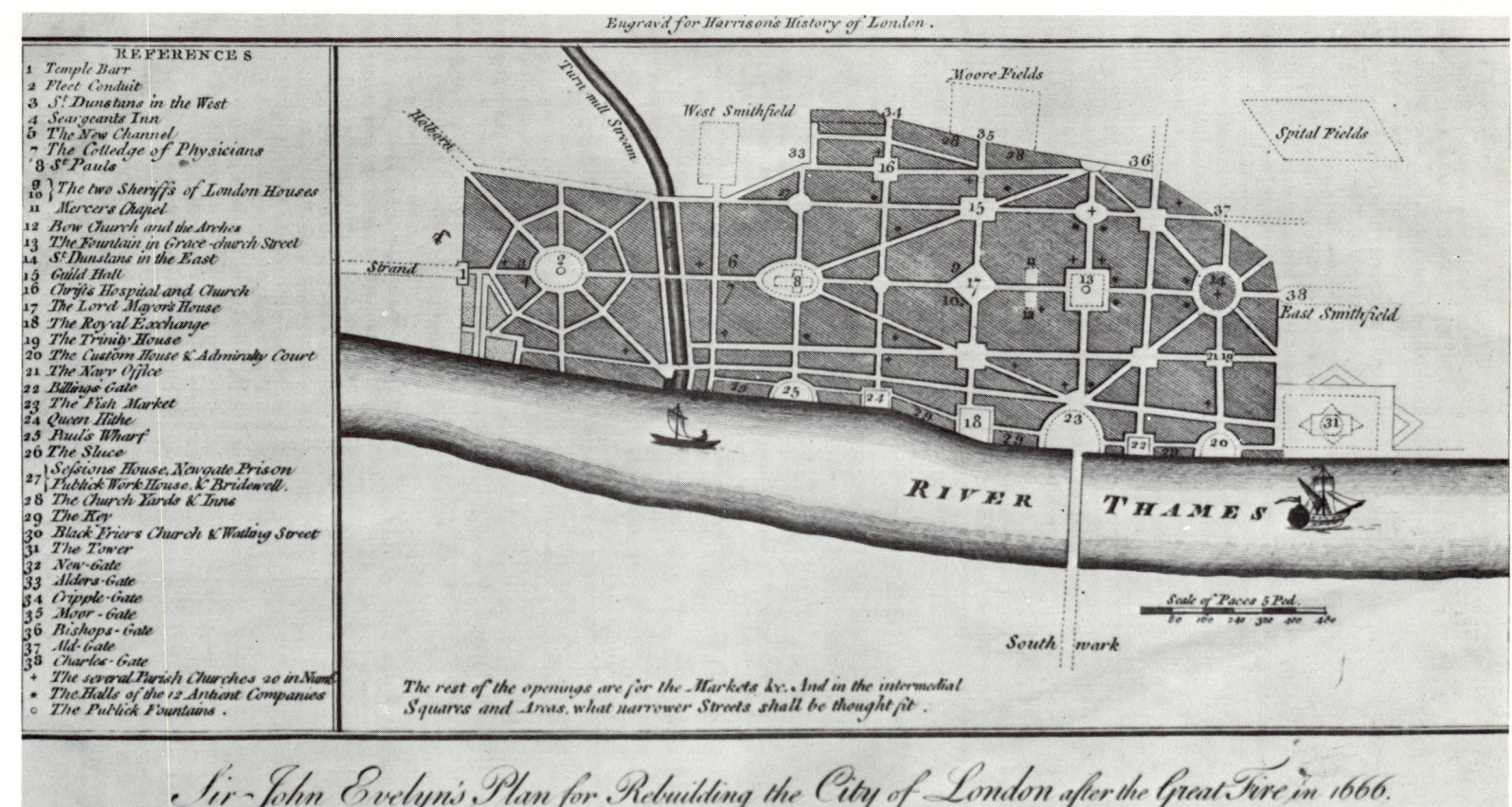

REFERENCES
1 Temple Barr
2 Fleet Conduit
3 S.t Dunstans in the West
4 Seargeants Inn
5 The New Channel
6 The New Channel
7 The Colledge of Physicians
8 S.t Pauls
9
10 } The two Sheriffs of London Houses
11 Mercers Chapel
12 Bow Church and the Arches
13 The Fountain in Grace-church Street
14 S.t Dunstans in the East
15 Guild Hall
16 Christs Hospital and Church
17 The Lord Mayor's House
18 The Royal Exchange
19 The Trinity House
20 The Custom House & Admiralty Court
21 The Navy Office
22 Billings Gate
23 The Fish Market
24 Queen Hithe
25 Pauls Wharf
26 The Sluce
27 { Sessions House, Newgate Prison
   { Publick Work House, & Bridewell.
28 The Church Yards & Inns
29 The Key
30 Black Friers Church & Watling Street
31 The Tower
32 New-Gate
33 Alders-Gate
34 Cripple-Gate
35 Moor-Gate
36 Bishops-Gate
37 Ald-Gate
38 Charles-Gate
+ The several Parish Churches 20 in Numb.
* The Halls of the 12 Antient Companies
o The Publick Fountains.

The rest of the openings are for the Markets &c. And in the intermedial Squares and Areas, what narrower Streets shall be thought fit.

Sir John Evelyn's Plan for Rebuilding the City of London after the Great Fire in 1666.

ment of London: the tradition of a planned lay-out – an inheritance from the Romans which still influenced the medieval city – and an agglomeration of villages surrounding it, and eventually amalgamated within it. Rasmussen stressed the latter element, the coalescence of small units, thus overlooking the fact that a residue of planning remained untouched through the centuries, and was revived and enlarged from the 17th century onwards.[23] Equally one-sided is the opinion of Olsen, who emphasized the unplanned elements in Paris, especially its medieval core, whilst stressing the regular evolution of the London squares, and overlooking the Paris *places* as centres of a planned environment.[24]

The lay-out of Paris remains comparatively simple, a medieval core, with formally planned later additions. London is more complex,[25] being based on two contrasting principles, the 'village sequence', and the regular plans as found in the Adams' Adelphi and Nash's sweep of Regent Street. Earlier, in 1766, John Gwynn (?–1786) suggested improvements for London and Westminster.[26] These were based on the introduction of a sequence of squares, which transformed the irregular pattern and led to the creation of new quarters, changing 'useless' parts into 'elegant' and 'commodious' ones, by removing Bethlem Hospital from Moorfields, for example. His taste was classical, and anti-Gothic, so he wished Westminster Hall to be entirely destroyed. He placed

John Evelyn, plan for rebuilding the City of London after the great Fire; from Harrison's History of London.
Note: *despite the original caption, Evelyn was never knighted.*

A. B. Hayward, Adam's Adelphi Terrace before 1872 (detail). Royal Institute of British Architects, London.

John Gwynn, plan of London (detail); from London and Westminster Improved.

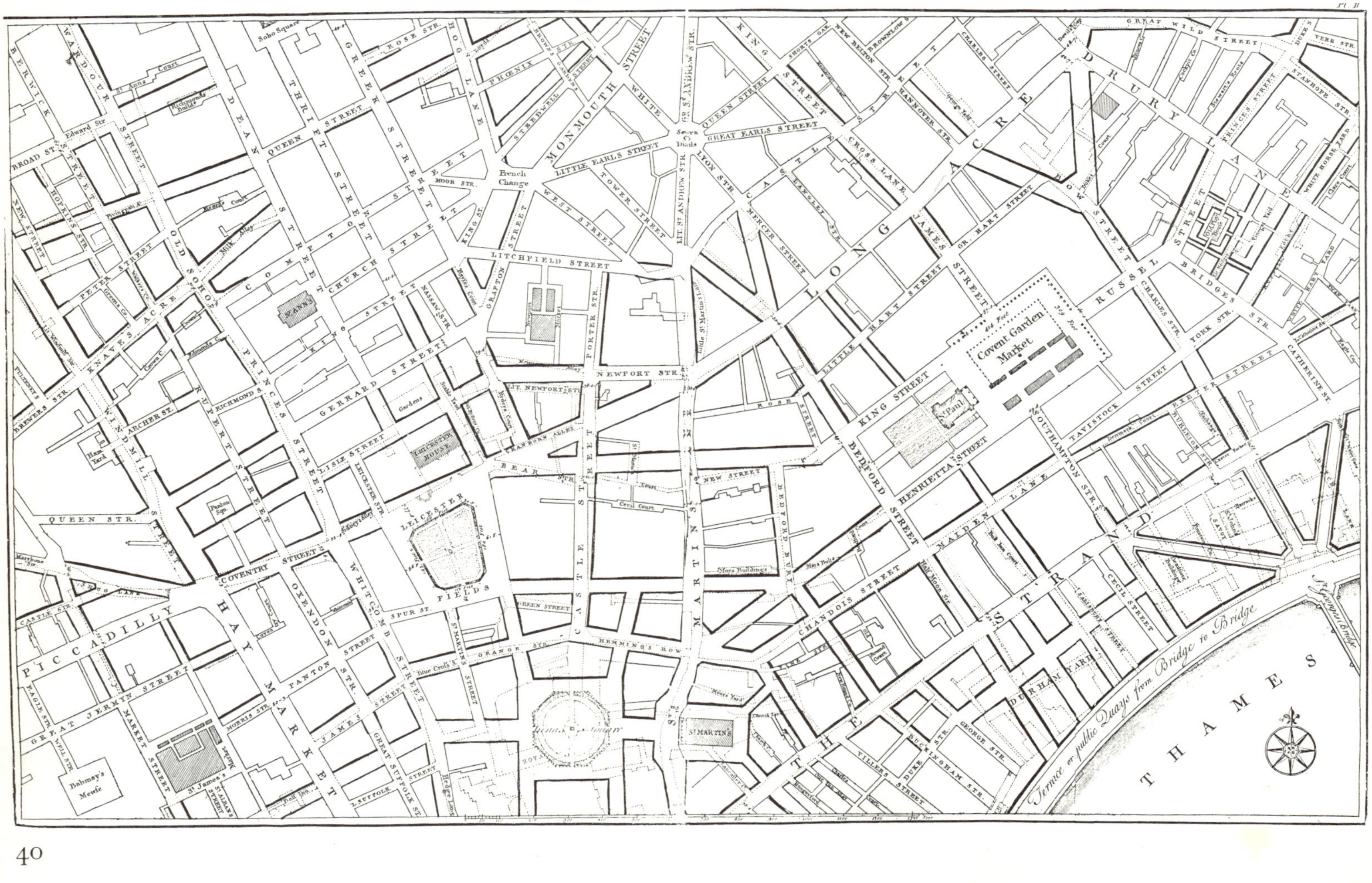

considerable importance on bridges and their approaches through regular *places* and wide unencumbered streets, in the French manner. Although his references to French art go back mainly to Louis XIV and his circle, it may nevertheless be assumed that he knew the work of the Abbé Laugier, whose influence appeared in the emphasis on a tidy lay-out. While Gwynn wanted wide streets for the dwellings of the rich, smaller spaces were also necessary for the habitations of the 'useful and laborious people'. His ideas emphasize the danger of what in modern parlance is described as zoning, pointing out that the poorer sections of the community, if separated, would be less industrious and less moral – a respectful view of the higher social orders totally at variance with the French critical attitude. Further, he feared that segregation could bring down the price of private property.

He deprecated the appearance of London, a commercial rather than a metropolitan centre, as being unfit for a great capital. For this reason, Gwynn wanted not only a royal palace in a huge park, uniting Hyde Park and Kensington Gardens, but he also favoured plans for improving the poorer quarters of the city. Where the displaced inhabitants were to go, once the district was developed, was a thought which did not occur to him, nor indeed to most of his contemporaries. The answers to such problems were left to a later period.[27] Gwynn also suggested that the growth of London should be restrained, and that for this reason the residence of Royalty should not be entirely confined to the capital – a thought perhaps of a prophetic nature.

The lay-out of London squares remained regular during the late 18th and early 19th centuries, and, to quote Olsen, 'the conscious planning of the estate offices was more often directed toward functional than toward visual ends'.[28] In this context the Adam brothers' Adelphi and London squares deserve special mention, as they catered for the aristocracy as well as for the middle classes. Furthermore, J. C. Loudon formulated a theory advocating more variety in the planting of shrubs because 'the public squares of London are a general concern'. Private property was thus regarded as a public obligation, an unusual attitude at the time.[29]

The plans for the redevelopment of the Regent's Park area by John Nash (1752–1835) were outstanding, combining not only the park itself with encircling dwellings for the rich, but catering also for the less affluent. The plan itself showed similarities with Ledoux's Hosten Estate, a speculative venture designed only for the wealthy in Paris. This was to include an 'English landscaped garden', while Nash's plan was more formalized, with a central ring in the inner grounds, reminiscent of the *Prix* designs of the French Academy.

Even more influential were the designs by Percier and Fontaine for the Champs Elysées, the Arc de Triomphe and the extension of the Rue de Rivoli. The most comprehensive and outstanding project was intended for Napoleon's infant son, the King of Rome. This consisted of a palatial residence, and a town connected with it, on the Mount of Chaillot. Here a comparison with the development of Regent's Park and Regent Street comes to mind. Although the formal differences with regard to the curving streets are well known, the use of circular and straight alignments shows a similarity of intention for city development on a grandiose scale. This is corroborated by statements made by the Prince of Wales, mentioned by Summerson, that it (the so-called

Marylebone plan) will 'quite eclipse Napoleon'. Another architect, James Elmes, refers to Percier-like interiors. It is also significant that Nash's partly executed plan of 1812 for Regent's Park includes a full circle at the centre and the periphery, now halved as Park Crescent. The use of the word *guinguette* for the refreshment pavilion further strengthens the suggestion of French influence.[30]

G. Dance the Younger, designs for London Bridge. Sir John Soane's Museum, London.

Some French influence was also reflected in the designs for the region adjacent to London Bridge by the architect George Dance the Younger (1741–1825), the London City Surveyor. This dates from between 1796 and 1800. One crescent north of the river was to be centred on the Monument, by Sir Christopher Wren, the other on the South Bank was to include a monumental obelisk, a part of which can still be seen near the former Bethlem Hospital, now the Imperial War Museum.[31] One is strongly reminded of Louis Combes' plans for the harbour of Bordeaux. They were famous all over Europe, and admired, among others, by Arthur Young, the well-known writer and traveller. As Dance does not seem to have visited that city himself, it is probable that Combe's designs were known to him through the engravings of the Brothers Varin. The arrangement of boats in Dance's design is reminiscent of the work of another Frenchman, Horace Vernet, whose paintings had been such an important factor in the development of marine pictures. The formal French element in Dance's plan becomes more apparent when it is compared with F. M. Eden's project for *Porto-Bello*, the harbour of London, published in 1798, in which the utilitarian aspect is pronounced and formal considerations appear minimal.[32] The bridge itself, as seen in a sketch, was a

See illustration on page 34, above

Eden, project for the Harbour of London; from Porto-Bello.

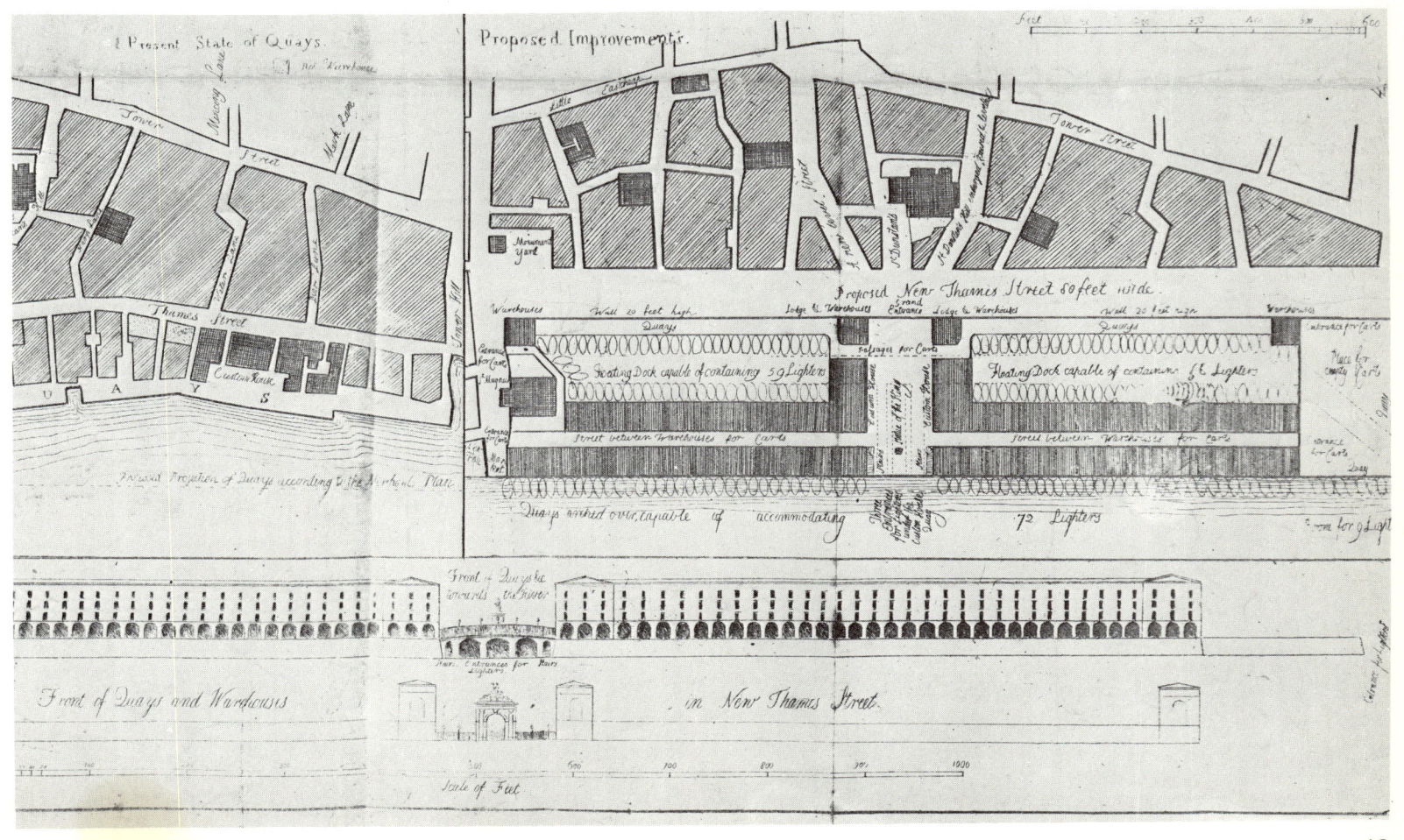

double drawbridge, intended to allow unimpeded passage to ships and traffic, as one part could be open while the other remained closed. This arrangement can be seen as an adaptation of a medieval concept to a functional and utilitarian purpose.[33] (The same principle has recently been adopted in dealing with transport problems in Bristol.)

A forerunner of Dance's scheme for the region of London Bridge can be found in his design for an engraving published in the *Gentleman's Magazine* of September 1786, which shows one monumental crescent, with a statue of the prison reformer, John Howard, as its focal point, the statue of the philanthropist thus taking the place of a traditional royal monument. However, the

View of a CRESCENT, as planned by Mr DANCE, and proposed to be built by Mr HEDGER in St Georges Fields, in Honour of Mr HOWARD.

project was abandoned on Howard's own wishes. Dance's scheme for the Minories should also be remembered; it was planned on a small scale and adapted a prototype from Bath for a humbler purpose in an unfashionable district. Even more interesting perhaps is the spatial development of Alfred Place, two large crescents enclosing a narrower main street, thus assuring privacy for the inhabitants.[34]

Housing in London at that time was concentrated on the private house, whether for the upper or the lower middle classes, but without any clear theoretical ideas for housing the poor. In Paris the Portiques du Temple of 1781 by Pérard de Montreuil went a step further. Landon stressed that this could not be fully appreciated as a private development, because it catered for a number of people, nor was it a public venture, as it was intended for the private citizen.[35] In this manner the Portiques du Temple set the programme for future evolution. The building, now unfortunately destroyed, was a rectangle, with semi-circular ends, and included arcades for shops, topped by two storeys of small lodgings. By contrast, the Hosten Estate by Ledoux and the *immeubles de rapport* mentioned above were speculative efforts, without a

G. Dance the Younger, design for a Crescent, including John Howard's Monument; from Gentleman's Magazine. British Museum, London.

See illustration on page 27

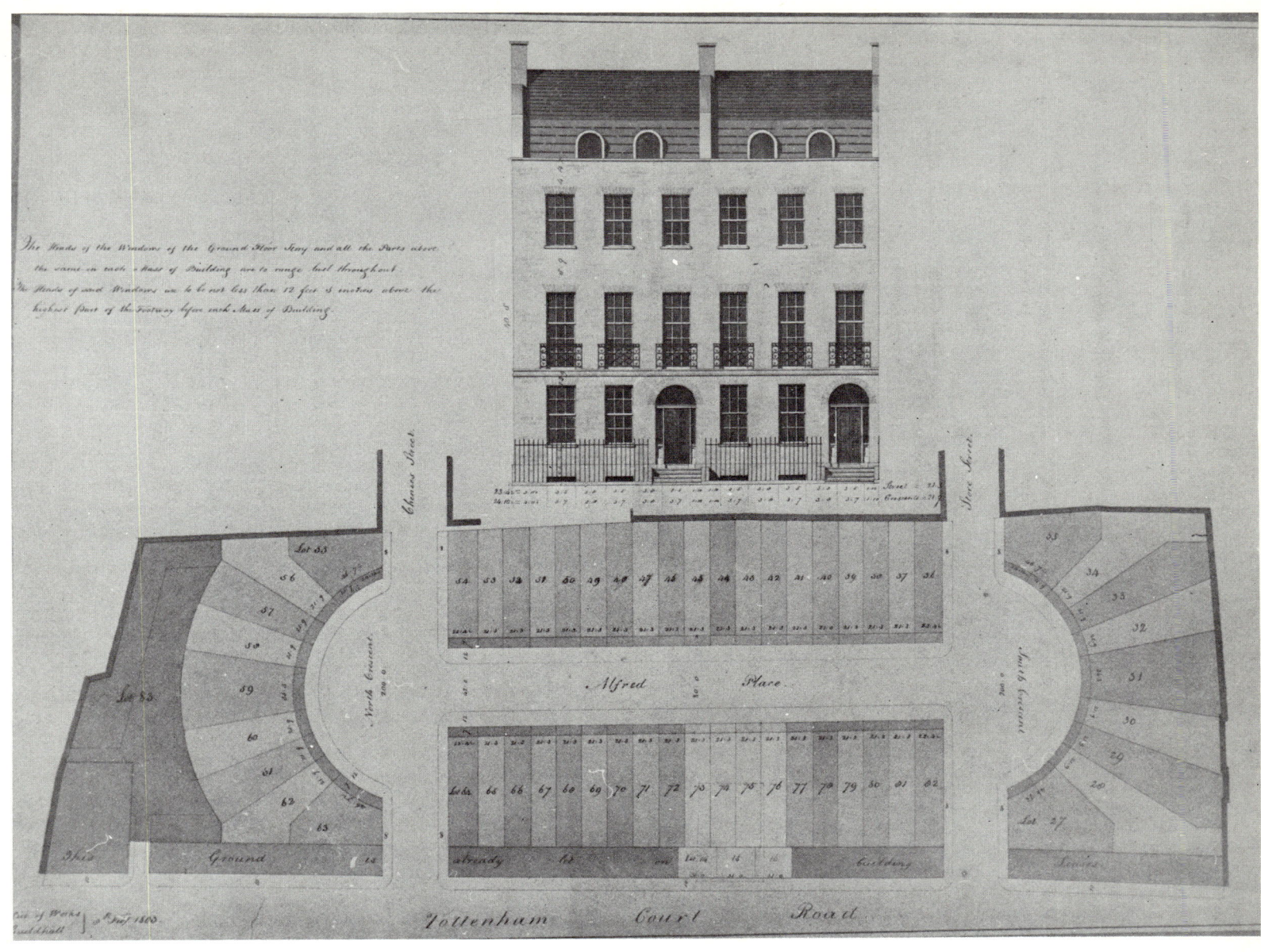

precise social aim and therefore only of marginal interest to us. It is in the Utopias that a more clearly defined social purpose appears, and they will be discussed later.

Ledoux's plans for Chaux have aroused much speculation, although his projects, including the oval plan, with their scanty provision for the housing of workers, were by no means particularly revolutionary or forward looking in a period when the new towns of Carouge and Versoix were built. Rooms to sleep four, and a communal kitchen, were the only amenities provided. Joseph Michael Gandy (1771–1843), of Huguenot descent, was influenced by the French tradition, particularly in his *Designs for Cottages* published in

G. Dance the Younger, Alfred Place. Sir John Soane's Museum, London.

See illustration on page 15

45

1805, shortly after the publication of Ledoux's *Architecture*. Gandy included plans for cottages which, in their emphasis on circular regularity, outstrip the French in their own field. Although these designs were not executed, they testify to French influence and French taste. Ledoux's book was in Soane's possession, and therefore possibly accessible to Gandy.[36] Other possible sources were the *Prix* designs and the *Recueil* by Durand.

The social reformer Robert Owen planned for an 'Establishment' of 1,200 inhabitants, and based his lay-out on a square, a traditional form of secular planning in England. Fourier, as has already been mentioned, criticized this type of plan, reinforcing the impression that social reformers are frequently Philistines as far as the arts are concerned.

Fourier's gradualist approach has already been pointed out, but it is important to remember that his interest in architecture was genuine and of

See illustration on page 21

46

long standing, as stated in his *Sommaire du traité de l'association*, etc., of 1823, where he emphasizes that the first thoughts on the subject occurred to him thirty-three years before, that is in or around 1790. He was impressed by the unifying effect of the Boulevard des Invalides, and by two small *hôtels* in adjacent streets, the Rue Acacias and Rue N. Plumet. These statements are expanded in the Fourier manuscripts published in the *Phalange* of 1849; they refer to an earlier date, after the foundation of Washington and the rebuilding of Moscow after the Napoleonic wars, a date somewhere between 1791 and 1812. Here, under the heading of *garantisme*, Fourier criticized the monotony of planned cities, and the anarchy of unplanned ones, and demanded a new approach. His new town was to be provided with four walls, some of them decorated. The second of these was to include the suburbs. Building, he thought, should favour collective living by the erection of large as against small houses, in order to cater for some thirty families in one unit. Here is the starting point of a type of thought which led to the fully planned, palatial *Phalanstère*, destined to accommodate 1,600 to 1,800 inhabitants.[37]

Planning was not only concerned with the living, but the dead, too, and showed a growing interest in cemeteries and cenotaphs. In the work of Boullée and his contemporaries this shows their understanding of all aspects of human existence and is not a sign of pessimism. On the contrary, it reveals an awareness of the fullness of life, transcending death. Indeed, Diderot, at an earlier period, especially in his correspondence with the sculptor Falconet, stressed an optimistic view, suggesting that the esteem of posterity could become the mainspring of cultural and artistic creation, thus replacing belief in the survival of the individual soul. This striving for, and belief in immortality through cultural achievements, left Falconet sceptical and incredulous, but Diderot's convictions remained unaltered.[38]

In the *Essay on Sepulchres* of 1809, by the famous anarchist William Godwin (1756–1836), French and English attitudes are combined in an optimism similar to Diderot's. Contemporary taste in cenotaphs favoured monu-

Boullée, Monument. Cabinet des Estampes, Bibliothèque Nationale, Paris.

W. Wood, Monument; from An Essay on National and Sepulchral Monuments.

mentality, as seen in Boullée's work and the monument in the form of a pyramid by William Wood, published in 1808. Godwin suggested simpler structures, of a more rural character, in fact rather in the English picturesque manner. In spite of this, his approach was rational, advocating an all-embracing plan, financed by subscriptions, for the erection of funerary memorials. They were to be run up cheaply, in timber, and not in expensive forms, such as pyramids. Here Godwin probably implied a criticism of French and English neo-classical architecture and sculpture. He countered objections by demonstrating the importance of history in the life of the nation: just as libraries were necessary, so were monuments to the dead, as mementoes, because, according to Godwin, 'man should be a virtuous and honourable creature' through study of the past. A map, 'the Atlas of those who have lived, for the Use of men Hereafter to be born', was to contain all the required monuments. It is significant that it is a collective, rather than an individualistic view which finds expression here, and this from a man who is usually regarded as the protagonist of an unrestrainedly personal approach.[39]

To sum up, it may be suggested that the theoretical basis of planning was more significant in France, but that social concern in England gave English planning equal historical importance. Neither country was a spiritual island in the late 18th and early 19th centuries.[40] In spite of political rivalries and wars, close contact was maintained, and the mutual influence exerted by one centre on the other was not only significant architecturally, but fostered the creation of a truly European style and consciousness.

1. M. Dumolin: *Etudes de topographie parisiennes*, 1st ed., 1929, *passim*. P. Lavedan, *Histoire de l'urbanisme*, Paris 1941, etc. Also P. Lavedan: *French Architecture*, 1956, *passim*. (Pelican books.) French original, Paris 1944.
2. M. Gallet: *Demeures Parisiennes*, Paris 1964, pp. 77 ff.
3. *The Ideal City*, pp. 78 and 88, and *Prix*, *passim*.
4. *Colvin*, p. 153.

5. N. Pevsner in *Architectural Review* XCIII, 1943, and *Studies in Art, Architecture and Design*, London 1967, pp. 18 ff.

6. F. M. Eden: *The State of the Poor*, I, 1797, pp. 553 f. and *passim*.

7. *Hautecoeur* IV, *passim. The Ideal City*, pp. 75 ff. and 108.

8. E. Frisch, Count de Fels: *Jacques-Ange Gabriel*, Paris 1924.

9. J. Gondoin: *Description des Ecoles de Chirurgie*, Paris 1780.

10. [M. A.] Laugier: *Essai sur l'architecture*, 1st ed., Paris 1753, p. 259. This point is not considered in W. Herrmann's important monograph: *Laugier and 18th Century French Architectural Theory*, London 1962.

11. P. Patte: *Monumens érigés en France à la gloire de Louis XV*, Paris 1765, 2nd ed. 1767.

12. J. Stern: *A l'ombre de Sophie Arnould, F.-J. Bélanger*, Paris 1930, I, pp. 130 f.

13. G. Bardet: *Naissance et méconnaissance de l'urbanisme*, Paris 1951, *passim*. The Moreau drawings are kept in the Cabinet des Estampes of the Bibliothèque Nationale.

14. *The Ideal City*, p. 75. *Hautecoeur* IV, pp. 148 f. On Combes, Professor G. Pariset in *Annales du Midi*, 76, 1964, pp. 543 ff. I wish to record my appreciation for the help given by him and M. Avisseau, the Municipal Chief Archivist, during my stay in Bordeaux. cf. A. Young in *Travels in France*, ed. by C. Maxwell, Cambridge 1929, pp. 58 ff. 'I have seen a design of the square and the streets.' The engraving by the Brothers Varin is dated 1785.

15. A good description of the *plan des artistes* and other 18th century plans for Paris are found in J. W. Simpson: *Essays and Memorials*, London 1923, pp. 75 ff.

16. L. P. Baltard: *Mémoires sur la réunion du Palais Impérial des Tuileries et du Louvre*, Paris 1811. The first plan was for a circular orangerie, the second for a circus or *place d'armes*, a long oval, open-ended on one side, similar to the circus reconstruction in *Boullée* (pp. 71 ff.), the third an *odeum* with a painted portico on the side of the Tuileries. cf. M. L. Biver: *Le Paris de Napoléon*, Paris 1963, and *Pierre Fontaine, premier architecte de l'Empereur*, etc., Paris 1964.

17. A. E. Brinckmann: *Stadtbaukunst*, Berlin 1920, pp. 87 ff.

18. *Boullée, passim.*

19. G. Levallet-Haug: *C.-N. Ledoux*, Strasbourg 1934, gives valuable references as to sources. The literature on Ledoux is enormous. Among the first to appreciate his importance was E. Kaufmann, whose thought is summed up in his posthumous publication: *Architecture in the Age of Reason*, Cambridge, Mass. 1955; M. Raval and J.-Ch. Moreux: *C.-N. Ledoux*, Paris 1945, gives a handy survey of illustrations. For a fuller bibliography see the present writer in *Gazette des Beaux Arts*, March 1964, pp. 174 ff.

20. J. F. Sobry: *De l'architecture*, Amsterdam 1776, pp. 170 f.

21. E. F. Sekler: *Wren and his Place in European Architecture*, London 1956, especially pp. 58 ff. V. Fürst: *The Architecture of Sir Christopher Wren*, London 1956. *Wren Society*, especially vols. XII, pls. XXIV, XXV. *Town Planning Review*, X, 1923, p. 71; XIV, 1931, pp. 13 ff; XVIII, 1939, pp. 155 ff. T. F. Reddaway: *The Rebuilding of London after the Great Fire*, London 1940.

22. J. Evelyn: *The Miscellaneous Writings*, London 1825, pp. 351 ff., p. 92 f. J. Evelyn: *London Revived*, ed. by E. S. de Beer, Oxford 1938. J. Evelyn: *Fumifugium*, 1st ed., London 1661, an influential treatise. This same concern is still implied in Jane Loudon's *Memoir* on the life of her husband, J. C. Loudon, in: *Self-Instruction for Young Gardeners . . . with a Memoir* by his Widow, London 1845.

23. S. E. Rasmussen: *London the Unique City*, London 1937.

24. D. J. Olsen: *Town Planning in London*, London 1964, *passim* and p. 15.

25. J. Summerson: *Georgian London*, London 1945, and *Architecture in Britain, 1530–1830*, London 1953.

26. J. Gwynn: *London and Westminster Improved*, etc., London 1766, p. 103 and *passim*.

27. Such examples are the destruction of the village of Trianon, in order to build the Trianon de Porcelaine, or the ruthless destruction by Haussmann of the Paris slums. English landowners were rather more enlightened, as seen in the rebuilding of Edensor by the 6th Duke of Devonshire. cf. M. S. Briggs: *The English Farmhouse*, London 1953, p. 202 and *passim*.

28. Olsen, op. cit., pp. 16 f.

29. Loudon on London Squares in *The Literary Journal*, 1803, cols. 739 ff. and not col. 789 as indicated in the List of Contents.

30. *The Ideal City*, p. 102 f. *Prix, passim*. Biver, op. cit. *Le Paris de Napoléon*, pp. 327 ff. and *passim*.

31. See Chapter III, note 27.

32. F. M. Eden: *Porto-Bello; or a Plan for the Improvement of the Port and City of London*, London 1798.

33. The present writer in the *Journal of the R.I.B.A.*, 1947, LIV, pp. 502 ff. *Colvin*, pp. 165 ff.

34. *Summerson, passim*, and p. 124 f. *Gentleman's Magazine*, 1786, part II, pl. 1 and pp. 723 ff. See also J. Aikin: *The Life of John Howard*, Philadelphia 1794, p. 92 f.

35. *Prix*, pp. 20 and 173.

36. Gandy worked for Sir John Soane who possessed Ledoux's *Architecture*, so he could easily have seen it. cf. also *The Ideal City*, p. 104. *Gazette des Beaux-Arts*, 1964, pp. 173 ff.

37. On cottage architecture in England cf. S. Blutman in *Architectural History*, XI, 1968, pp. 25 ff. *Phalange*, 1849, pp. 18 ff. *Oeuvres complètes*, IV, p. 457 f. *Publication des manuscrits de Ch. Fourier*, Paris 1968. I owe a number of valuable suggestions to Mr. S. G. Pembroke.

38. Diderot: *Oeuvres Complètes*, ed. J. Assézat.

39. W. Wood: *An Essay on National and Sepulchral Monuments*, London 1808. On Godwin, cf. the distinguished and unsurpassed work by H. N. Brailsford: *Shelley, Godwin and their Circle*, 2nd ed., Oxford 1951, especially p. 17.

40. The European and international outlook is epitomized in Vaudoyer's *Maison d'un cosmopolite*, first published in the *Annales du Musée*, II, 1802, pp. 123 ff. also H. M. Fletcher in the *Journal of the R.I.B.A.*, 1935, pp. 774 ff. Kaufmann, op. cit., p. 185.

3
Hospitals

An increasing interest in hygiene and concern with disease developed in the late 18th century, based on the scientific study of infection. This development, however, did not proceed unhindered, as the medieval heritage frequently persisted in buildings and staffing arrangements. In England, voluntary and secular help played a large part in the care of the sick, whilst in France the emphasis remained on the religious orders, especially the Sisters of St Vincent de Paul: even during the French Revolution nursing by nuns was still permitted.[1]

The buildings, of a monumental nature, intended for charitable purposes were handed down to the 18th century. Especially notable are the Hôtel des Invalides in Paris built under Louis XIV, and the Hospitals for soldiers and seamen erected in London under Charles II, James II, and William and Mary.[2] The large late Medieval and Renaissance hospitals – these included not only institutions for nursing the sick, but new homes for the poor and infirm – were usually based on enclosed cloisters, with a commanding church either in the centre, or located towards the east. This style is still reflected in Philibert de l'Orme's ground-plan for an Hôtel-Dieu, reproduced in the rare posthumous editions of his *Oeuvre entière* of 1626 and 1648. However, the original text of his *Architecture* of 1567–8 already suggested an interest in hospitals. 'God willing . . . rich citizens, merchants, financiers and others . . . should immediately set about building and founding some hospitals or colleges to help the poor and for the public good, instead of erecting magnificent houses, which produce only annoyance and misfortune.' The appeal here is primarily to the wealthy, rather than to the King or the nobility.[3]

Traditional buildings proved unsatisfactory from the hygiene point of view and were superseded by experimental buildings, favouring pleasant location, privacy and fresh air, requisites which were considered essential, particularly for 'lunatics'. The concern for problems of health was fostered by the growth in city population and in consequence the increasing dangers of infection.[4] So physicians influenced not only the development of medicine, but also provided a significant impact on the evolution of architecture. These facts are recorded by J. R. Tenon, a physician and surgeon (1724–1816), who in his *Mémoires sur les hôpitaux de Paris*, published in Paris in 1788, made a complete survey of the problems involved and suggested improvements. His interest was centred on the Hôtel-Dieu, the oldest and most important hospital in Paris. Here fourteen wards were to be arranged in pairs, one side for male and the other for female patients, located along a main axis culminating in a monumental church.

According to Tenon, the foremost theorist of this movement, the best arrangement – the pavilion type – was found in England, especially in the Royal Naval Hospital at Stonehouse, near Plymouth. The institution was referred to as 'this noble hospital' in John Howard's book on *Lazarettos*. It consisted originally of a central building containing the chapel, surmounted by a turret. There were two pavilions on each side, to which a further six were symmetrically added along the main axis at a later period, all connected by an arcade. John Howard published a view and ground-plan of this hospital in 1784 in the third edition of his work on *Prisons*, and these buildings were then complete, although only eight were shown in the view accompanying

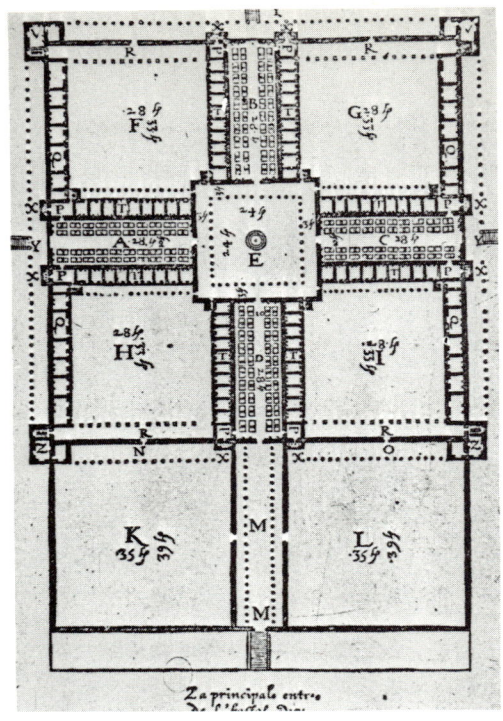

Philibert de l'Orme, Hospital; from Oeuvre entière.

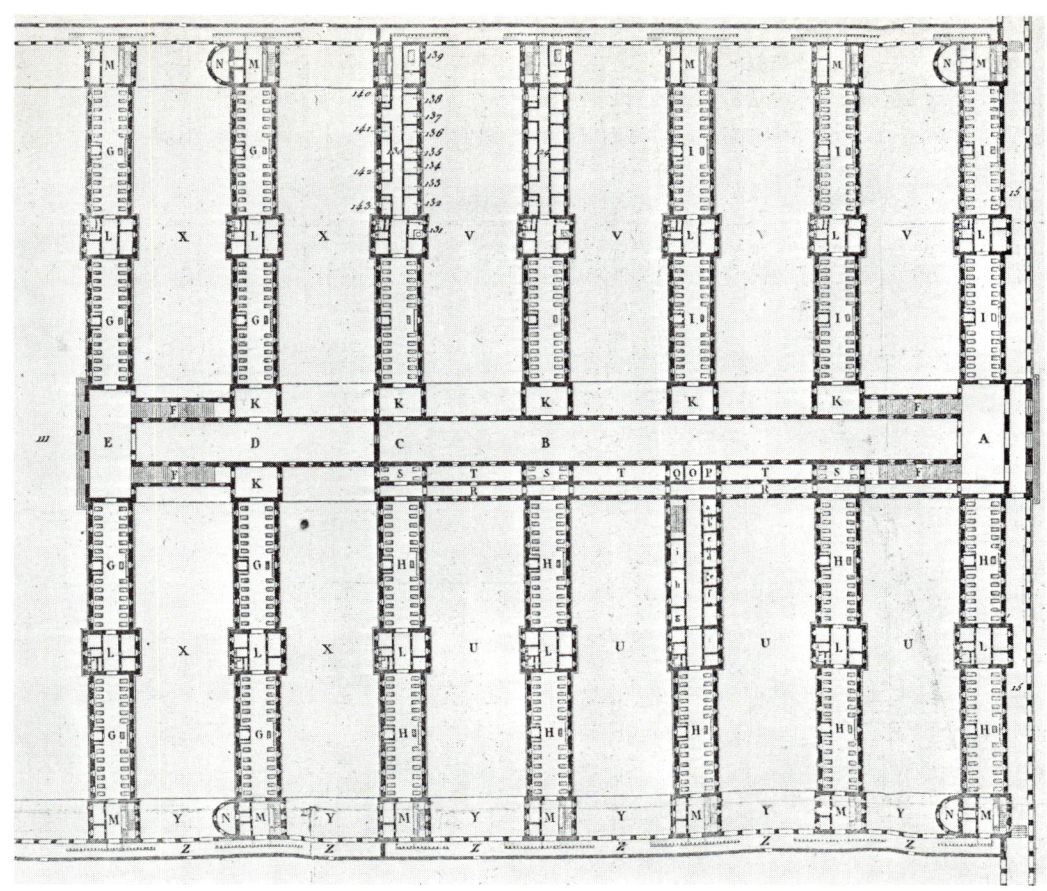

Tenon, Hospital for La Roquette; from his Mémoires.

The Royal Naval Hospital, Plymouth; from Howard, The State of the Prisons.

his text.[5] The arrangement in small units was presumably intended to diminish the risk of infection. The architect's name is uncertain, but according to Tenon, it was thought to be Rovehead; the overseer, according to Colvin, Rouchard or Ronchart.[6] The buildings were opened to patients in 1762. Tenon advised that in France also, hospitals should consist of separate pavilions, allowing for privacy, efficient nursing and ventilation. These were to be planned 'like the tents of a camp, or the pavilions at Marly', Marly being perhaps the most popular of Louis XIV's palaces.[7] This is an interesting

The Palace of Marly, after Rigaud.

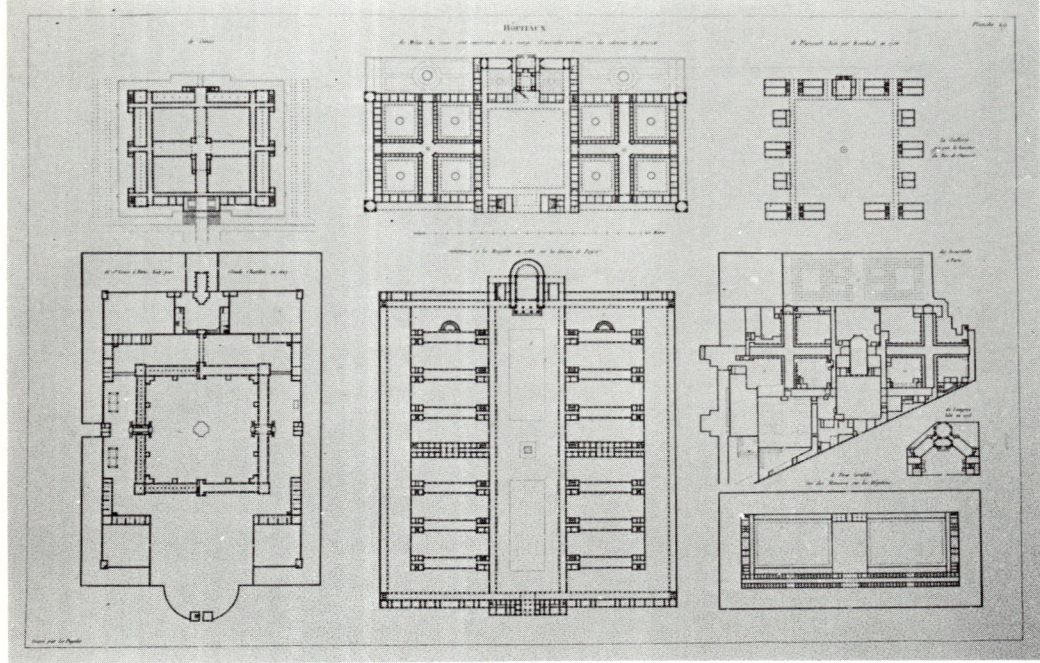

Survey of Hospitals; from Durand's Recueil.

example of the adaptation of a traditional structural type to a new purpose,[8] and was considered remarkable enough for the Plymouth Hospital to be included in Durand's *Recueil*. Tenon produced his own plan for a new hospital at La Roquette, in Paris, following the principles outlined above. The ground-plan was drawn by Poyet, who took account of the irregularities of the site whilst following his patron's requirements. He therefore located the chapel in a separate building, and thus was able to plan seven symmetrical wards in pairs along a main axis.

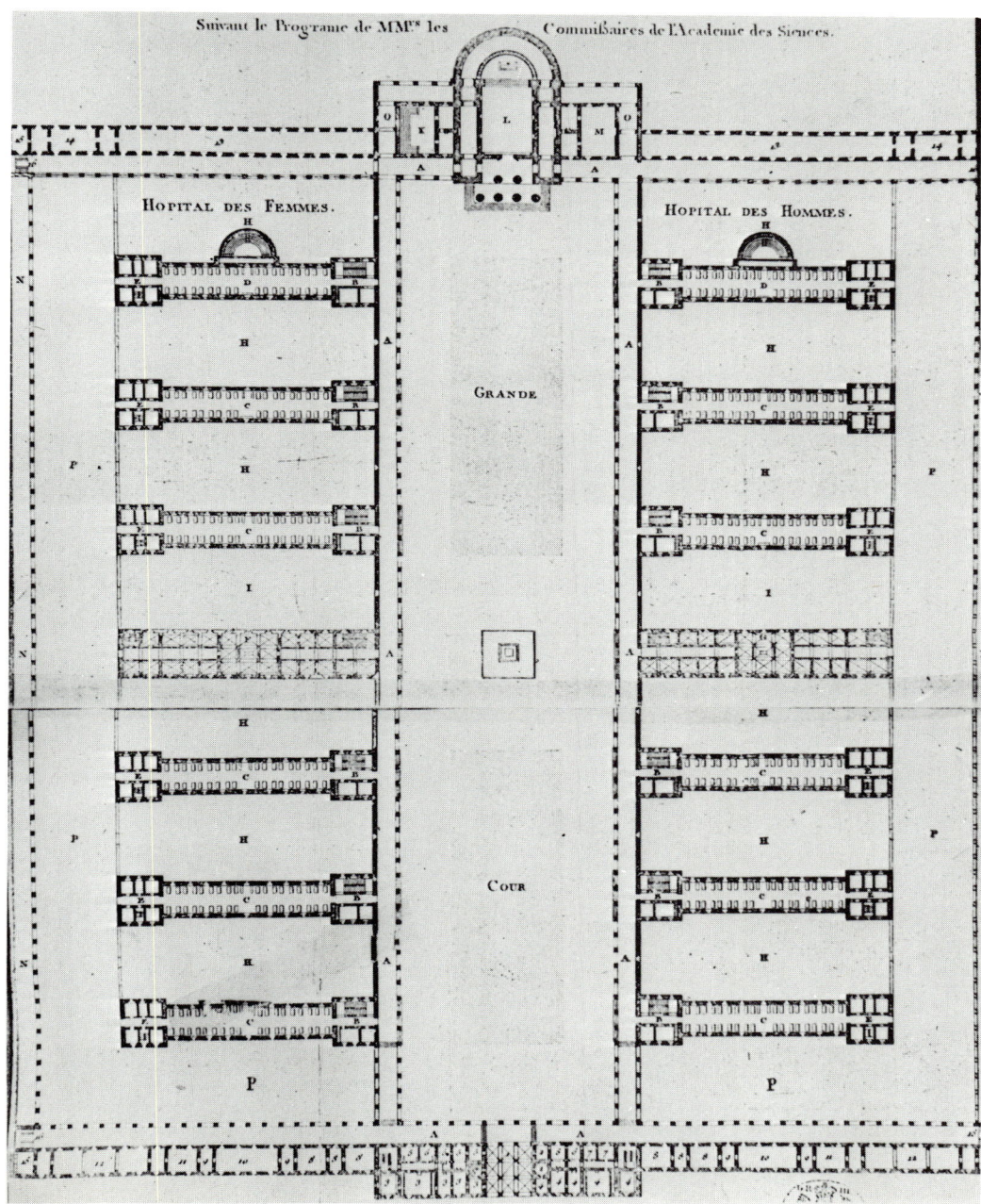

Poyet, Hospital plan; from Rapport.

Poyet also supplied a model design for the *Second Rapport des Commissionnaires chargés par l'Académie des projets relatifs à l'établissement des quatre hôpitaux* in 1786, of which the plan for La Roquette, inspired and published by Tenon, is an adaptation. The pavilion type is also seen in Charles-François Viel's project for the Hôtel-Dieu which he wished to transfer to the Ile des Cygnes. This design included individual ventilation shafts for each sick bay. Although the plans were published in 1787, Viel asserted that he designed them earlier, in 1780, that is one year before he became the architect

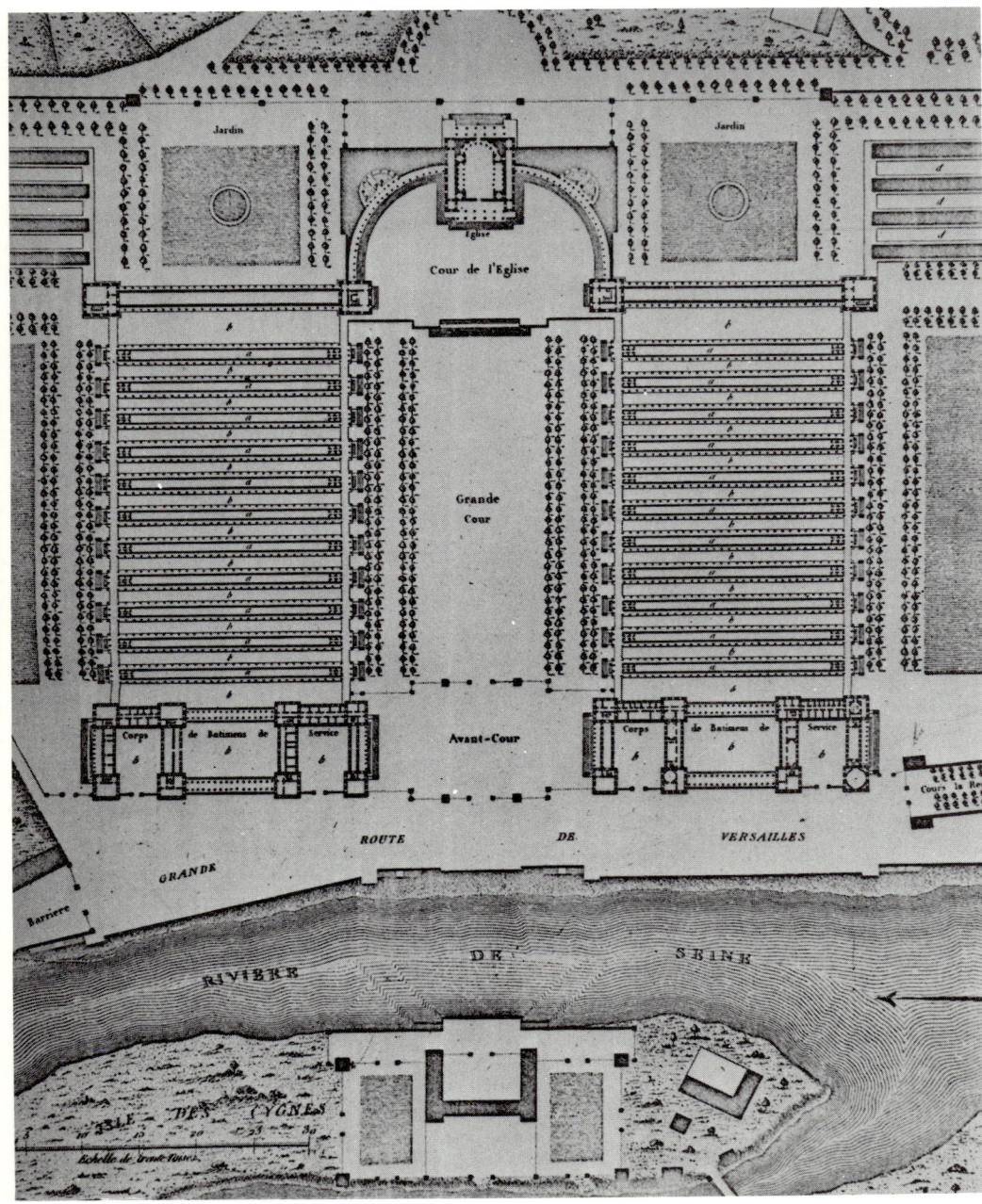

Viel, project for a Hospital, from Le Roy's Précis d'un ouvrage sur les hôpitaux.
This page: Site plan.
Opposite page, above: Plan and section of a single ward.

of the Hôpital Général, and earlier than Poyet's plans, discussed below. This claim seems unlikely, as Viel was more of a traditionalist than an innovator.[9]

Nicholas-Marie Clavareau (1751–1815), the official architect of the Paris hospitals, should be mentioned here. He was responsible for the new entrance to the Hôtel-Dieu of 1803, an impressive contrast to the neighbouring cathedral of Notre-Dame. His *Mémoire sur les hôpitaux civils de Paris*, published in 1805, includes an ideal plan for 2,000 patients, based on Tenon's programme of symmetrical parallel wards along a main axis. Clavareau's

Below left
Entrance of the Hôtel-Dieu, Paris. Photograph by Jacques Buchholz, Paris.

Below right
Clavareau, Hôtel-Dieu, Paris; from his Mémoire.

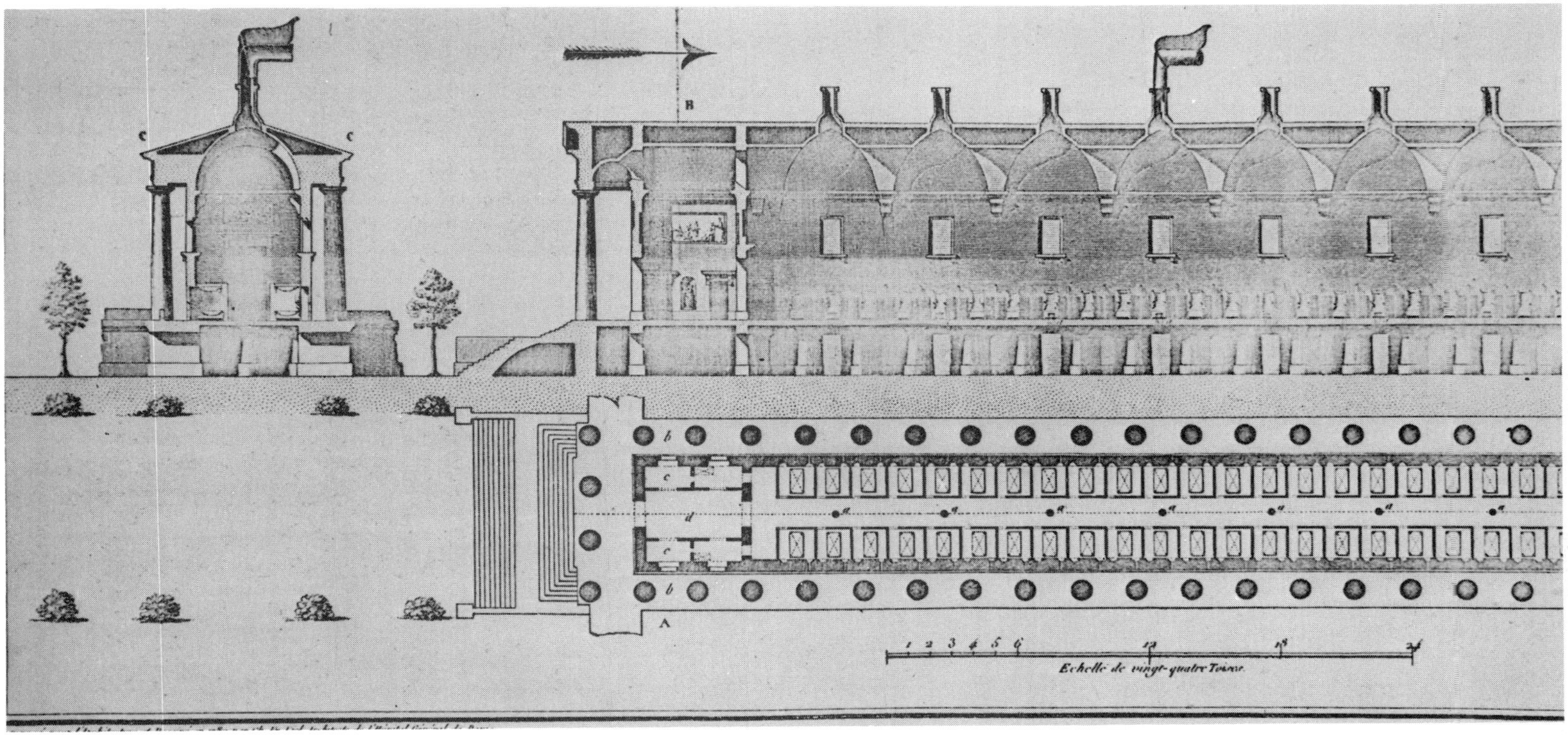

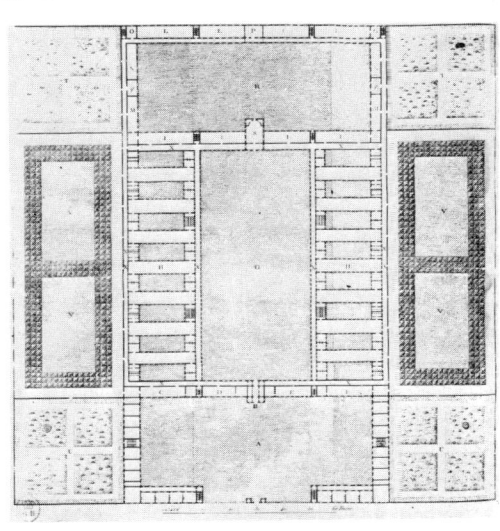

fame was such that he was invited to visit Russia, which he refused to do, although he was acquainted with England and Italy. He commented in his treatise on the humid conditions found in England, which necessitated the raising of the ground floor levels of hospitals. Clavareau advocated the building of hospitals in new townships, which were sadly lacking in this facility. It should be emphasized that hospital building in Paris was centralized under his guidance,[10] a marked contrast to the conditions prevailing in London.

The plans for hospitals and lazarettos found in the *Prix* designs followed the prototype of parallel wards. J.-Ch.-A. Moreau's Lazaretto of 1784 is exceptionally carefully sited within a landscape. By doing this, he followed a practice severely discouraged by the jury of the Academy who wanted the buildings to speak for themselves: they therefore demanded concentration on the purely architectural aspects of design.[11]

More revolutionary, if less influential, were the slightly earlier designs by the surgeon Antoine Petit (1718–94), one of the outstanding pioneers in hospital planning. When he published his *Mémoire sur la meilleure manière de*

J.-Ch.-A. Moreau, Lazaretto; from Prix.

construire un hôpital de malades in 1774, Petit was aware of the prevailing opinion in Paris, which was shocked by the insanitary conditions then in existence, especially at the Hôtel-Dieu. Furthermore, a fire there in 1772 had made the problems more pressing. Radical reform was necessary, according to him, and a new type of building was to be developed on a healthy and, if possible, hilly site, outside Paris. He pointed out that hospitals had previously had to be located near the cathedrals which provided financial assistance, while in his own period such establishments possessed funds of their own. He rejected a location proposed earlier by Patte, adjacent to the Seine at the Ile des Cygnes, in favour of the hills of Belleville, north-east of Paris, and, at that time, outside the city. For the sake of convenience, however, Petit wished to retain the equivalent of a casualty department in the centre of Paris.[12] Having discussed the importance of healthy air and a hilly site, in order to avoid infection, Petit proceeded to point out the two main principles on which, in his view, hospital building should depend: easy access and maximum accommodation for patients. For these reasons, a square lay-out was to be

Petit, Hospital plan; from his Mémoire.

Petit, Hospital elevation. Cabinet des Estampes, Bibliothèque Nationale, Paris.

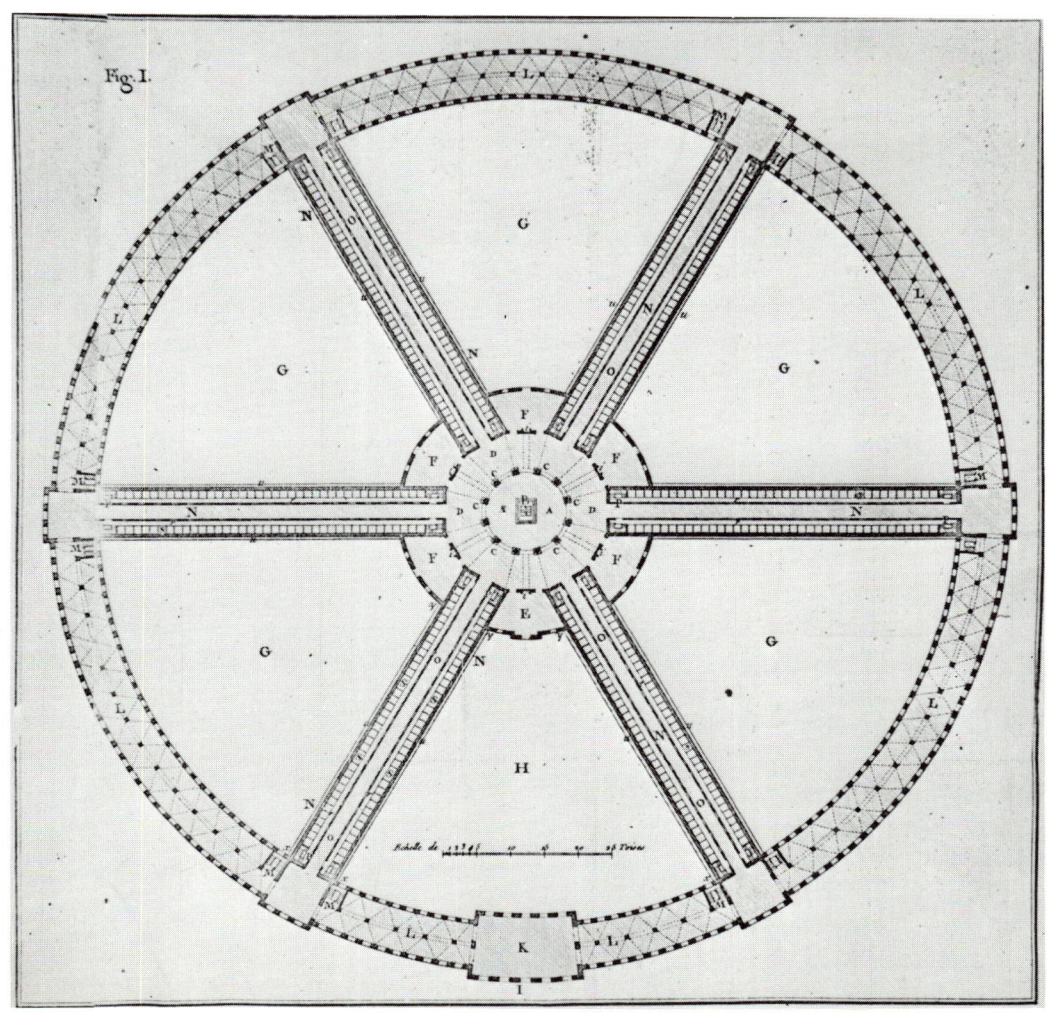

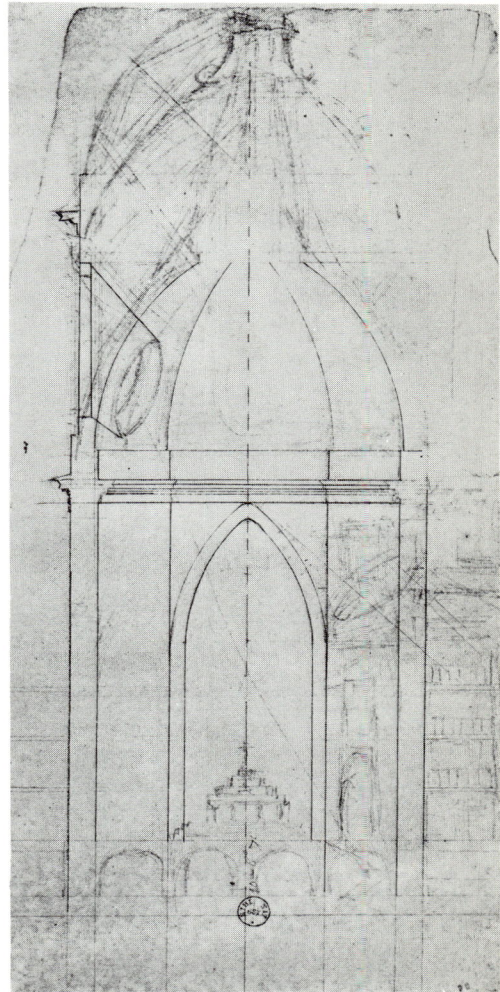

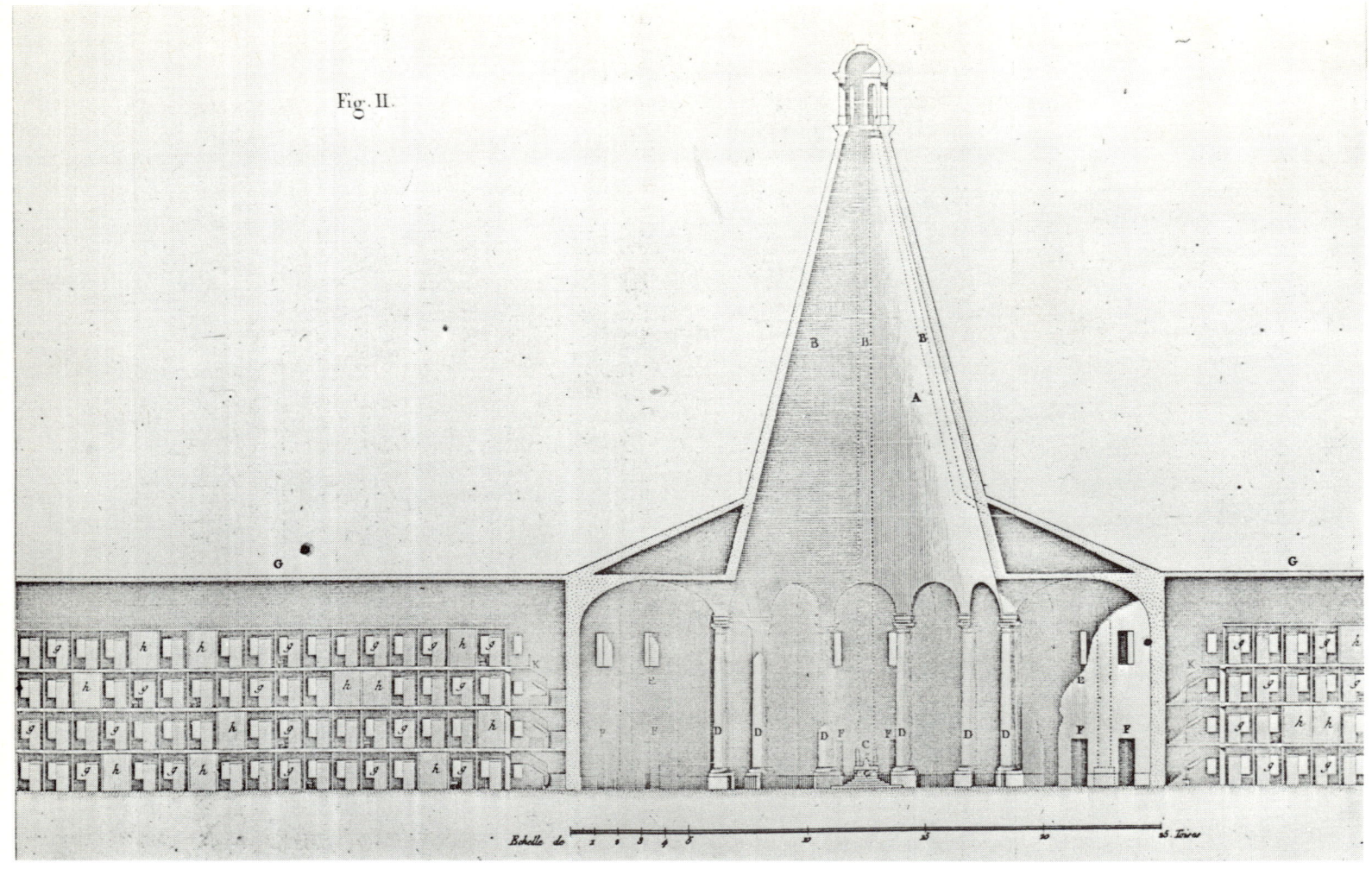

Fig. II.

Petit, Hospital elevation; from his Mémoire.

avoided as it wasted time and space and also made communications difficult. The arrangement was to be based on functional, rather than æsthetic considerations.

Petit advocated a circular plan enclosing six radial wings with a surrounding colonnade, and quoted the architect Prunneau de Mont-Louis in support of his views. A vertical central cone was to allow for satisfactory ventilation, and within it the chapel was to be housed. An alternative elevation of a Baroque design is found in the Cabinet des Estampes at the Bibliothèque Nationale.[13] The patients were to be protected from cross-infection by subdivision of the large wards, placed on four storeys: these were to be partitioned into small *loges*, with individual cubicles. The excrements of the sick were to be ejected out of the windows, into a drain at ground-level, a seemingly primitive, but all the same effective arrangement, allowing for the quick removal of contagious matter.

Petit was responsible for the basic design of the proposed hospital and his text was accompanied by engravings executed by Pierre-Claude de Lagardette,

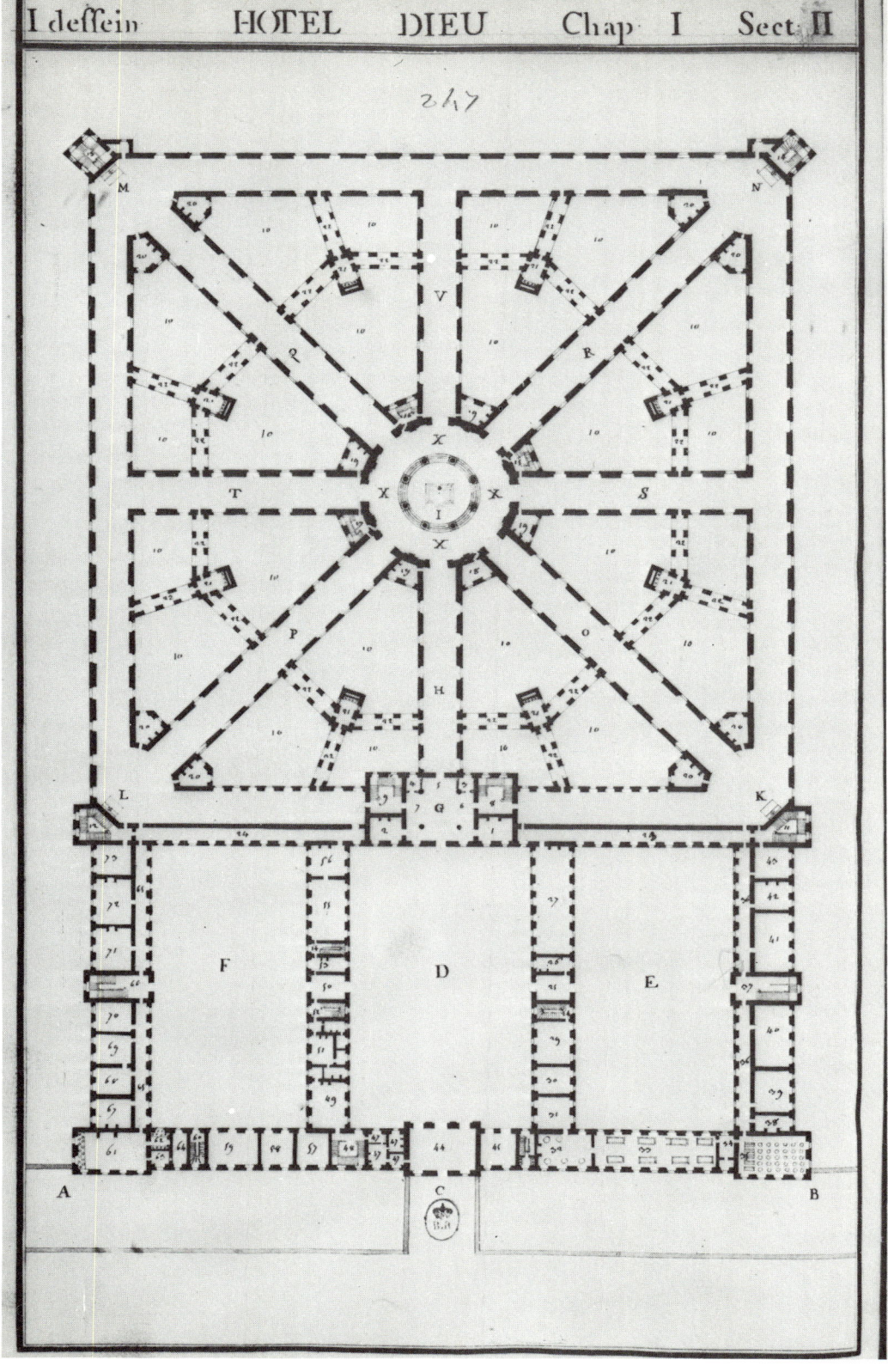

Desgodets, *plan for a Hospital. Cabinet des Estampes, Bibliothèque Nationale, Paris.*

engravings which clarified the project and added to its quality. Whereas the radial arrangement was Petit's own contribution, the colonnade was indebted to the Halle aux Blés. An earlier unpublished radial plan by Desgodets (1653–1728), now in the Bibliothèque Nationale, is based on the subdivision of a square, and includes four side-altars, as well as a central one. It was certainly unknown to Petit, but is mentioned by Tenon in his *Mémoires*.[14]

Although Petit's treatise failed to achieve popular recognition, his main points were successfully propagated by Claude-Philippe Coquéau, a versatile thinker, and his associate, the architect Bernard Poyet. In their *Mémoire sur la nécessité de transférer et reconstruire l'Hôtel-Dieu de Paris* of 1785 they imitated the circular plan, replacing Petit's six radial wards by sixteen, however, and eliminating the separate cubicles for patients, whilst retaining the chapel as a central feature. The surrounding colonnade was to be replaced by wards and the lay-out is therefore more cramped and less hygienic than Petit's spacious project.[15]

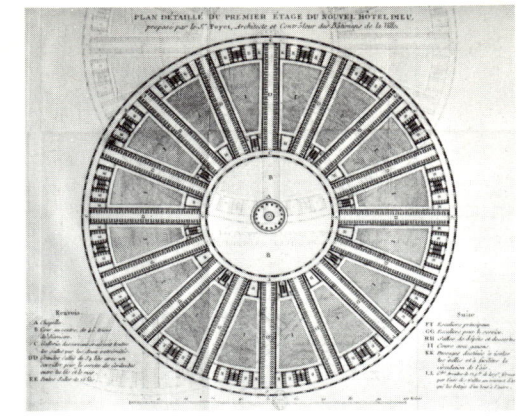

Poyet, Hospital ground-plan and elevations (below); from his Mémoire.

Vue perspective du nouvel Hôtel Dieu proposé par le Sr Poyet, prise du Chemin de Versailles.

Coupe en perspective de la Cour du centre et des Salles du nouvel Hôtel Dieu

Petit's hospital was intended for about 2,000 patients, Poyet's for approximately 5,000. This was not a sign of architectural megalomania, as suggested by Lemonnier as a characteristic of the period, but was due to an increasing awareness of the rising tide of population in Paris, which planners and architects had to recognize. (These trends are particularly apparent in Mercier's *Tableau de Paris* and Poyet's numerous writings.) It is important to remember

Poyet, Hospital, site plans, from his Mémoire.

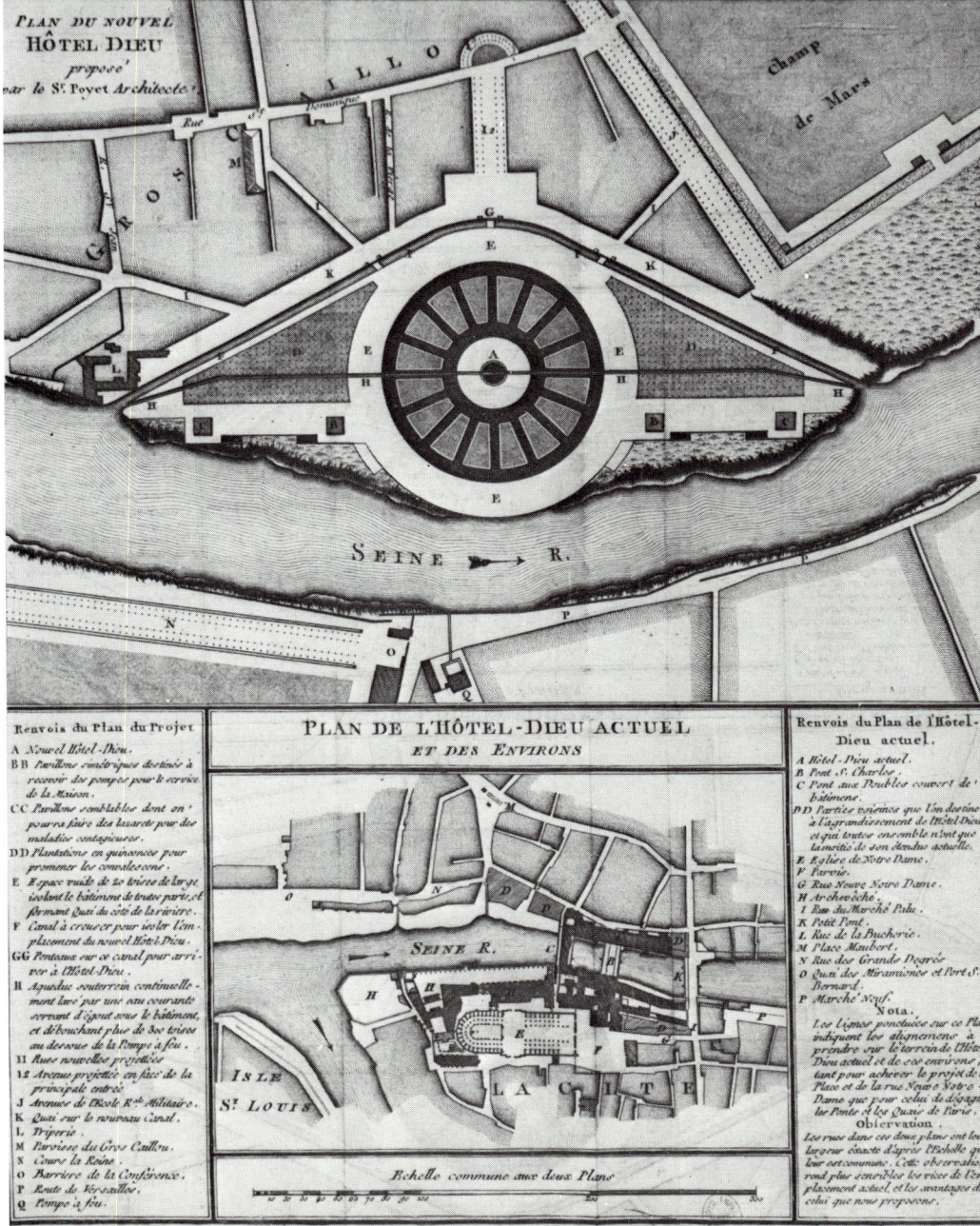

that in the Hôtel-Dieu patients were admitted according to need and without fees, and this procedure was regarded by Petit as essential for the practice of good medicine. His concern was with the citizen, following a tradition expressed by Montesquieu in *De l'esprit des lois*, especially in the chapter on hospitals. Here the obligation of the state to provide 'assured subsistence' for all is stipulated.[16] It is also worth noting that the original meaning of the word hospital does not relate solely to housing the sick, but that it designated a building where help and comfort could be found, whatever the circumstances. It is in this sense that Ledoux used the expression when he praised England for multiplying hospitals, while he regretted over-concentration in France.[17]

Circular planning in this field proved abortive, however, partly because it was too advanced, but also because little building took place in Paris during the Revolution. Even Tenon's more modest plans, based on the official Report on Hospitals of 1786, were shelved and his personal experiences in England, especially his visits to Portsmouth and Plymouth, disregarded. He nevertheless made a significant contribution to planning by advocating decentralization, and the establishment of four hospitals in the Northern, Southern, Eastern and Western districts of Paris. Supplies were to be centralized in one administrative building, and, following Petit's earlier recommendation, Tenon wished to establish a *hospice*, a sort of out-patients' department on the site of the Hôtel-Dieu.[18] Tenon is thus representative of advanced thinking on hospital planning in Paris, his main contribution being the classification of patients, facilitated by separate parallel wards.

Compared with the Hôtel-Dieu, the newly established 18th century hospitals in Paris were small. Among them was the one founded by Madame Necker for 120 patients in 1788 in which twelve Sisters of Charity undertook the nursing.[19] The older hospitals remained old-fashioned, like the Hôpital St Louis with its ground-plan still centred on a cloister.

Among the foundling hospitals, the Hôpital des Enfants-Trouvés built by Boffrand in Paris in 1747 was outstanding, although it was criticized by Laugier as being too sumptuous for its purpose, and, therefore, infringing the laws of *bienséance*.[20] Nevertheless, this hospital with its simple façade and high roof was one of Boffrand's most successful architectural commissions. It was well known, as its designs were published in J. F. Blondel's *Architecture Françoise* of 1752–56. However, Boffrand's authorship was sometimes overlooked, because the designs could not be included in his earlier publication of 1745, *Architecture ou principes de cet art*. For the same reason, his *place* designs for the statue of Louis XV were also left out. The Hospice Beaujon, built by Girardin in 1784, only catered for indigent girls and boys, twelve of each sex, who were kept in comparative luxury, possessing their own beds and blankets,[21] a fact which aroused strong opposition.

The Foundling Hospital in London, of approximately the same date as the one for the Enfants-Trouvés in Paris, was built to the designs of the amateur architect, Theodore Jacobsen, between 1742 and 1752, and unfortunately demolished in 1928. It was not only a monumental building but also showed excellence of detail. As Sir John Summerson has pointed out, it was a work of art in itself, but also provided a rallying point for music and painting. It is well known that Hogarth was one of the institution's patrons, and painted

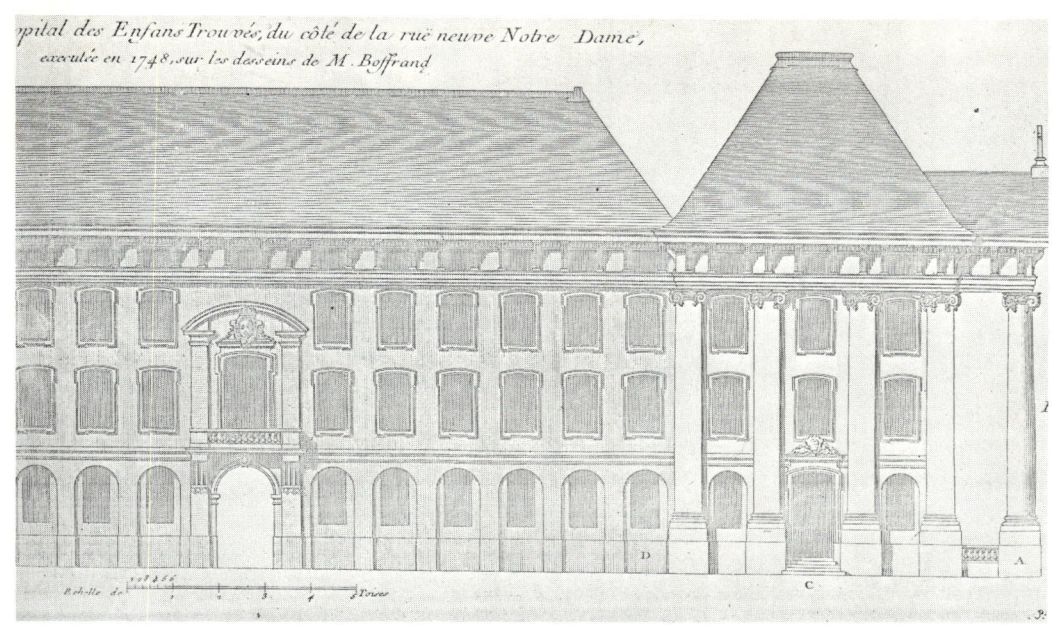

Hôpital des Enfans Trouvés, du côté de la rue neuve Notre Dame, executée en 1748, sur les desseins de M. Boffrand.

Echelle de ... d Toises

Boffrand, Hôpital des Enfans Trouvés, elevation; from Architecture Françoise.

Foundling Hospital, view, after Boitard.

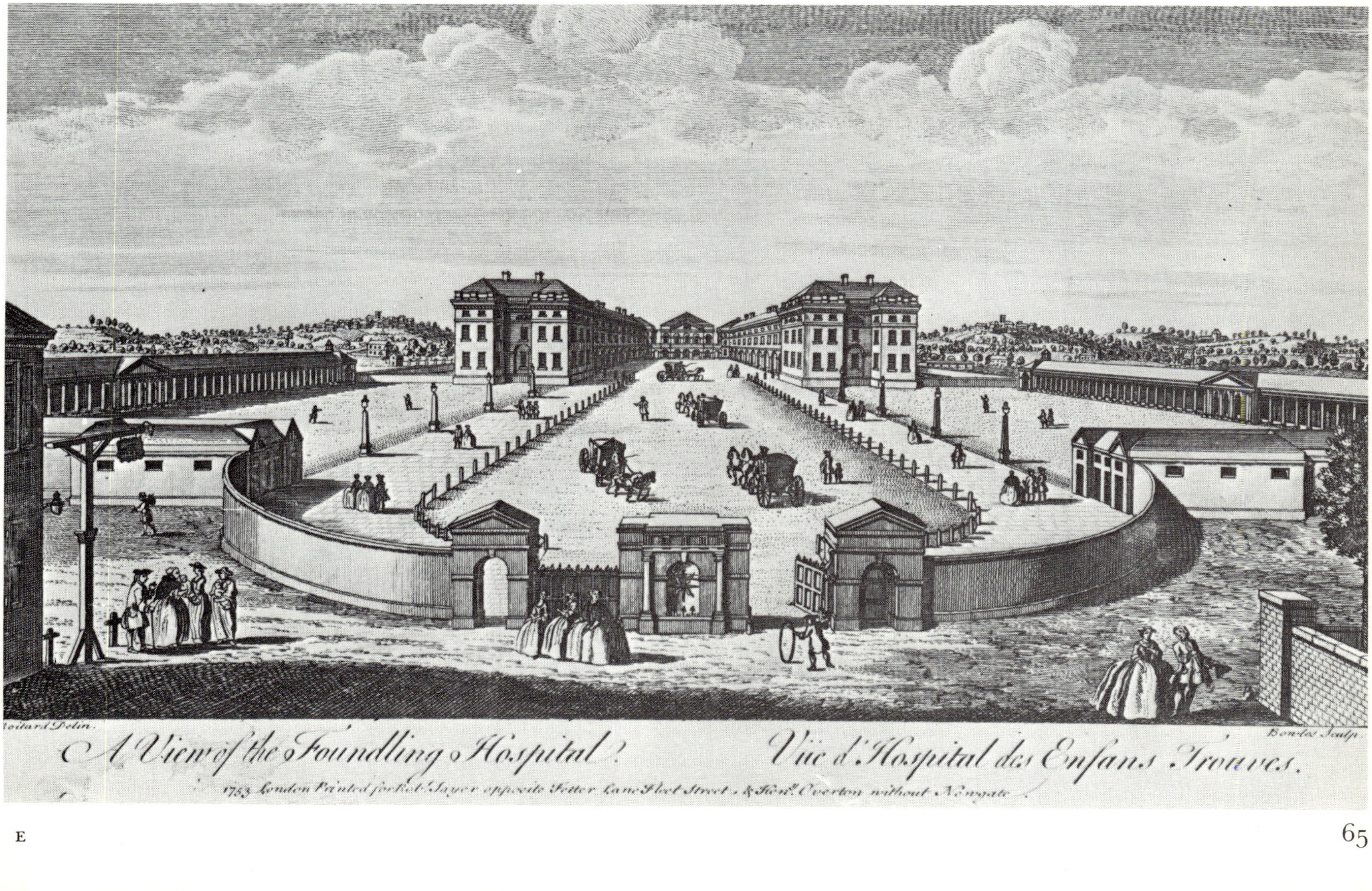

Boitard Delin.

Bowles Sculp.

A View of the Foundling Hospital.   Vüe d'Hospital des Enfans Trouvés.

1753 London Printed for Rob.t Sayer opposite Fetter Lane Fleet Street, & Hen.r Overton without Newgate.

pictures for its collection, including the portrait of the founder, Captain Coram. Situated in an open field, outside London at that time, it complied with the demands of the period for a healthy site. The number of children admitted varied, but it was never intended to be very large, and for this reason branch hospitals were built in the country after 1759.[22]

It is not possible here to deal with hospital building in London comprehensively, but an attempt is made to select the most significant 18th century buildings from the view-point of social purpose and future impact. In this connection Mr Guy's Hospital has first claim, the London, St George's and Middlesex Hospitals following later. An 18th century foundation incorporating classical features, Guy's nevertheless preserved the lay-out of medieval cloisters, in the guise of colonnades, an architectural arrangement which was to leave its

Guy's Hospital, 1815; from an engraving by J. Pass.

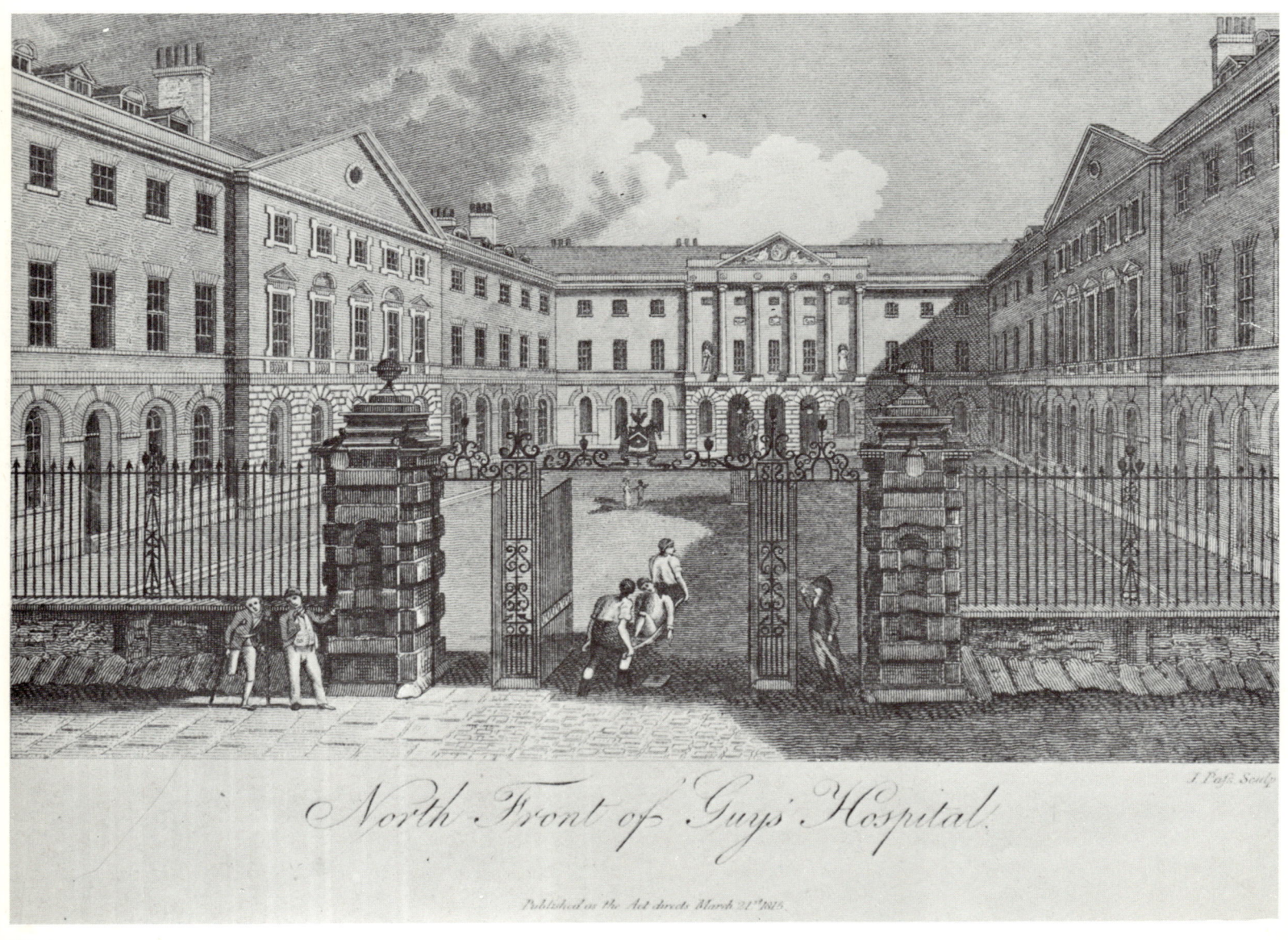

North Front of Guy's Hospital.

Published as the Act directs March 21st 1815.

mark on future developments. Thomas Guy (1645–1724) started his hospital plans in 1720, founding a new institution in 1721 which represented an early example of the voluntary system. Originally it was intended to admit incurable patients, who were classed as inadmissible by other hospitals. Thomas Guy thus provided an early example of that enlightened benevolence which characterized the later 18th century. Thomas Dance was responsible for the plan, the east wing being erected by James Steer.[23] Similar in lay-out was St Bartholomew's, a medieval foundation largely rebuilt in the 18th century by James Gibbs.[24] John Bacon's monument to the founder of Guy's, showing as the background a fairly accurate relief of the elevation of the hospital, may be seen not only as a personal tribute, but also as a means of glorifying the ideal of charity.

In France the tendency at that time was to treat the insane in general hospitals, Philippe Pinel's activities from 1793 onwards at Bicêtre and the Salpétrière leading to the release of patients from their chains.[25] In England, on the other hand, an early attempt was made to provide accommodation for these patients in separate institutions, especially Bethlem and St Luke's Hospitals in London.

George Dance's St Luke's Hospital for the Insane, built between 1782 and 1784 and unfortunately now demolished, was less privileged than the new

G. Dance the Younger, St Luke's Hospital elevation and section. Sir John Soane's Museum, London.

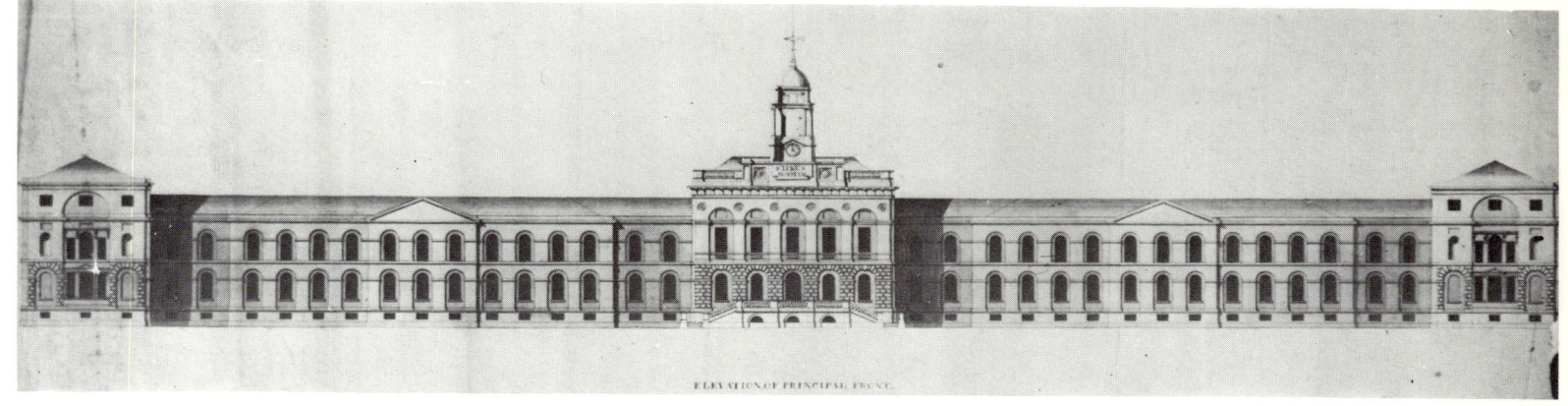

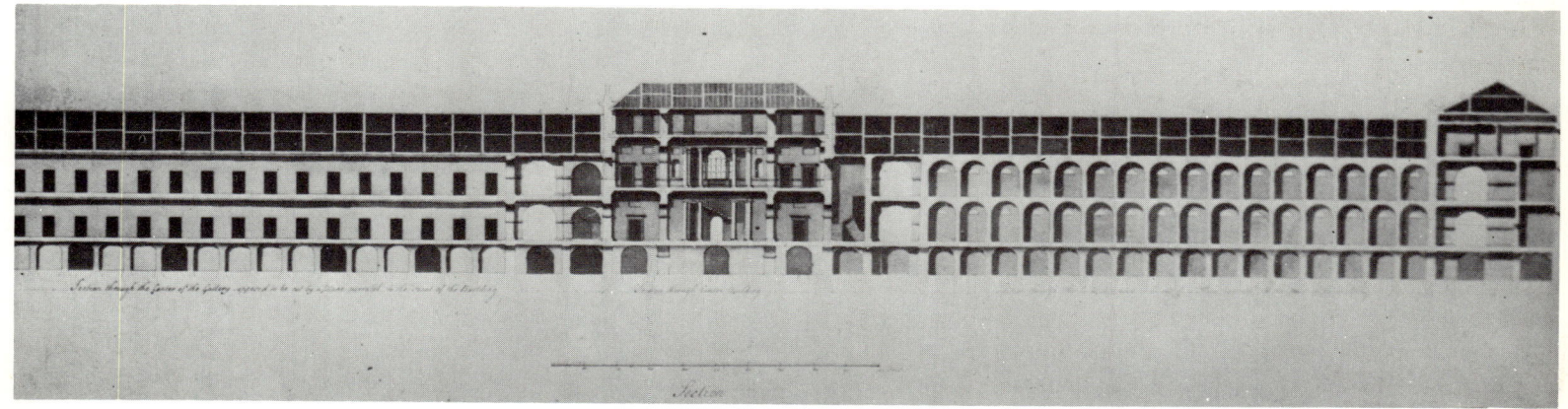

Bethlem, as far as site was concerned.[26] Here the arrangement of large wards made classification difficult; thus it was regarded as old-fashioned, a fate which also threatened the same architect's Newgate Gaol of 1770–78 from its inception.

Robert Hooke's earlier Bethlem Hospital in Moorfields (1675–76) was mainly intended for lunatics, but soon proved too small and inconvenient. It was replaced between 1812 and 1815 by the spacious and well-situated new Bethlem Hospital built by James Lewis in St George's Fields.[27] It was located on what were then the outskirts of London, thus ensuring quietness and fresh air. (The architecture of the new Bethlem Hospital will be more fully discussed below.) In this period also nearby St George's Circus was planned, in conjunction with the rebuilding of London Bridge, plans which then proved abortive.

New Bethlem Hospital, after Shepherd.

Drawn by Thos. H. Shepherd.   Engraved by J. Tin...

NEW BETHLEM HOSPITAL, ST. GEORGE'S FIELDS.

The two hospitals, the new Bethlem and St Luke's, vied with each other as far as cures were concerned, the treatment at St Luke's being regarded as slightly more humane than at Bethlem. The latter building, now the Imperial War Museum, has been substantially changed and enlarged. Here the provision of cells rather than wards expressed a new trend in medical and architectural thought, and Bethlem was therefore regarded as a model institution. Both hospitals represented the progressive endeavours of the age, and although patients were still chained, when it was considered necessary, they expressed a challenge to the crammed and cruel conditions shown up by Hogarth in *The Rake's Progress*. Their architecture formed a contrast to designs for small country Retreats, of which the one connected with William Tuke was outstanding.

Hospital development in London crystallized around the competition of 1810–11 for the new Bethlem. According to O'Donoghue, thirty-six competitors entered sets of designs, and one such set is still in the possession of the Bethlem Royal and Maudsley Hospitals at the time of writing. These designs, sent in under the motto *Dum spiro, spero*, were, according to an accompanying slip of paper, the work of John Gandy, later Gandy-Deering, better known by his signature John P. Gandy, the form which is found for example in his *Unedited Antiquities of Attica* of 1817.[28]

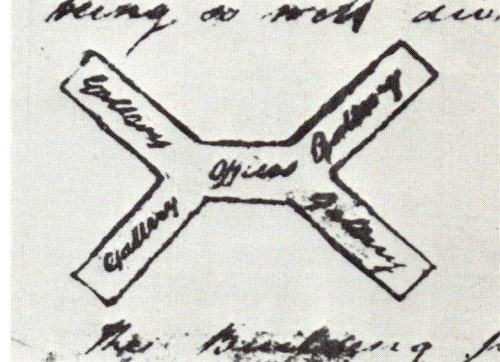

One type of ground-plan shows an oblong with projecting wings at right angles, whilst another, with an accompanying explanatory note, contains the sketch of a rectangle with double diagonal spurs at both ends. Particularly

John P. Gandy, sketch of plan for New Bethlem Hospital, and motto of submission. Archives of the Bethlem Royal and Maudsley Hospitals, London.

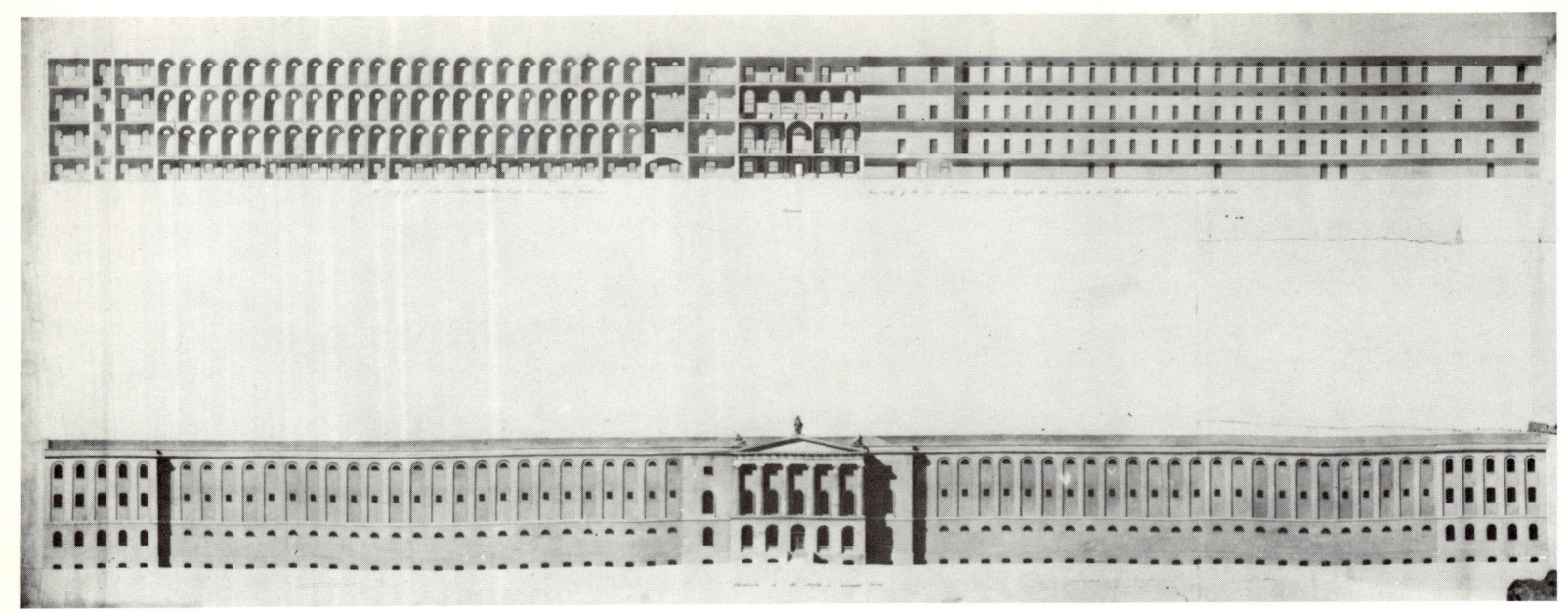

interesting is the elevation, which shows an arrangement of thin pilaster strips and a central Doric portico supporting a pediment. The cells were to open on a corridor, which in turn opened into arcades, a traditional feature already found in the Hôtel des Invalides in the 17th century. O'Donoghue mentions as a source the predecessor of Bethlem, the Moorfields Hospital, which had also followed a French prototype. The building, finally erected by James Lewis, keeps the main arrangement of the Gandy-Deering plan, but reverses the location of the façade and replaces the Doric by the more conventional Ionic style.

Also connected with Bethlem Hospital was the enquiry found in *Reports* of 1814–15 and 1816 to Committees of the House of Commons, dealing with the

John P. Gandy, section, elevation and west elevation for New Bethlem Hospital. Archives of the Bethlem Royal and Maudsley Hospitals, London.

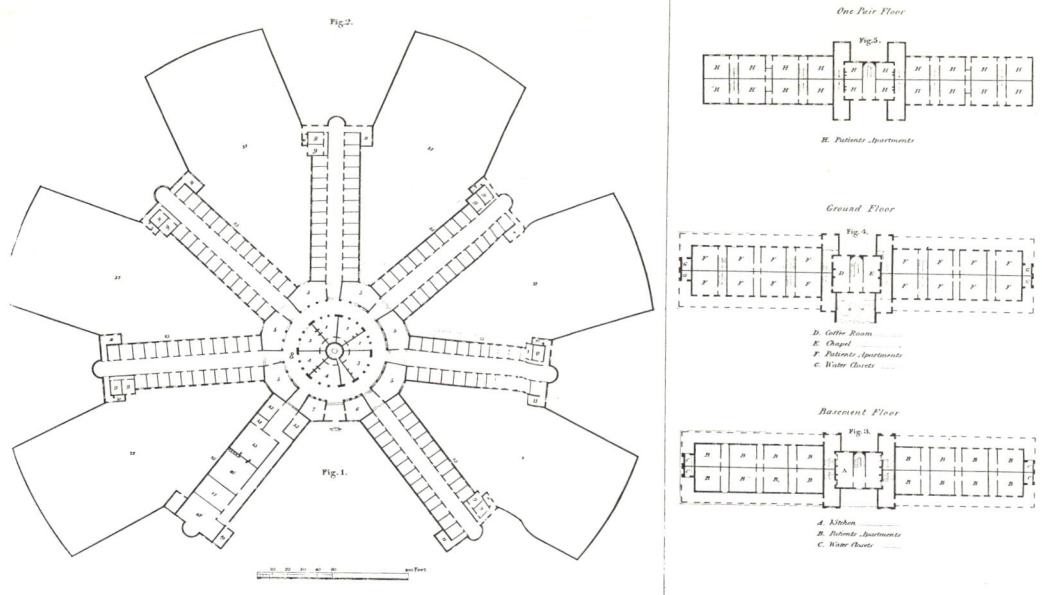

Bevans, Asylum ground-plan and details; from Report . . . to the House of Commons.

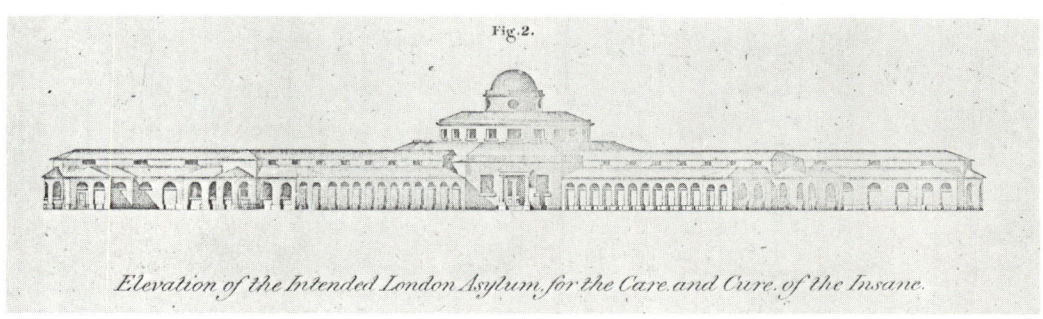

Bevans, elevation of Asylum; from Report . . . to the House of Commons.

care of the poor and insane and the desirability of improving their conditions. James Bevans, an architect whose work has been forgotten, submitted a Panopticon-like design in 1814–15 for an asylum to be erected in London.[29] The Glasgow Asylum, the work of William Stark, was also considered as a

Stark, Asylum for Glasgow, elevation and ground-plan, from Remarks.

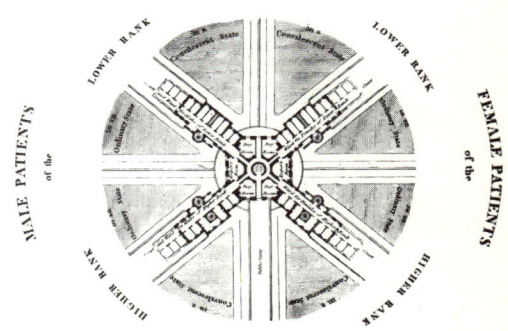

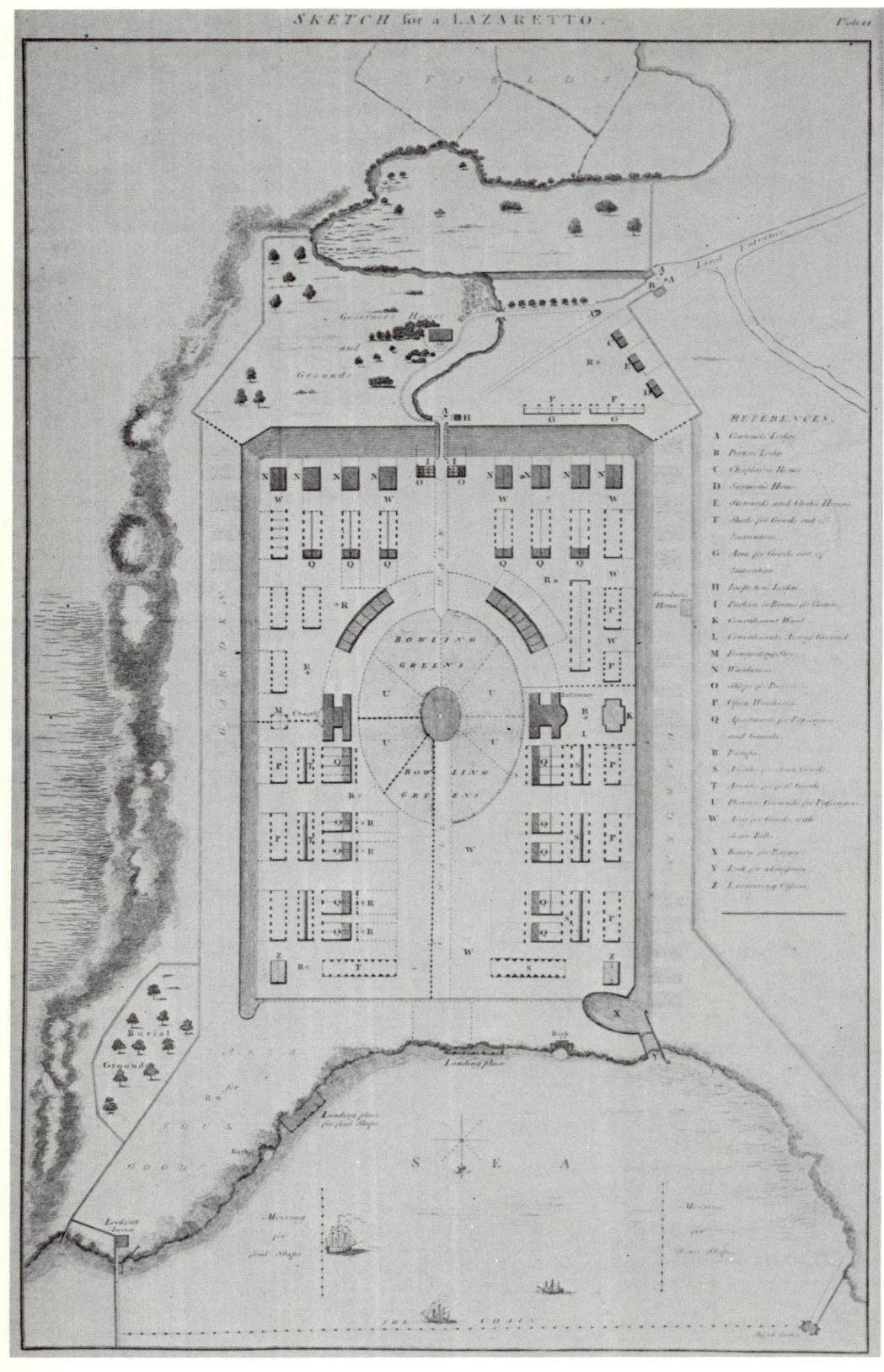

SKETCH for a LAZARETTO.

Howard, Lazaretto; from Lazarettos.

possible model in 1816. Because of this the two illustrations to his book, *Remarks on the Construction of Public Hospitals*, published in 1810, were included in the *Report*.[30]

On a more theoretical level, John Howard had published his ideal plans for a model Lazaretto in his treatise on the subject. This Lazaretto in a peaceful setting on an open stretch of coast-line has a regular lay-out with an inner garden and complete isolation of patients from outside contacts as well as from each other. (Jeremy Bentham's adaptable Panopticon will be more fully discussed in the context of prisons.)

As we have seen, architectural planning for the mentally sick was widely discussed, and the benefits of different structural types were contrasted. The foremost advocate of better conditions for paupers was Samuel Tuke.[31] The Retreat in York, founded by his grand-father, William Tuke, catered for only about twenty-four patients. It opened in 1796 and looked more like a country

Tuke, Retreat in York, after Atkinson; from Description.

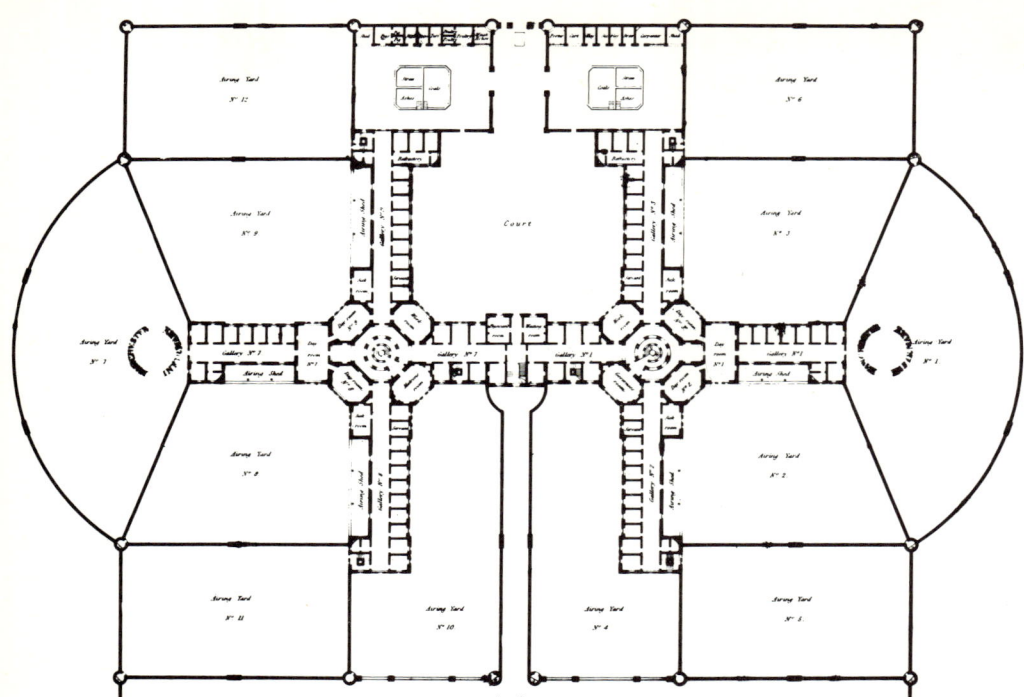

Wakefield Asylum; from Watson and Pritchett,
Plans, Elevations, *etc.*

estate than a medical institution. This asylum was intended for patients who
could afford to pay, or had sponsors looking after them. By contrast, the
Asylum in Wakefield built with the help of Samuel Tuke's advice, between
1816 and 1818 by Watson and Pritchett, was intended for the indigent and
those without means of support. Tuke advocated moderate size asylums,
although he considered plans for possible extensions right from the start. He
criticized the Glasgow Asylum because it reflected the architectural influence
of Ipswich prison in its compact lay-out and he stressed the difference in
function between curative and punitive establishments. He advocated fourteen
day galleries for the patients to walk in, twelve airing yards, and accessible
windows with a cheerful view, a challenge to the prevailing prison atmosphere
in lunatic asylums. He favoured the principle of inspection, made popular by
the Panopticon. Knowing the abuse of power to which warders tended to be
prone, he encouraged servants and officers to spy on each other, in order to
prevent ill-treatment of patients. Tuke's idea of dividing the inmates, 150 men
and 150 women, into three classes, unequal in size, was based on the symptoms
of their illness: the incoherent, those still able to feel 'rational enjoyment', and
therefore capable of doing some work, and the convalescent. For the violent,
a fourth category had to be added, and separate accommodation was provided
for them. Tuke was an optimist, as far as recovery was concerned. His attitude
was based on the twin concepts of care and cure. In his own words he represented a growing trend of enlightened opinion: 'The change which has taken
place in the general sentiments, in regard to the attentions due to deranged
persons, has produced a striking change in the mode of treatment.'[32]

Lastly, William Stark's Asylum in Glasgow may be mentioned again,
because its provisions sum up the official thought of the period. By combining

See illustration on page 84

See illustration on page 71, below

the shape of the cross with four radiating wings it was possible to completely segregate the different classes of patients. They were divided into male and female, curable and incurable inmates, and the socially higher ranks were separated from the lower. Stark explained his ideas in his book on hospital building, drawing on earlier experiences and especially on the writings of Samuel Tuke. One does not envy the medical staff who made the decisions on curability or otherwise, but it is likely that those treated as incurables remained mentally sick, whereas there are doubts about the recovery of the so-called curables.

Guy's Hospital, in accordance with Guy's wishes, was especially intended for incurables. This was an exceptional arrangement, and was soon altered even in this instance. It is quite astonishing to see, when perusing London hospital accounts, how high the rates of recovery were. This can best be explained by an admissions procedure, which only provided for the curables,[33] a division absent in the Hôtel-Dieu in Paris, and indeed elsewhere in France. This explains the lower figures of recovery found there, and indeed testifies to a more humane, if perhaps less efficient attitude towards the mentally sick.

To sum up, one can say that in the field of new hospital building France remained mainly traditional, but excelled in comprehensive ideal plans, based on a centralized design or on parallel wards. England on the other hand achieved outstanding progress in the building of lunatic asylums, in the classification and isolation of patients, and indeed developed a comprehensive architectural programme for the care of the sick. Hospital building in England was regarded as a model, not only in France, but also throughout Europe.

1. P. Vallery-Radot: *Paris d'autrefois, ses vieux hôpitaux, deux siècles d'histoire hospitalière*, Paris 1947. *Dix siècles d'histoire hospitalière Parisienne, 651–1650. L'Hôtel-Dieu de Paris*, Paris 1961. Sir Henry Burdett: *Hospitals and Asylums of the World*, London 1891–93. H. Rosenau in *Zeitschrift für Kunstgeschichte*, 1964, pp. 228 ff. A. Goodwin: *The French Revolution*, London 1953, pp. 98 ff. and excellent bibliography, p. 186.
2. C. Dainton: *The Story of England's Hospitals*, London 1961. *Hautecoeur* II, 1, pp. 518 ff. L. Dimier: *L'Hôtel des Invalides*, Paris 1910, p. 10.
3. *Le Premier Tome de l'Architecture de Philibert de l'Orme:* Pleust à Dieu, et à ma volonté, que les riches bourgeois, marchands, financiers et autres . . . s'adonnassent aussi tost à faire et fonder quelques hostels-dieu, ou colleges pour le soulagement des pavvres, et utilité du bien publique, que édifier un tas de superbes et magnifiques maisons qui ne leur servent que d'ennuie et malheur.' Livre V, Paris 1568, p. 130.
4. K. Jones: *Lunacy, Law and Conscience, 1744–1845*, London 1955.
5. J. Howard: *An Account of the Principal Lazarettos in Europe*, 1789, p. 187, and *The State of the Prisons in England and Wales*, Warrington 1784, pls. 21 and 22.
6. *Colvin*, p. 515. It may be suggested that these are in fact varied versions of the same name, which is found as Ranchard in J. G. Legrand's *Essai sur l'histoire générale de l'architecture*, Paris 1809, p. 202. A short history is found in J. M. Reese: *The Royal Naval Hospital, Plymouth, 1762–1962*. A. E. Richardson and C. Lovett Gill: *Regional Architecture of the West of England*, London 1924, pp. 56 ff.
7. J. R. Tenon: *Mémoires sur les hôpitaux de Paris*, Paris 1788, pp. XII, VII and *passim*.
8. This process, which deserves wider study, has been more fully appreciated in the field of iconography than of architecture.
9. See J.-M. Pérouse de Montclos in *Bulletin de la société de l'histoire de l'art français*, 1966, published 1967, pp. 257 ff. Patte, op. cit., p. 213, refers to the Ile des Cygnes. See Chapter II, note 1.

10. The first names of Clavareau are given according to Bauchal and Thieme-Becker. Clavareau's *Mémoire*, pp. 205 ff. and *passim*.

11. *Prix*, pp. 46–48, 25–27, 51–53.

12. A. Petit: *Mémoire sur la meilleure manière de construire un hôpital de malades*, Paris 1774, *passim*. Tenon, op. cit., pp. VI and XII, p. 385. Tenon was well-informed with regard to European developments, as shown in his reference to the famous writer and physician Hunczowsky, whose name he mis-spells, however. The *Narrenturm*, or Fool's Tower, of the Vienna General Hospital of 1783, was a circular building without wings. cf. D. Leistikow: *Ten Centuries of European Hospital Buildings*, Ingelheim 1967, pp. 73 ff.

13. Bibliothèque Nationale, Cabinet des Estampes, Hd mat 15.

14. J. Duportal in *Revue de l'art ancien et moderne*, vol. 36, 1914–1919, pp. 153 ff. Tenon, op. cit., p. IV f.

15. C.-Ph. Coquéau and B. Poyet: *Mémoire sur la nécessité de transférer et reconstruire l'Hôtel Dieu de Paris*, published in Paris in 1785.

16. Charles Louis de Secondat de Montesquieu: *Oeuvres complètes*, II, Paris 1956, pp. 712 ff.

17. *L'Architecture* I, p. 215.

18. Tenon, op. cit., p. XXXVIII f.

19. M. Gambier-Parry: *Madame Necker*, etc., Edinburgh and London 1913, pp. 175 ff.

20. W. Herrmann, op. cit., p. 32.

21. A. Masson: *Un mécène bordelais Nicolas Beaujon*, Bordeaux 1937, pp. 127 ff.

22. On the Foundling Hospital cf. R. H. Nichols and F. A. Wray: *The History of the Foundling Hospital*, London 1935, *passim*. Summerson, p. 120. Colvin, p. 312 f.

23. H. C. Cameron: *Mr Guy's Hospital, 1726–1948*, London 1954, *passim*.

24. Sir D'Arcy Power and H. J. Waring: *A Short History of St Bartholomew's Hospital*, etc., London 1923, *passim*. Also *Royal Commission on Historical Monuments, London IV, The City*, pp. 123 ff.

25. Ph. Pinel: *Traité médico-philosophique sur l'aliénation mentale ou la manie*, Paris 1801. Also Francis Tiffany: *Ph. Pinel, 1745–1826*, Paris 1898. Scipio Pinel: *Traité complet du régime sanitaire des aliénés*, Paris 1936. The plans still show the influence of the *Prix* type of design.

26. C. N. French: *The Story of St Luke's Hospital*, etc., London 1951, p. 41 and *passim*. H. Rosenau in *Journal of the R.I.B.A.*, LIV, 1947, pp. 502 ff.

27. E. G. O'Donoghue: *The Story of Bethlehem Hospital*, etc., London, Leipzig 1914, pp. 302 ff. and *passim*. For the background of the treatment of the insane cf. F. Antal: *Hogarth and his Place in European Art*, London 1962, especially pp. 15 and 221, notes 67–70.

28. I wish to express my appreciation to Miss Patricia Allderidge, the Archivist of the Bethlem Royal and Maudsley Hospitals, for placing her material on Gandy at my disposal. *Colvin*, p. 222.

29. See especially *Fourth Report. Minutes of Evidence taken before The Select Committee . . . for the Better Regulation of Madhouses in England*, 26 June 1815, Vol. IV, Sessional Paper No. 296, and *Third Report from the Committee on Madhouses in England, etc. with an Appendix*, 11 June 1816, Vol. VI, Sessional Paper No. 451. It should be noted that the 19th century building of the North London Hospital, now University College Hospital, still followed the Panopticon type.

30. W. Stark: *Remarks on the Construction of Public Hospitals*, etc., Glasgow 1810.

31. S. Tuke: *Description of the Retreat, an Institution near York*, etc., York 1813. M. S. Langfitt: *William Tuke's Contribution to the Humane Treatment of the Insane*, Pittsburgh 1937, *passim*.

32. S. Tuke in Watson and Pritchett: *Plans, Elevations, Sections and Descriptions of the Pauper Lunatic Asylum lately erected at Wakefield*, York 1819, *passim* and especially p. 5.

33. See note 23.

4
Prisons

During the late 18th century the connection between prisons and hospitals was close. Not only were the two kinds of buildings intended to foster the improvement of their occupants, either morally or physically, but their functions also tended to overlap. The sick had to be provided for, even during a period of punishment, and some forms of illness, such as lunacy, led to residential confinement. The Bethlem Hospital, as seen in Hardwick's ground-plan, published by O'Donoghue, gives a clear indication of this fact.[1] Here two prisons, housed in symmetrical isolated buildings, were added next to the airing grounds.

In both France and England discontent with prison conditions was marked, but whereas this country produced an unrivalled pioneer in the field of reform in John Howard, in France the emphasis was political, concentrating on abuse by officials and the venality of the judiciary.

One of the earliest establishments of a humane nature in 18th century France was a prison for galley-slaves, a *bagne* near Brest, designed in about 1757 in conjunction with the building of three berths for ships, by the architect A. Choquet de Lindu (1712–90). Engravings of the projected buildings appeared in Choquet's *Description des trois formes du Port de Brest*, published in Brest in 1757. Subsequently he erected some of them, and described them in the *Supplément* of the *Encyclopédie* of 1776; his illustrations were adapted to appear in the accompanying plates of 1777. The *bagne* was a prison for former galley-slaves, who had been removed from the hulks in 1748. It is interesting to note not only the scale of the project, intended for 20,000 prisoners, but also the emphasis given to sanitary arrangements, such as

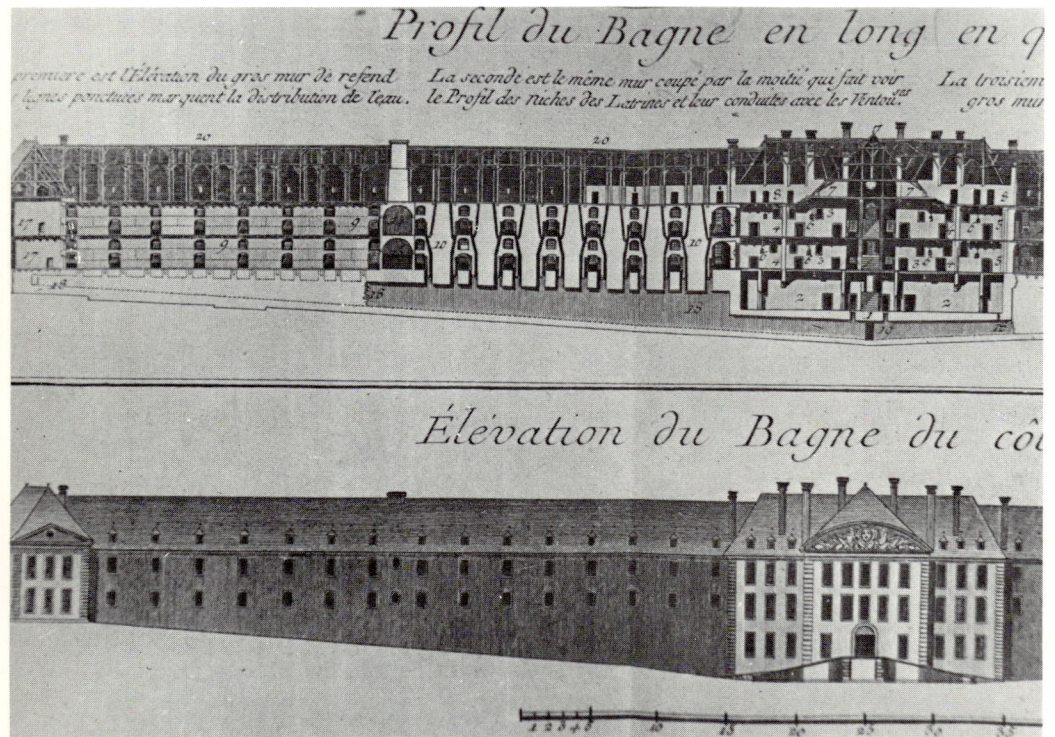

Prison for galley slaves near Brest (details); from Encyclopédie.

latrines, piped water and conduits. The growth of social conscience in the equipment of prisons was developed shortly after in Beccaria's study on *Crimes and Punishments*, first published in a French translation in 1766.[2] A century later it inspired Victor Hugo's romanticized version of the subject in *Les Misérables*, in which the hero is a galley-slave. The contrast between the sumptuous central mansion of the commanding officer and his staff and the prisoners' wards in Brest expresses the traditional attitude of the period, but the spacious quarters for the prisoners and the concern with hygiene reveals the growth of humanitarian considerations.

In England, the hulks on the Thames and other rivers were still maintained and John Howard criticized these in his treatise on *Lazarettos*. Although he did not entirely condemn them,[3] he regretted the length of sentences and the lack of hygiene.

The most significant change in the planning of prisons is represented by the Maison de Force in Ghent, with its octagonal plan based on the outline of an ancient citadel. John Howard reproduced it in a half-completed stage in his book on *Prisons*, and it did in fact remain unfinished. The building, planned in 1771, was erected between 1772 and 1775, owing to the initiative of Vilain XIIII, as he styled himself. He advocated the moral improvement of prisoners, especially through learning a trade, and may, therefore, be regarded as a thinker on parallel lines with Beccaria, but with a more practical approach.[4] It is a sign of the high esteem in which the Maison de Force was held, that J.-N.-L. Durand included it in its complete form as a model in his *Recueil*, published in Paris in the year IX of the Revolutionary calendar.

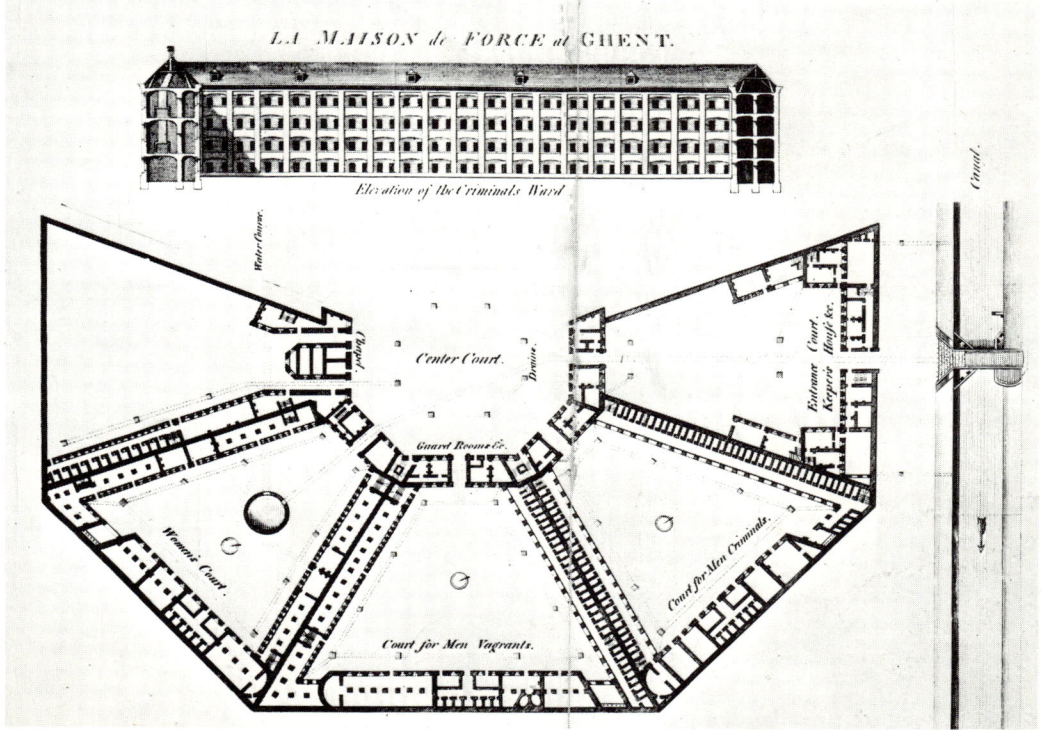

Maison de Force, Ghent; from Howard's State of Prisons.

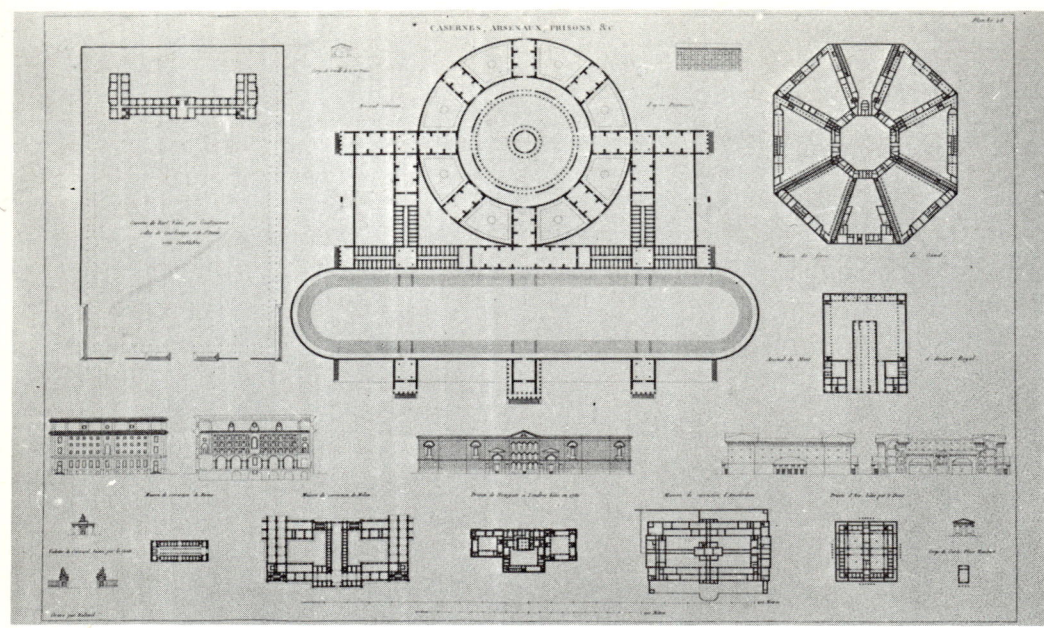

Durand, Survey of Prisons; from Recueil.

The Maison de Force must have been known to Samuel and Jeremy Bentham, and may be regarded as an architectural source for the polygonal ground-plan of the Panopticon, published by the latter in 1791.[5] Another model for the Panopticon, especially as regards the elevation, is provided by the House of Correction, a prison for women founded under Catherine the Great in St Petersburg. This building was mentioned as nearly finished in the third edition of Howard's book on *Prisons*, published in 1784, and first illustrated in the first edition of his *Lazarettos* of 1789. The compact lay-out and the two-storey elevation surmounted by a dome show a marked similarity to the Panopticon. The flat dome has been raised and the crenellation discarded in Bentham's design.[6] The relationship is probably not fortuitous, as the newly completed building could have been known to the brothers Bentham from reproductions and was probably seen by one or both during their travels in Russia. Unfortunately no further information on this prison has become

Howard, House of Correction in St Petersburg; from Lazarettos.

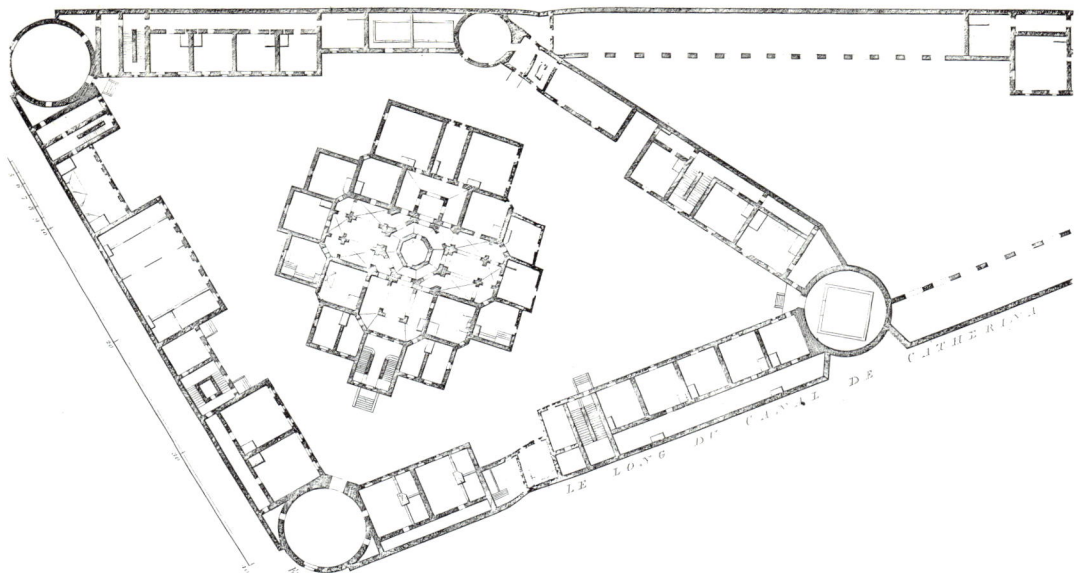

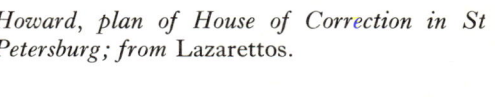

Howard, plan of House of Correction in St Petersburg; from Lazarettos.

available through the Soviet authorities and none can be obtained in England.

Jeremy and Samuel Bentham's invention of the Panopticon, the prototype for a multi-purpose building, was primarily intended as a prison, allowing supervision by warders from the centre. The traditional arrangement was thus reversed: instead of the inmates looking inwards towards an altar in the centre, the warders were looking out, supervising them. Samuel Bentham was particularly interested in a wide range of possible adaptations of his scheme,

See illustration on page 20 (left)

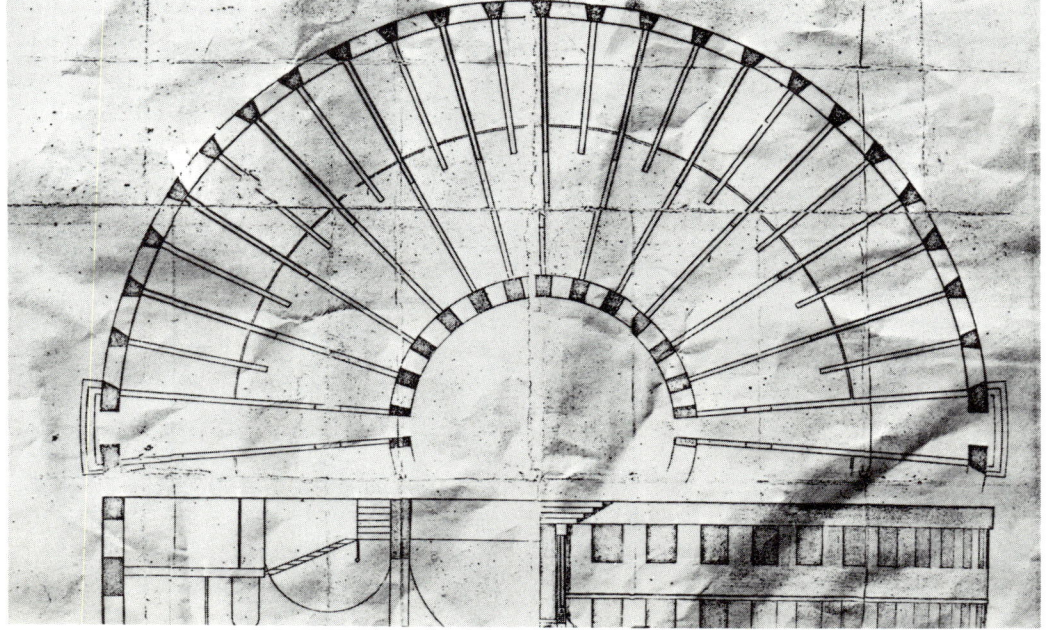

Bentham, section of Panopticon; from Panopticon.

but it was primarily intended for prisons.

It was John Howard, the philanthropist and reformer, who was most influential in the amelioration of prison conditions. He demanded better food for the convicts, cleanliness and hygiene, and expected that an improvement in character would result from enforced isolation in single cells, especially at night.[7] However, the separation of prisoners was not a complete innovation. Particularly dangerous prisoners – or those regarded as such – had been isolated at all times. What was new was the prophylactic and humanitarian as opposed to punitive approach to the problem of crime.

Although John Howard was a great prison reformer, he was not remarkable for his architectural vision. He included a design for a County Gaol to accommodate debtors and felons in his work on *The State of Prisons in England and Wales*, first published in 1777. His prevailing interest in hygiene is shown here, the prisons proper being elevated above a colonnade, a motif based, according to him, on the market in Halifax. Furthermore this arrangement, besides providing covered walks, was also intended to make escape more difficult, if not well nigh impossible. Males and females, debtors and felons, young and old, were to be completely separated and facilities for voluntary work provided.

A further plan, found in Howard's book on *Lazarettos*, first published in 1789, is for a penitentiary for criminals condemned to forced labour – a substitute for deportation. Again it is not architecturally distinguished, show-

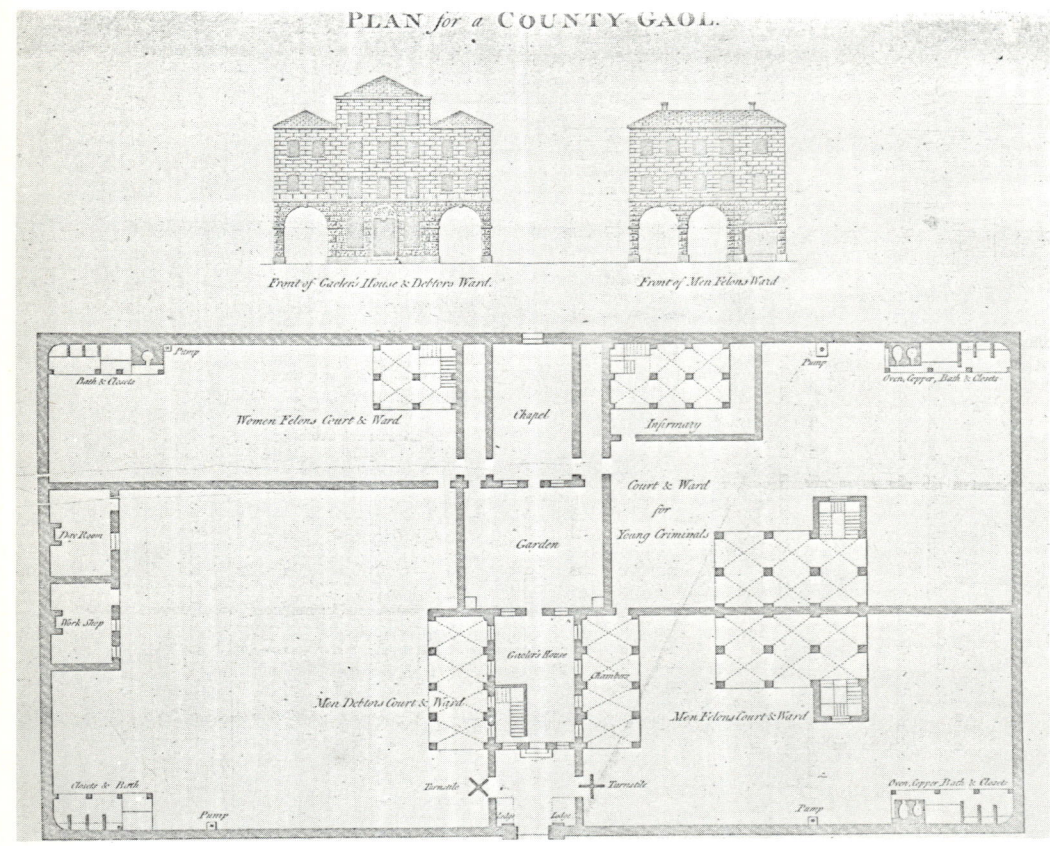

Howard, design for County Gaol; from State of Prisons.

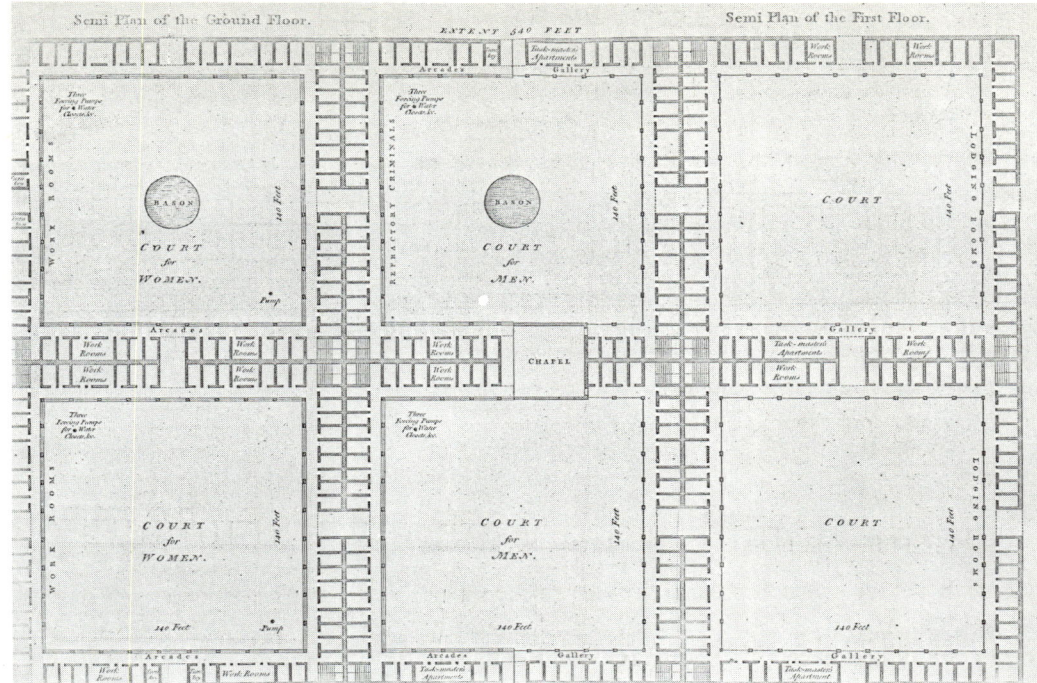

ing courtyards enclosed by wings at right angles, with a small chapel in the centre block. This design, modelled on the earlier one, included arcades and demanded strict classification and separation of prisoners. It will be remembered that John Howard was an advocate of individual cells, and these were to be provided in all prisons, especially for use during the night. But his advocacy of solitary confinement did not necessarily extend to the daytime, as prisoners were to exercise in common, although they were forbidden to speak to each other. This may seem harsh to us, yet it represented at the time an attempt at humane treatment.

One further reason for Howard giving so much thought to conditions in penitentiaries was his conviction that only terms of long imprisonment – more than two years – could prove beneficial. His plans were his own, uninfluenced by William Blackburn's well-known ideas, although he referred to the latter as an 'ingenious' architect on frequent occasions in his book on *Lazarettos*:

rather faint praise when compared with his rapturous references to Sir William Blackstone and other dignitaries. The influence of John Howard's thought on prison reform is reflected in an Act (*see* Appendix) which led to an architectural competition in prison design in 1782.

The Act appointed supervisors for the erection of two Penitentiary Houses for hard labour, which were to be 'plain, strong and substantial Edifices', to be built outside inhabited areas, on waste ground, but with due regard to 'Healthiness, and the Accommodation of Water'. They were to cater for a variety of requirements, including the possibility of isolating offenders. One building was to be allocated to 600 male, the other to 300 female prisoners – perhaps a reflection on the lower criminal incidence in women. William Blackburn (1750–90) won the prize in the competition of 1782. Unfortunately, his designs cannot now be traced, either at the Home Office or the Public Record Office,[8] so it may therefore be assumed that they were returned to the architect. Such a procedure was at any rate established at the Royal Academy, where the prize-winning designs remained the personal property of their owners. This practice is contrary to the French system, as can be seen in the collections of the Ecole des Beaux Arts in Paris, which still possesses practically all the prize-winning academic drawings.

Little is known at present of Blackburn's life. What we do know is mainly connected with designs for prisons, completed after the competition of 1782 for a Penitentiary. His plans for Ipswich gaol consisted basically of a central Greek cross with four wings attached at the angles in diagonal directions – a system which facilitated expansion. The centre was occupied by a staircase, and the four adjacent rooms were the governor's room, the committee room, the kitchen and the parlour. Double rows of single cells were located in the wings, along a middle corridor, so that the inmates were kept apart.[9]

Sir John Soane (1753–1837) was another competitor for the Penitentiary prize, although he published his designs as late as 1828. They are of an academic nature and form a compact lay-out, the Penitentiary for men being an unusual irregular hexagon with an elongated base, and the Penitentiary for women being inscribed in a circle. No social involvement is apparent: more interest is shown in the æsthetic aspects than in the welfare of prisoners.[10] The great similarity between James Elmes' and Soane's prison projects is notable, both being dependent on a compact lay-out. Elmes, better known as the father of the architect of St George's Hall, Liverpool, H. L. Elmes, published a book, *Hints for the Improvement of Prisons*, in the year 1817, showing his awareness of current trends on the subject. According to Colvin, he had personal contact with Soane, so it is possible that he had some knowledge of the latter's designs.[11] Like Soane, he designed separate buildings for men and women, as laid down in the rules of the competition; the one mainly for women was a square with triangular extensions and the other for men, triangular. Elmes' approach was more functional than Soane's because, though he retained a centrally situated chapel, he increased the prisoners' segregation by providing separate sections for different classes of delinquents. He also added towers to his designs, thus emphasizing the fortress-like character of the proposed structures.

John Howard's influence is also apparent in Charles Middleton's *Plans*,

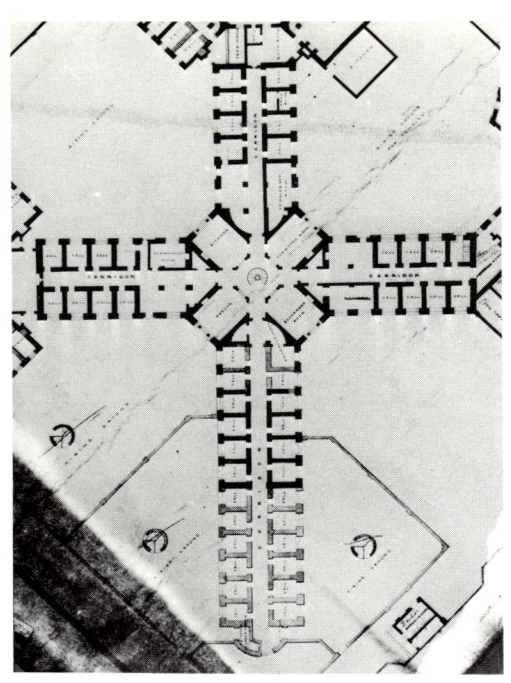

Ipswich Gaol, detail of ground-plan. Ipswich and East Suffolk Record Office.

Opposite page:
Above
Sir John Soane, Penitentiary designs; from Designs for Public Improvements.

Below left
James Elmes, Prisons; from Hints.

Below right
C. T. Middleton, House of Correction, section; from Plans, Elevations, etc.

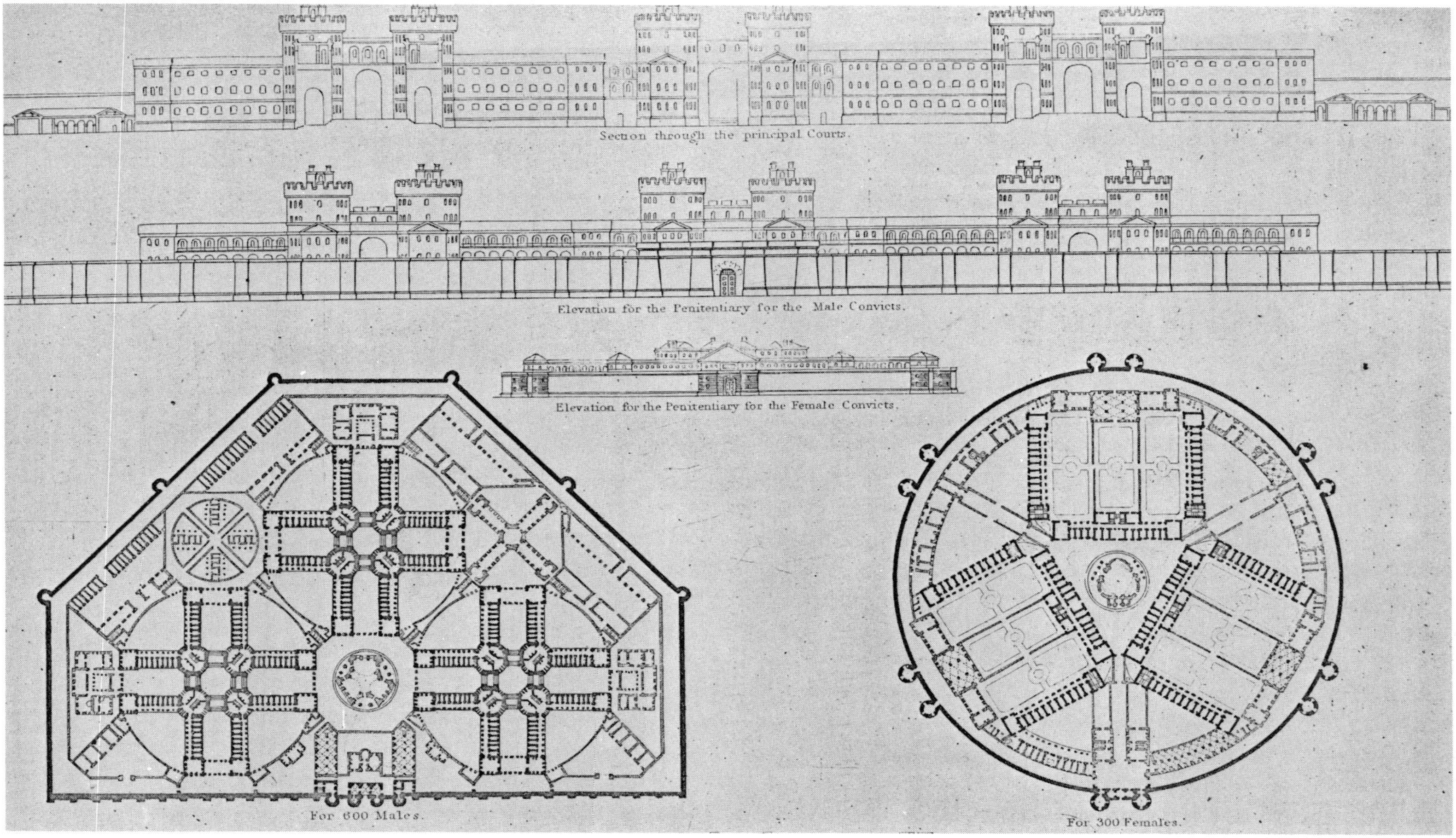

Section through the principal Courts.

Elevation for the Penitentiary for the Male Convicts.

Elevation for the Penitentiary for the Female Convicts.

For 600 Males.

For 300 Females.

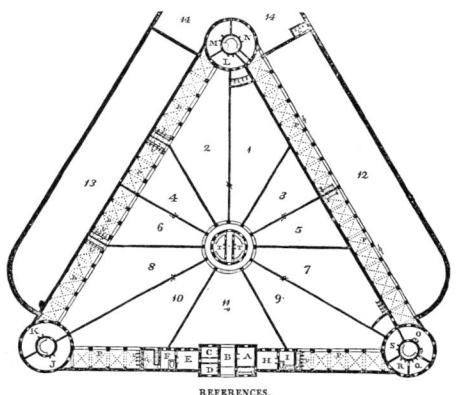

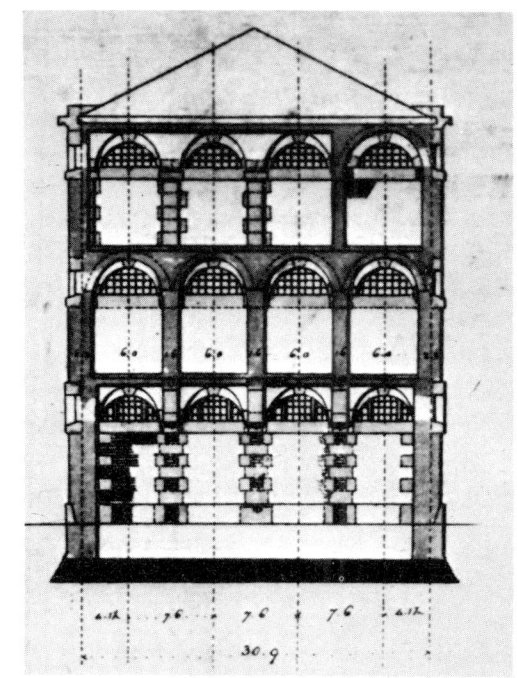

REFERENCES.

A. Governor's parlour.
B. Public entrance.
C. Governor's office.
D. Turnkeys' room.
E. General kitchen.
F. Bake-house.
G. Store room for ditto.
H. Laundry and Cold bath.
I. Hot bath. Oven for tainted clothes, &c. Room for examining felons.
J. Work room for class 10.
K. Ditto ditto———— 8.

L. Work room for 20 male felons of the best class.
M. Dining room, &c. for the debtors.
N. Common room for ditto.
O. Public kitchen. Copper for ditto.
PPP. Piazzas under the cells for each class.
Q. Living room for cook or superintendant.
R. Sleeping room for ditto.
S. Work room for female debtors.
T. Turnkeys' rooms, with stairs to chapel for different classes.
UUUU. Privies, &c. to every class.

1. Extra court for felons of the best class.
2. Court and ward for 20 felons of the best class.
3. Court for criminals condemned to hard labour.
4. ———— for 12 felons of the second class.
5. Court for male debtors to work, &c.
6. Court and ward for 12 felons of the worst class.
7. ———— for female debtors only.
8. Court and ward for 20 deserters, King's evidences, &c.

9. Court and ward for 18 female felons.
10. ———— for 18 young criminals, and for assaults, misdemeanours, &c.
11. Court for turnkeys, state prisoners,&c.
12. Court and wards for the debtors.
13. An Extra court for gardens, work and rope grounds, &c.
14. Ditto ————————&c.

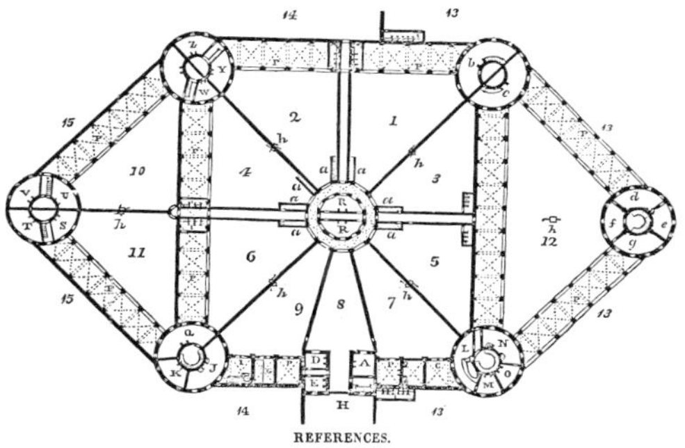

REFERENCES.

A. Gaoler's parlour.
B. ————k tchen.
C. Felons' public kitchen.
D. Turnkeys' room.
E. ———— office.
F. Room for examining felons,&c.
G. Cold bath.
H. Fore court and entrance.
I. Oven for tainted clothes, warm bath, &c.

J. Laundry.
K. Store room for clothes.
L. General bake-house.
M. Bakers' living room.
N. Public kitchen for debtors.
O. Cooks' living room.
P. Piazzas to every class.
Q. Day room for class 6.
R R. Turnkeys' rooms with chapel over them.

S. Day room for class 11.
T. Second day room or work room for same class.
U. and V. Day and work room for No. 10.
W. and X. do. do. for No. 4.
Y. and Z. do. do. for No. 2.

aaaa. Stairs to the separate divisions of the Chapel from the different wards.—b. Day and work room for No. 1.—c. Tap-room for debtors.—d. and e. Day rooms for debtors.—f. Male debtors' work room.—g. Female debtors' work room.—hhh. Pumps.—iiii. Privies and urinals.

1. Court and ward for 18 felons of the best class.
2. ————for 18 ————second class.
3. Extra court for felons of the best class.
4. Court and ward for 18 felons of the worst class.
5. Extra court for such female debtors as prefer associating by themselves, and from which males are excluded.
6. Court and ward for ditto.
7. Kitchen, baking and brew-house yard.
8. Court for turnkeys, state prisoners, &c.

9. Court for laundry, drying ground, and bath yard.
10. Court and ward for 22 criminals, as deserters, assaults, &c. or for King's evidences.
11. Court and ward for 22 boy felons and for those who are to be punished for misdemeanours.
12. Court and work yard for debtors.
13. Airing ground, &c. for debtors.
14. Rope ground.
15. Yard for hard labour for felons.

85

Elevations and Sections of the House of Correction in Cold Bath Fields, etc., published in 1788. Here individual cells were provided for most prisoners in a building with a palatial emphasis on heavy columns. The arrangement of the vaults and chimney of the Infirmary reveal a mastery of design, possibly based on drawings by Sir Robert Taylor. The text of the treatise is, however, clearly utilitarian, emphasizing hygiene in general, and the provision of privies and drainage in particular. The Infirmary especially is illustrated in meticulous detail. (The House of Correction, erected in 1794, was demolished in 1889.)[12]

Left
Westminster Penitentiary; from R. Ackermann's Repository of Arts, *1817.*

Right
C. T. Middleton, House of Correction Infirmary, section; from Plans, Elevations, *etc.*

Below right
Bullar, House of Correction for 200 prisoners; from Remarks.

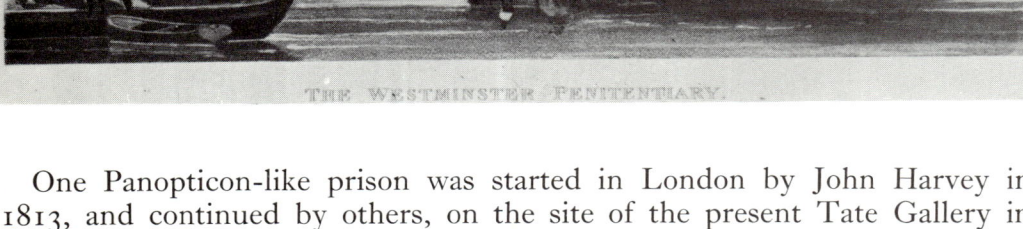

THE WESTMINSTER PENITENTIARY.

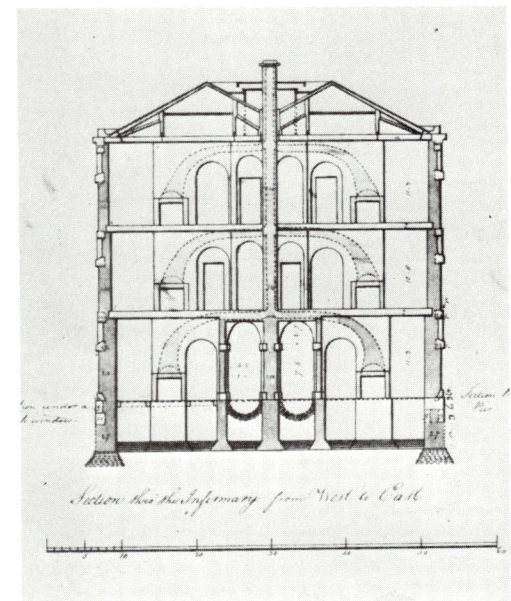

Section thro the Infirmary from West to East

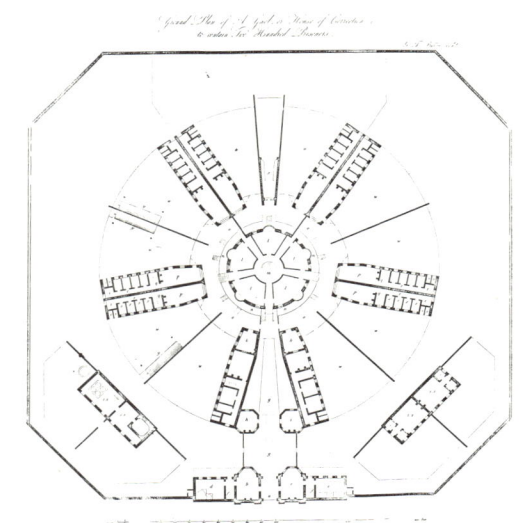

One Panopticon-like prison was started in London by John Harvey in 1813, and continued by others, on the site of the present Tate Gallery in Millbank. It was regarded as unhygienic as well as unsatisfactory as far as supervision was concerned, but the plan was influential enough to be imitated in the so-called model prison of Pentonville in 1840–42.[13]

Perhaps the most important historical treatise on prison design in England was due to the Committee of the Society for the Improvement of Prison Discipline. This was published in 1826 under the chairmanship of the philanthropist Samuel Hoare, with the title *Remarks on the Form and Construction of Prisons with Appropriate Designs*. It provides a survey of buildings with their ground-plans and elevations, and makes a fair assessment of Blackburn's significant contribution. The publication includes, among others, a modern gaol or House of Correction for 200 prisoners by G. T. Bullar which may have influenced the plans for La Roquette in Paris.

In view of the developments suggested earlier, it appears that the architectural form of the Panopticon idea was deeply indebted to the late 18th century tradition, especially in France, and that there was in fact little new about it

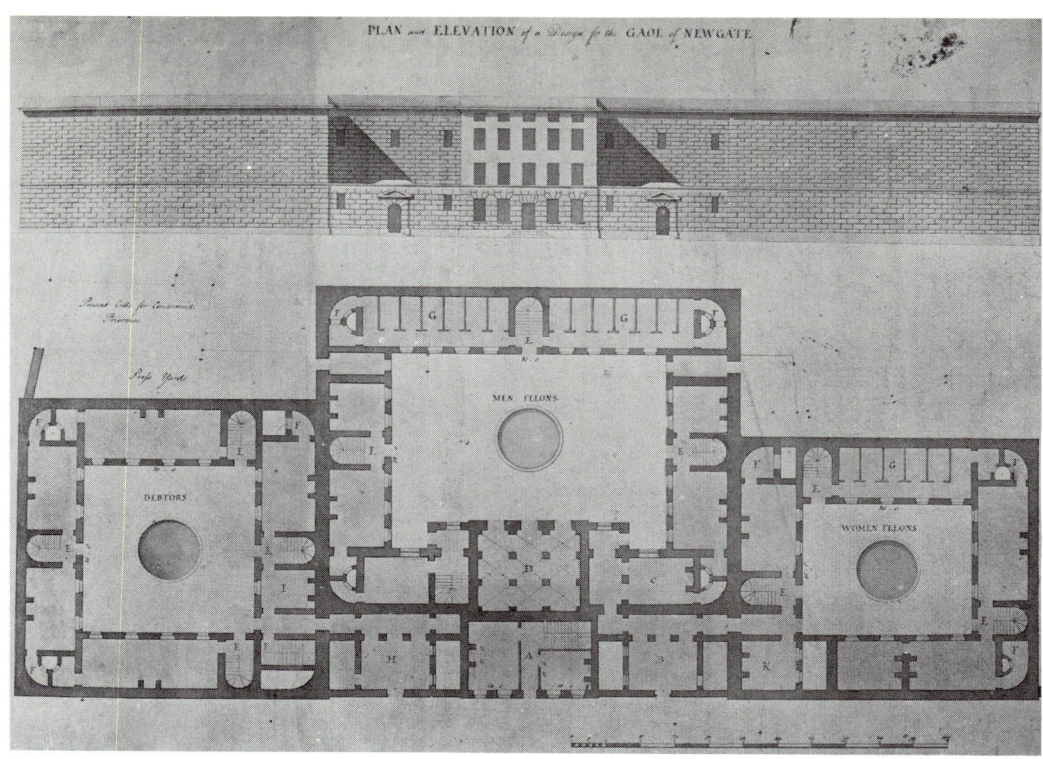

G. Dance the Younger, Newgate Gaol, elevation and ground-plan. Sir John Soane's Museum, London.

G. Dance the Younger, Newgate Gaol, view. Sir John Soane's Museum, London.

architecturally. However, when the Panopticon was first conceived, the older type of prison building, containing wards instead of individual cells, was still prevalent. George Dance the Younger's prison designs for Newgate Gaol (1770-78) were antiquated at the time of building, by comparison with Howard's novel ideas. They made isolation and classification of prisoners difficult. Dance believed prison should be a deterrent, and the formal idiom of heavy rustication, borrowed from Piranesi, clearly aimed at this effect. But he later changed his mind in view of criticism, and headed an enquiry into prison conditions which was published in 1816. In this *Report* on inspection, with Committee of Aldermen, of several gaols of this kingdom, he had become converted to Howard's views.[14]

During this period in France the influence of new ideas on penology was slight, if not altogether absent. Boullée and Ledoux both designed prisons intended to terrify the prisoners, the former locating the actual prison symbolically below the Palace of Justice, the latter in his plans for Aix designing

Boullée, Palais de Justice and Prison. Cabinet des Estampes, Bibliothèque Nationale, Paris.

a separate and threatening building. Austere and unadorned surfaces, small windows and bare walls characterize these schemes, which are reminiscent of Piranesi in scale, but show no similarity to him in their rational simplicity. Piranesi's *Carceri*, although stimulating to the imagination, were too fantastic to have a precise influence on prison design, although their impact was felt in mood and scale. A kindred type of composition, using Gothic arches, was a prize design by Houssin, probably of 1795. In none of these cases is the well-being of the prisoners considered, as is made particularly clear by the suppression of open courts for their exercise.[15]

Ledoux, Prison project for Aix; from L'Architecture.

Pl. 2.

Coupe et élévation d'une prison d'Etat par M. Houssin. *Prieur fecit*

Houssin, Prison; from Prix.

The political dissatisfaction with prison conditions in Paris had little influence on actual prison construction during the Revolutionary period. The Fall of the Bastille was a political event,[16] but led to no drastic change in architecture; this took place later, mainly through American influence, although this was originally indebted to Blackburn and Bentham. On the theoretical level the influence of John Howard's teaching was paramount and widely acknowledged. Marquet-Vasselot, the penologist, expressed in his three volumes on prison reform and penal changes his admiration for Howard, while advocating stricter conditions.[17]

L. P. Baltard's *Architectonographie des prisons* of 1829 influenced the development of prison architecture.[18] Baltard bestowed high praise on the modernization of older religious establishments, such as St Lazare, used as a prison during the Revolution, Ste Pélagie and the Madelonnettes. On the other hand he was strongly critical of a model prison plan on the Panopticon principle, which, according to him was in the process of being erected. He must have been referring to the prison for young offenders at La Roquette,

Baltard, Prison design; from Architectonographie.

La Roquette, Prison; Ville de Paris Collection.
Photograph by Jacques Buchholz, Paris.

built by H. Lebas from 1826 onwards. He criticized the plan, a wheel of six spokes, for the large distances involved, the lack of supervision from a remote centre, the wings, too near together at the core, but wasteful of space at the periphery. He also regretted the angularity of the enclosure which replaced the traditional circular *chemin de ronde*, for this hampered visibility. According to modern requirements, however, the provision of workshops and the space between the wings is outstanding. These humane provisions were abandoned shortly after in the prison of Mazas, a Maison d'Arrêt built on a cellular plan. The model here, for solitary confinement during day and night, was based on the principles of the American 'Cherry Orchard', the Eastern State Penitentiary in Philadelphia.

Indeed, 19th century penology was far removed from the more humane approach of Howard. He tempered severity with compassion, and saw the need to spend appropriate sums on prison comforts, while the early 19th century penologists stressed solely the deterrent aspects of prisons and wanted them to be run on the cheap.

In spite of his polemics, Baltard was aware of the quality of some of the smaller French prisons, such as that of Lorient, and also of new developments

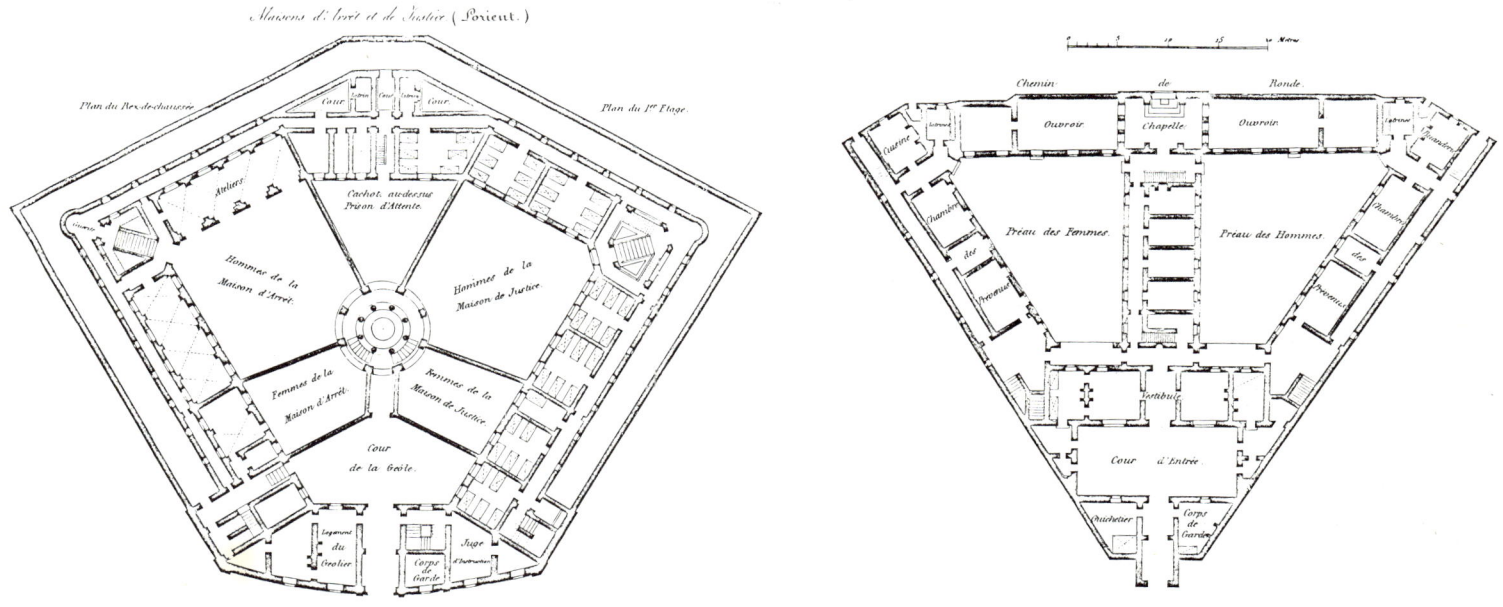

in England. He reproduced approvingly the plan of Bury Gaol, built by George Byfield on Blackburnian lines. Rather illogically, he saw no objection to the six wings found there, in spite of his strictures of the 'model prison' of La Roquette, the reason being presumably that his own work in this field was patching up the old, rather than designing the new.[19] Baltard also quoted copiously from La Rochefoucauld-Liancourt's treatise on prisons in Philadelphia, and gave a measure of approval to the latter's *prison d'essai*, a scheme for prison reform.[20] La Rochefoucauld-Liancourt's concern was of a wide and searching nature. He attempted to deal with the incidence of begging and pauperism in France in general, and with the relief accorded through the Hôpital Général in Paris in particular, pointing out the complexity of this

Lorient Prison; from Baltard's Architectonographie.

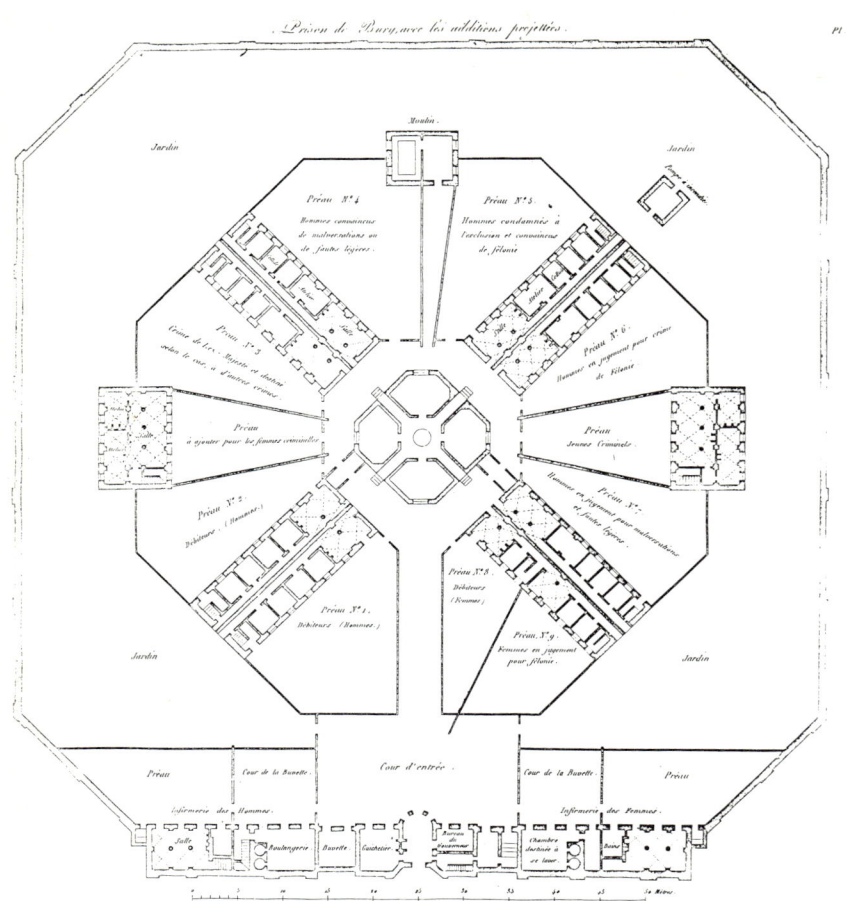

institution, which included a store, called the Maison de Scipio, the hospitals of La Pitié, of Bicêtre and the Salpétrière, three foundling hospitals and other branches. These catered for approximately 15,000 people, some paying, some admitted without fee, some being organized and sent out to beg.[21] La Rochefoucauld-Liancourt's ideas on improvement and rationalization proved abortive and failed to make an architectural impact, although his suggestion for fewer buildings and more efficient administration contained hints which could have led to structural improvements.[22]

So it becomes clear that the French type of circular architectural form permeated English prison design, and that the latter in turn influenced French design. Howard's own specific contribution – the isolation of prisoners in individual cells – was suggested by hospital building, the fear of spiritual contamination replacing the dread of bodily infection. The influence of Howard was unsurpassed in France, where he was acknowledged as an undisputed leader. Indeed, in the field of European prison reform the English ascendancy found full recognition, until the established provisions were challenged, systematized and brutalized in the United States in the 'Cherry Orchard' Penitentiary of Philadelphia, which isolated prisoners during the day, as well as during the night.[23]

1. O'Donoghue, op. cit., p. 306.

2. Marquis C. Beccaria Bonesana: *Dei delitti e delle pene*, Monaco 1764, and *Traité des délits et peines*, 1766, translated by A. Morellet. For a brilliant elucidation, cf. H. Mannheim: *Pioneers in Criminology*, London 1960.

3. J. Howard, op. cit., pp. 216 ff.

4. J. T. P. Vilain XIIII: *Mémoire sur les moyens de corriger les malfaiteurs*, etc., published 1771 and 1775, new ed. Brussels 1841. The Maison de Force was completed in 1825 by L. Roelandt: *Promenades historiques et topographiques . . . de Gand*, Gand 1883, pp. 137 ff.

5. cf. J. Bentham: *Panopticon; or The Inspection House . . .* , London 1791; French ed., Paris 1791. A possible source for Bentham can further be found in fortifications; cf. the Marquis de Montalembert's *La fortification perpendiculaire*, I, Paris 1776, *passim*.

6. D. L. Howard: *The English Prisons*, etc., London 1960. J. H. Hamilton: *The Art and Architecture of Russia*, Harmondsworth 1954; *The Pelican History of Art*, p. 189, fails to mention this building, which is also omitted in Réau's *L'art russe*, Paris 1922, and other studies on art and architecture. The design is possibly due to the influence of Y. Velten, who was attached to the Imperial Office of Building, and favoured flat domes and crenellation. Hamilton, pp. 219 ff. Thieme-Becker, XXXIV, p. 209.

7. On John Howard cf. especially J. Aikin: *A View of the Character and Public Services of the late John Howard*, London 1792.

8. I wish to take the opportunity of thanking these Authorities for searching their records, although unfortunately without success.

9. On the architecture of prisons see Th. Markus in *Architectural Review*, CXVI, October 1954, pp. 251 ff. *Colvin*, p. 77. *The Builder*, XXVII, 1869, p. 781. Wasmuth's *Lexikon der Baukunst*, II, Berlin 1930, col. 587 ff.

10. When dealing with Soane it must be remembered that he habitually re-issued his plans under various titles. The most convenient collection of some of his designs is found in *Designs for Public Improvements in London and Westminster*, 2nd imp., London 1828. See p. 27, pl. 41.

11. J. Elmes: *Hints for the Improvement of Prisons*, etc., London 1817. *Colvin*, p. 193; cf. also J. Adshead: *Prisons and Prisoners*, London 1845, *passim*.

12. W. Kent: *An Encyclopaedia of London*, under 'Prisons of the Past', numerous editions. *Colvin*, p. 387.

13. On Millbank, cf. H. Mayhew and J. Binny: *The Criminal Prisons of London and Scenes of Prison Life*, London 1862. D. L. Howard: op. cit., pp. 42 ff. On Pentonville and the model prison: D. L. Howard, op. cit., p. 63 and Adshead, op. cit., pp. 225 ff.

14. Society for the Improvement of Prison Discipline, London 1826. H. D. Kalman in *Architectural History*, 12, 1969, pp. 50 ff.

15. *Prix*, p. 41 and pls. 116 and 117. It was not unusual for cells to be located under the courts; for example, Rembrandt's realistic rendering in his 'Christ presented to the People' in the British Museum.

16. E. Seligman: *La Justice en France pendant la Révolution, 1789–1792*, Paris 1913.

17. L. A. A. Marquet-Vasselot: *Examen historique et critique des diverses Théories Pénitentiaires*, etc., Lille 1835.

18. [L. P.] Baltard: *Architectonographie des prisons*, etc., Paris 1829. Baltard, op. cit., pl. 21, and pp. 31 ff., and *passim*. Gourlier, Biet, Grillon and Tardieu: *Choix d'édifices publics*, etc., Paris 1825, etc., Part VII.

19. Baltard, op. cit., pl. 21, and pp. 28 and 34 ff. J. Adshead: *Prisons and Prisoners*, London 1845. L.-M. Moreau-Christophe: *De la réforme des prisons en France*, etc., Paris 1838, especially pp. 215 and 378. Ph. M. Alhoy and L. Lurine: *Les prisons de Paris*, etc., Paris 1846, p. 532. Also *Hillairet*, II, p. 502 f.

20. On the Prison d'Essai cf. Ferdinand Dreyfus: *Un philanthrope d'autrefois, La Rochefoucauld-Liancourt, 1747–1827*, Paris 1903.

21. The Duke de La Rochefoucauld-Liancourt: *Des prisons de Philadelphie*, etc., Philadelphia 1796. According to the text, this treatise was written in 1794.

22. cf. the first *Rapport fait au nom du Comité de mendicité*, etc., of 1789, as well as the second report of 1790.

23. The Philadelphia system was replaced by the so-called Auburn system, which isolated prisoners only at night, but allowed them to work silently in groups during the day. Although the Auburn prison was older than Cherry Orchard, the former completed in 1825, the latter in 1829, its arrangements slowly gained general acceptance. cf. the relevant articles in *The Encyclopaedia of the Social Sciences*, which deal with the psychological implications of this change. cf. also notes 9 and 19 of this chapter.

Appendix

Extracts from *An Act to explain and amend the Laws relating to the Transportation, Imprisonment, and other Punishment, of certain Offenders.*
Public General Acts 19, Geo. 3, Cap. LXXIV, pp. 1387 ff.

And whereas, if many Offenders, convicted of Crimes for which Transportation hath been usually inflicted, were ordered to solitary Imprisonment, accompanied by well-regulated Labour, and religious Instruction, it might be the Means, under Providence, not only of deterring others from the Commission of the like Crimes, but also of reforming the Individuals, and inuring them to Habits of Industry; be it therefore further enacted, That it shall and may be lawful for His Majesty, in His Privy Council, to appoint Three Persons to be Supervisors of the Buildings to be erected in pursuance of this Act, and from Time to Time to remove them, or any of them, and appoint others in the Place of such as shall be so removed, or shall die, or resign their Trust; and the said Supervisors, or any Two of them, shall, as soon as conveniently may be, Fix upon any Common, Heath or Waste or any other Piece or Pieces of Ground, which may be lawfully purchased under the Powers of this Act, and which shall be situated within any One of the Counties of *Middlesex*, *Essex*, *Kent*, or *Surrey*, upon which they, or any Two of them, shall erect, or cause to be erected, Two plain, strong, and substantial Edifices or Houses, which shall be called The *Penitentiary Houses*, for the Purpose of confining and employing in Hard Labour, in One of the said Houses, such Male Convicts, and in the other, such Female Convicts, as, in pursuance of the Powers hereinafter contained, shall be ordered to Imprisonment and Hard Labour: Provided always, That in fixing upon such Piece or Pieces of Ground as aforesaid, Regard shall be especially had to Healthiness and the Accommodation of Water, avoiding, as far as possible, any Place where other Buildings are or may be erected continuous to, or within a small Distance from the outward Fence or Inclosure of such Houses, or a Situation within any populous Town: Provided also, That the Situation and other Circumstances of such Piece or Pieces of Ground shall be reported to and approved of by the Lord Chancellor, the Speaker of the House of Commons, the Justices of the Courts of King's Bench and Common Pleas, the Barons of the Coif of the Court of Exchequer, and the Lord Mayor of London, for the Time being respectively, or by any Eight or more of them, before the same shall be finally fixed upon, or any Purchase made of the same . . .

And be it further enacted, That the said Supervisors, or any Two of them, shall contract with proper Persons for erecting such Penitentiary Houses, together with the several Buildings and Inclosures thereunto belonging, and shall superintend the Erection of such Houses and Buildings, and the due Performance of such Contracts as shall be entered into touching the same; and the said Penitentiary Houses shall be made sufficiently large to contain, the One of them Six hundred Male Convicts, and the other of them Three hundred Female Convicts;

and each of such Houses, or the Buildings and Inclosure thereunto belonging, shall contain proper Storehouses, Warehouses, Workhouses, and Lodging-rooms, an Infirmary, a Chapel and Burying-ground, a Prison divided into dark but airy Dungeons, a Kitchen Garden, and also proper airing Grounds, Yards, Offices, and other necessary Apartments for the several Officers and Servants herein-after directed to be appointed: Provided always, That before any such Contracts shall be made or entered into by the said Supervisors, the Plan of such Houses and Buildings, with the Estimates of the Expence of erecting the same, shall be laid before, and approved of by, the same Persons to whom the Approbation of the Piece or Pieces of Ground whereon the same are intended to be erected is herein-before referred, or by any Eight or more of them: Provided also, That the Expences of purchasing the said Ground, of erecting the said Buildings, and of making a proper Compensation to the said Supervisors for their Trouble and Charges, being previously examined and settled, from Time to Time, by the Justices of the Peace of the County or Place wherein such Ground shall be situated, at their Quarter or other General Session, and approved and allowed by the Justices of Assize, at their then next subsequent Assizes, or, if in Middlesex, by the Justices of the Court of King's Bench, shall from Time to Time be defrayed by Warrants from the Commissioners of His Majesty's Treasury, or the High Treasurer for the Time being, and shall be provided for in the Manner herein-after mentioned.

And be it further enacted, That it shall and may be lawful for His Majesty in His Privy Council to nominate and appoint Three Gentlemen, or other creditable and substantial Persons, as and for a Committee to superintend the said Houses, and from Time to Time to remove all or any of the Persons composing the said Committee, and appoint others in their Stead, or in the Stead of such as shall die or resign; which Persons so composing the said Committee, shall be intitled to such Allowance *per Diem* for their Trouble and Expences, in every Day's actual Attendance on the Duties of their Office, as the said Justices of the Peace, at their Quarter or other General Session, with the Approbation and Allowance of the Justices of Assize, at their then next subsequent Assizes, or, if in *Middlesex*, by the Justices of His Majesty's Court of King's Bench, shall from Time to Time order and direct; and the said Committee, or any Two of them, shall and may appoint a Clerk, to continue during their Pleasure, with such Salary as they shall judge to be reasonable; which Clerk shall keep regular Minutes of the Proceedings of the said Committee; and the said Committee, or any Two of them, are also hereby authorised and required to appoint stated Meetings, giving Two Days Notice thereof, and from Time to Time to adjourn the same, and at such stated and adjourned Meetings, and not otherwise, nor in any less Number, to carry this Act into Execution; and at every such Meeting the Chairman of such Committee shall not only have a single Voice or Vote, but, in case of Equality of Numbers, a decisive or casting Vote.

And be it further enacted, That when the said Penitentiary Houses shall be erected, and so fitted up as to be ready or nearly ready for the Reception of the Offenders herein-after directed to be sent thereto, the Committee shall elect such Officers as are herein-after directed, and shall make Provision for Stock and Materials for the Use and Employment of the Offenders to be confined in the said Penitentiary Houses; and also shall make Orders for the Regulation of the said Houses, and of such Offenders, in such Cases as are not by this Act particularly provided for; which Orders of Regulation, being approved of by the said Justices of the Peace, at their Quarter or other General Sessions, and confirmed and allowed by the Justices of Assize at their then next subsequent Assizes, or, if in Middlesex, by the Justices of the Court of King's Bench, shall be carried into Execution; and the said Committee shall, in like Manner, from Time to Time, as often as they shall think necessary, make any other Orders of Regulation, as well for Repeal of such Orders before made, as by way of Addition thereto, which, before they are carried into Execution, shall also be approved of, confirmed, and allowed by the Justices aforesaid.

And be it further enacted, That for the Regulation and Management of each of such Penitentiary Houses, and previously to the Opening thereof for the Reception of Offenders, there shall be elected and appointed by the said Committee, a Governor, a Chaplain, a Surgeon or Apothecary, a Storekeeper, and a Task-master; and also, in the House set apart for Female Convicts, a Matron; and in each of them, such other Officers as the said Committee, with such Approbation, Confirmation, and Allowance, as aforesaid, shall judge necessary; and such Officers shall from Time to Time be removeable by any Order of the said Committee; and when any Vacancy shall happen, new Officers shall be elected by the same Authority; and such Salaries and other Allowances shall be made to the said Officers, with such Approbation, Confirmation, and Allowance, as aforesaid, and also such of them from whom the said Committee may deem it proper to require Security for the due and faithful Execution of their Offices, shall give such Security accordingly . . . And no Person, except the Officers and Servants of the House and such Persons as shall be authorised by Order of any Two of the Committee aforesaid, shall be permitted to go at any Time into such Lodging-rooms, or to see or converse with the Offenders; and every Night in the Year the Doors of all such Lodging-rooms shall be locked, and all Lights therein extinguished, after the Hour of Nine; and a Watchman shall patrole each of such Penitentiary Houses at least Twice in every Hour during the Night, and until Return of the Time of Labour in the Morning of the next Day.

Provided always, That it shall and may be lawful for any Justice or Justices of the Peace, acting for the County or Place wherein such Penitentiary Houses, or Places of Confinement, to be provided in pursuance of this Act, shall be situated, at all seasonable Times, to visit and inspect every Part of such Penitentiary Houses, or Places of Confinement, in order to make Report to the Quarter Sessions, or give Notice to the Inspector, herein-after mentioned, of any Abuse or Mismanagement which he or they may observe therein.

And be it further enacted, That the Chaplain shall read Morning and Evening Prayers, in the Chapel of each of such Penitentiary Houses, and preach a Sermon both Morning and Afternoon, on every Sunday in the Year, and also on every *Christmas-day* and *Good Friday*; and all the Offenders confined in such House, who shall not be disabled by Illness, shall attend the said Prayers and Sermons, which shall also be attended by the resident Officers, and by the Servants of such House, or such of them as can be spared from their several Employments, and shall not be prevented by Illness; and the said Chaplain shall visit, with the Leave of the Governor, any of the Offenders, either sick or in health, that may desire or stand in need of his spiritual Advice and Assistance, provided that such Visitation, to such of the Offenders as shall be in Health, shall not interfere with their stated Hours of Labour.

And be it further enacted, That there shall be, adjoining to each of such Penitentiary Houses, One or more large and airy Yards or Places, inclosed and properly secured, in which, and on the Top of such House, if the Building will admit such a Convenience, the Offenders ordered to be confined in such House shall be permitted to walk and air themselves, for such stated Time as their Health may require, and the Governors shall respectively permit; and if proper Employment can be found, such Offenders may also be permitted to work in such Yards, instead of their Lodging-rooms or Work-rooms; but such airing or working in such Yards shall never be permitted unless in the Presence or within the View of the Governor or Task-master, or some of their Servants or Assistants.

5
Educational Institutions

One of the most significant tenets of the late 18th century was that of the perfectibility of man. Inevitably the need for wider education of greater numbers was appreciated, and the period fostered educational progress. The forms of education were manifold, but schools and libraries played a decisive part in the process.

Until the late 18th century schools remained on the whole traditional, especially in England. The public schools had become establishments for the privileged, although they were originally intended to be charitable institutions. The connection with charity was clearly expressed by Lord Burlington in his drawings for a school flanked by alms houses in Sevenoaks. These drawings were engraved by William Kent in *Designs of Inigo Jones, with some Additional Designs*, first published in 1727, and re-issued in 1770 and 1825, now to be found in the Royal Institute of British Architects.[1]

Education for the nobility in France had made great strides under Louis XIV. The establishment of St-Cyr, by Madame de Maintenon, for the education of young impoverished and aristocratic ladies was a sign of such progress.[2] The Ecole Militaire in Paris, inspired by secular principles, was

Lord Burlington, School in Sevenoaks; after Kent's Designs of Inigo Jones.

Ecole Militaire, Paris, after Landon; Ville de Paris Collection. Photographed by Jacques Buchholz, Paris.

erected by Jean-Jacques Gabriel about 1750. Built on a monumental scale, it incorporated the latest trends in hygiene by providing single rooms instead of dormitories for its aristocratic pupils. This measure was consciously taken to avoid infection.[3]

La Chalotais (1701–85) advocated the training of élites on a secular basis; at the same time he was also profoundly convinced of the necessity to keep the poor without education and in total ignorance. The reason for this was to maintain their willingness to perform menial jobs. Johann-Heinrich Pestalozzi (1746–1827) perhaps the foremost thinker on the subject of education, sympathized with the poor and the orphans, and regarded home life and the mother's influence as outstanding factors. In his hard and tormented life, he served his ideals, whenever and wherever possible, but his first loyalty was to the underprivileged. He had to make do with such buildings as were allotted to him by a variety of authorities to house his pupils. His lack of funds and his emphasis on the home precluded his taking an active interest in architecture. By comparison with Pestalozzi, Rousseau's importance in the field of mass education appears secondary. The latter dealt with the well-to-do child taught by a private tutor in isolation. Therefore his *Emile* could only provide guidance for a minority, however significant and influential.[4]

Education according to social stratification was widely accepted during the 18th century, except in revolutionary circles. This is perhaps best illustrated in Hofwyl, founded and directed by Philip Emanuel von Fellenberg, who erected a school for the rich and one for the poor side by side, without incurring any difficulties or criticism.[5] Goethe in his novel *Wilhelm Meister* ignores the problem of equality of opportunity in his section of the *Pædagogical Province*. Indeed, this issue has remained unresolved up to the present time.

In the period of Enlightenment, revolutionary thinkers regarded the training of élites and the necessity of singling out the gifted from all classes as both simple and urgent. Selection was for the purpose of extending schooling, the problem of the 'late developer' being as yet undiscovered.

Condorcet (1743–94), the best known educational theorist of the Revolutionary period, dealt with education in all its stages, from primary to secondary and advanced level. Lakanal (1762–1844) inaugurated the first plans for primary education and teachers' education. The Committee of Public Instruction of the Convention were concerned with the matter and methods of learning but uninterested in architectural achievements. This is also true of earlier thinkers, such as Helvetius, whose references to education were numerous; he demanded boarding schools in the country without, however, considering their architectural form. His ideas were ultimately based on the appreciation of nature found in Rousseau's *Emile*, but, contrary to Rousseau, he advocated education for the masses, and not merely for the privileged individual. Lepelletier-de-St Farjeau (1760–93) followed Helvetius' example and wanted to make boarding schools free and compulsory for all; they were intended for boys from five to twelve years of age and for girls from five to eleven, the scholars to be maintained by taxes. These writers, although influential in educational theory, had little effect on architectural development in schools.[6]

Therefore Ledoux's design for a school, published in his *Architecture* of

Ledoux, School; from L'Architecture.

1804, is of special interest. Quite a small venture, this *maison d'éducation*, set in the open countryside, was to cater for thirty resident students as well as for their teachers. Beds for the former were provided in separate cell-like units, thus continuing the arrangements of the Ecole Militaire. The staff were allowed more spacious quarters, including bedrooms and sitting-rooms. The central feature of the establishment was a chapel, which demonstrates the essentially traditional nature of Ledoux's approach. His school design has no apparent connection with his plans for the development of Chaux, especially Chaux II, and it must therefore be assumed that the school is of a later date. The text accompanying the engraving deals with generalities only, such as the beauty of nature and the passing of the four seasons. No particular interest in education emerges, but it must still be to the architect's credit that he dealt with this rare architectural subject at all. A further design, this one executed, was for an agricultural school at Meilland, again a boarding institution, and emphasizing the connection between nature and education.[7]

In general, schooling during the Revolutionary period was provided in improvised surroundings. The Ecole de Mars, a military school for the underprivileged, was intended as a counter to the aristocratic Ecole Militaire. It was located in cheap tents in the Sablons on the outskirts of Paris. These tents were laid out in regular patterns, but the school operated for only a few months on its site in 1794. In Paris itself schooling often took place in existing buildings, for example the Ecole Polytechnique, also founded in 1794, was transferred to the ancient Collège de Navarre in 1805.[8]

Schools were not usually dealt with in architectural treatises. C. L. Stieglitz' comprehensive study of school building in his *Encyklopädie der Bürgerlichen*

Ecole de Mars, aquarelle. c. 1794. *Cabinet des Estampes, Bibliothèque Nationale, Paris.*

Baukunst, which appeared between 1792 and 1798, was unusual. He differentiated between town and village schools, demanding an increase in educational provision related to the rise in population, and also insisted on workshops and agricultural training in the countryside.[9]

Quatremère de Quincy in the volume *Architecture* in the *Encyclopédie méthodique* of 1801 took up the educational theme, demanding that the instructor should live in the village school, whilst in the towns the director at least and preferably some of the staff should reside on the premises. He then discussed university buildings, the Ecole de Chirurgie by Gondoin of 1769, the Ecole de Droit of 1771 opposite the Panthéon by Soufflot, and the Ecole Militaire by Gabriel, contrasting them favourably with the 'old fashioned' Cambridge and especially Oxford colleges.[10]

It was Fourier who continued the Revolutionary tradition in France, and insisted in his numerous writings on the collective up-bringing of all children in his Phalanstères. They were to be divided into different sets, the *séries* uncontaminated by parental influence, which he regarded as pernicious. The Phalanstères made provision for this, isolating the children from their parents, and developing separate quarters for them.[11]

See illustration on page 20 (right)

It has been shown in previous chapters how the functions of 18th century institutions are loosely defined and tend frequently to overlap, especially in England. This is clearly demonstrated in Christ's Hospital, London, where a new wing for the school was added in 1793. (The buildings were demolished in 1902.) The architect, probably James Lewis, erected an imposing structure of three stories, the main accents being the rusticated ground floor and giant orders at the centre and as ornamental endings at the sides.[12] The elevation

Christ's Hospital, elevation. Probably by James Lewis.

foreshadows the similar appearance of Bethlem Hospital, built by the same architect.

In the late 18th and early 19th centuries two contrasting theories on education were current, either based on individualized family teaching, or alternatively the *école mutuelle* in France and the monitoring system in England. The basis for learning was instruction by several pupil teachers under the supervision of only one master. It was claimed that up to a thousand pupils could be taught in such groups and this system necessarily required large halls. The arrangement commended itself for cheapness and efficiency, and was therefore regarded as a suitable means of instruction for the masses. Its greatest drawback was learning by rote, rather than by intelligent understanding. To put it in the words of Charles Lamb, there existed at Christ's Hospital only 'an imaginary line' between different classes of scholars.[13]

According to the Baron Prony the system of the *école mutuelle* was first introduced in France at the Ecole des Ponts et Chaussées in Paris, founded in 1747. Its first director was Rodolphe Perronet (1708–94), best known as the builder of bridges. Independently from this venture, the monitoring system was developed in England first by Andrew Bell, and then further adapted by Joseph Lancaster. It gained great popularity in England and this in turn spread back to France.[14] Marlet showed such a school in action, in two lithographs, one based upon the other. The first print, which is presumably earlier, realistically depicts a lesson given in a disused church or church hall, the second, probably later, represents children teaching Napoleon's soldiers, a contribution to the Napoleonic legend. In England prints of this nature are rare, but one example shows a monitoring school in a barn-like structure, the pupils neatly lined up at long desks.

It represents the interior of the Royal Free School, Borough Road, and clearly shows the pupils teaching. Further light is thrown on this method in a print belonging to a series published for the British and Foreign School Society. That this is a realistic setting is clear from the ground plan for a Paris monitoring school, published by Gourlier and his associates, showing similar arrangements.[15]

These endeavours reached their fullest development in the project for a

Enseignement Mutuel.

Marlet, Enseignement Mutuel; from Tableaux de Paris. Musée d'Histoire de l'Education, Paris.

École d'Enseignement mutuel d'Metz

Marlet, Enseignement Mutuel in Metz. Musée d'Histoire de l'Education, Paris.

Interior of the Royal Free School, Borough Road. Archives of the Greater London Council.

Below left
School, published by the British and Foreign School Society. Archives of the Greater London Council.

Elementary School; from Gourlier et al., Choix d'édifices publics.

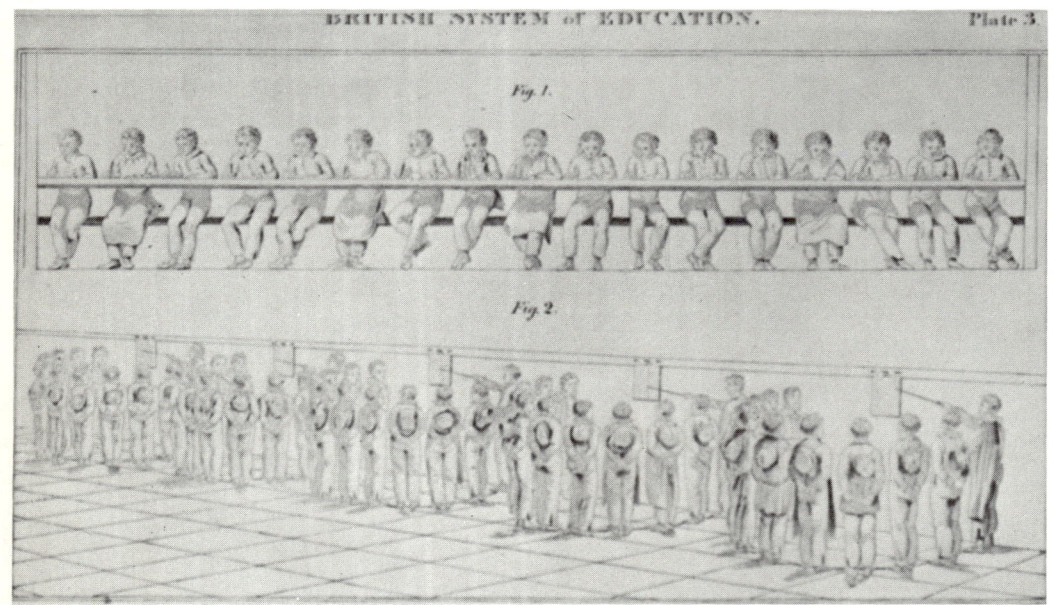

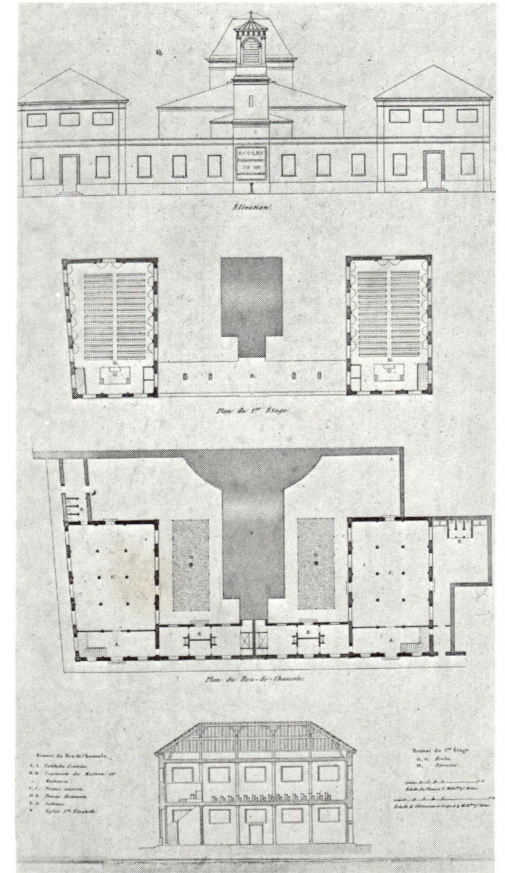

Chrestomatic School, which Jeremy Bentham wished to found near Leicester Square in 1815. It was intended to benefit the middle classes, thus showing an extension of the original purpose of educating the poor. Naturally, for Bentham, the Panopticon, intended to be multi-purpose, was to supply the architectural prototype for the venture. Residential accommodation was to be provided separately for 600 boys and 400 girls. It was to be designed so that scholars would be unable to look out through the windows, thus ensuring their constant attention. To Bentham's disappointment, the necessary financial backing for the project failed, and the plans proved abortive.[16]

The representation of school interiors in painting and the graphic arts gives some further insight into the prevailing attitude towards the subject. In Jan Steen's picture of a school the sentimental and realistic elements are about equally balanced. The sensuous aspects were stressed during the *ancien régime*, as in the case of Fragonard, who painted a young boy half naked, perhaps his son, in the picture of *The Schoolmistress* (in the Wallace Collection). Characteristically this school is set in a bare room, with an enormous blackboard. George Morland's expression of genteel snobbishness in his rather elegant *Visit to a Boarding School*, probably of *c.* 1790, gives a telling example of English taste. The skit by E. F. Burney on a finishing school of the early 19th century shows, in his *Elegant Establishment for young Ladies*, a girl suspended from the ceiling in order to stretch her neck. A large room crammed with activities is evoked, and although the work belongs to the realm of caricature rather than fact, it nevertheless emphasizes the lack of privacy generally taken for granted in early 19th century teaching.

Interest in education extended to the establishment of new orphanages, such as the Asylum for Female Orphans, Lambeth, with an exterior in severely classical style, and an interior characterized by the typically large dining hall. Similar in style, although simpler, was the Asylum for the Deaf and Dumb in Kent Road, built in 1807. More sumptuous is the Royal Military Asylum for Soldiers' Children founded in 1801 by the Duke of York. The original

Asylum for Female Orphans, Lambeth, aquarelle, c. 1820. Archives of the Greater London Council.

· ASYLUM · FOR · FEMALE · ORPHANS · LAMBETH ·

Pugin, Asylum for Female Orphans; from Microcosm.

Asylum for the Deaf and Dumb, Kent Road; from Gentleman's Magazine, *1812.*

Royal Military Asylum for Soldiers' Children, 1811. Archives of the Greater London Council.

façade still exists, although the building has been substantially altered in both function and appearance.

Turning to university buildings, the conception of a university as a democratic institution had been submitted by Diderot to Catherine the Great when he visited Russia in 1773. These plans were characteristically unconcerned with architecture.[17] It was Piranesi who executed the first comprehensive design, published in his *Opere Varie* of 1750. Considering the compactness and

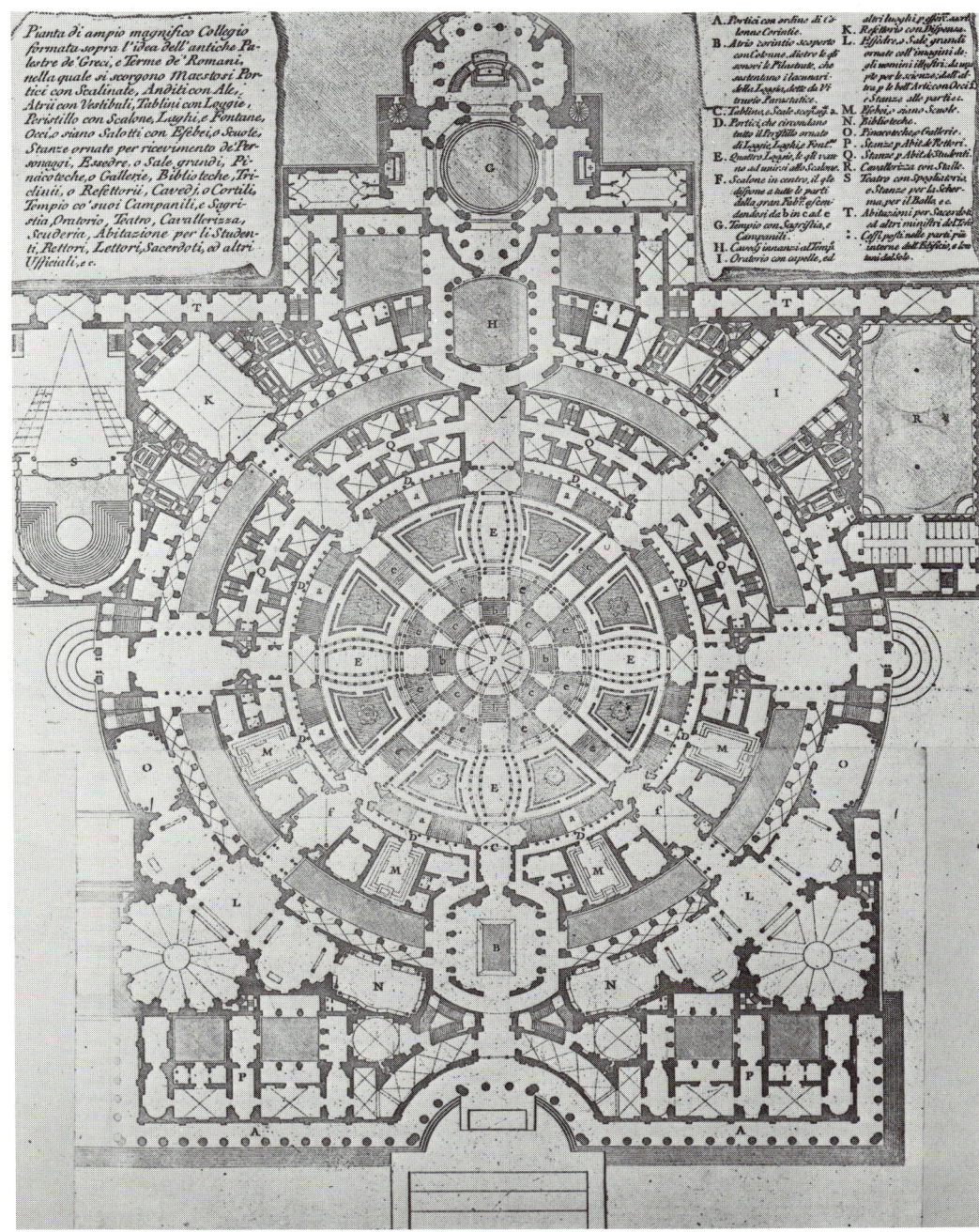

Piranesi, plan for a University; from Opere Varie.

intricacy of this lay-out it is significant that, perhaps for this very reason, it remained of academic interest only. On the other hand, Robert Adam's plan for Edinburgh University, begun in 1789, and of simple form based on a monumental inner court, presents a historical landmark then unparalleled

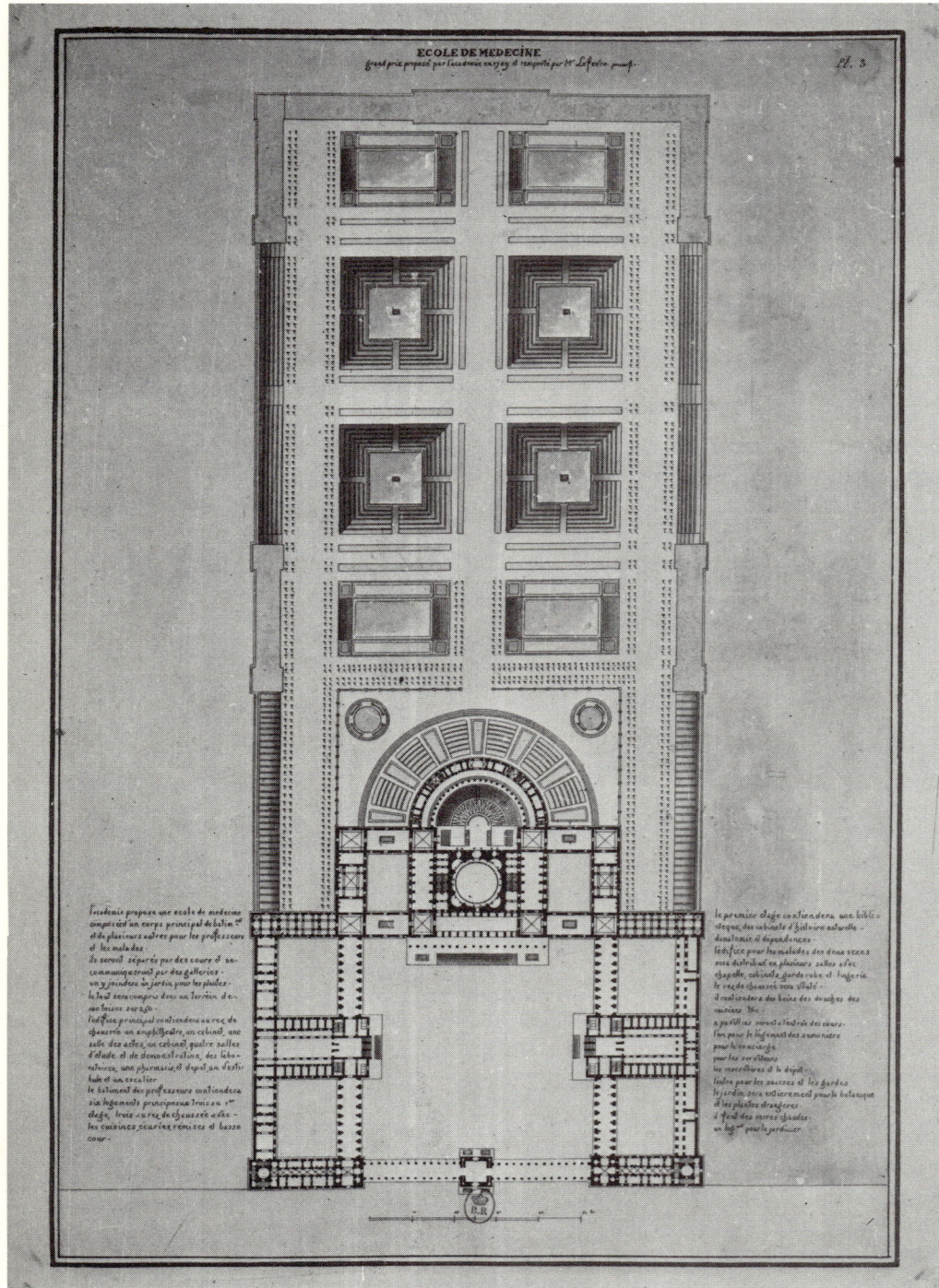

Lefebure, Medical School, 1789; from Prix.

in England.[18] The plan for a medical school by Lefebure of 1789, one of the *Prix* designs, should be remembered.[19] It enlarged on the plan for the Ecole de Chirurgie in Paris by Gondoin, including not only an amphitheatre for lectures, but also a circular library building, and botanical gardens divided into square plots.[20]

Charles Kelsall's little known plans, published in 1814, for a secular university to be built in the county of Stafford, epitomize the aspirations of an

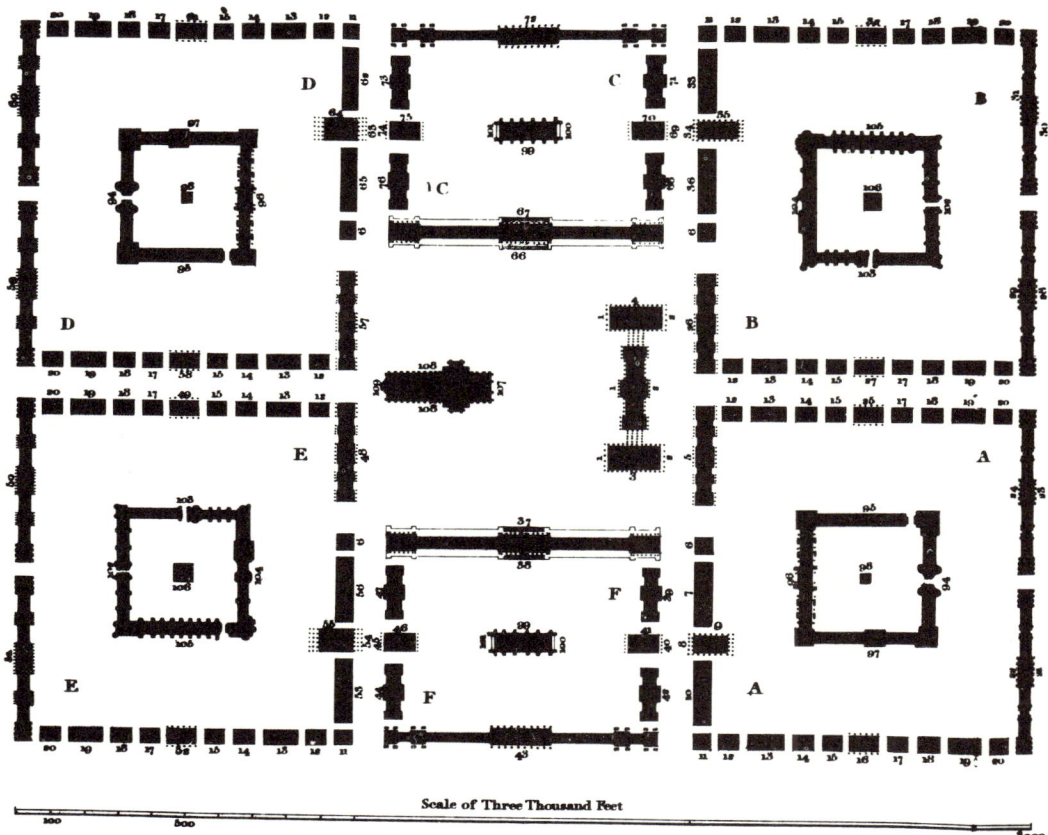

Kelsall, project for a University, plan; from Phantasm.

Scale of Three Thousand Feet

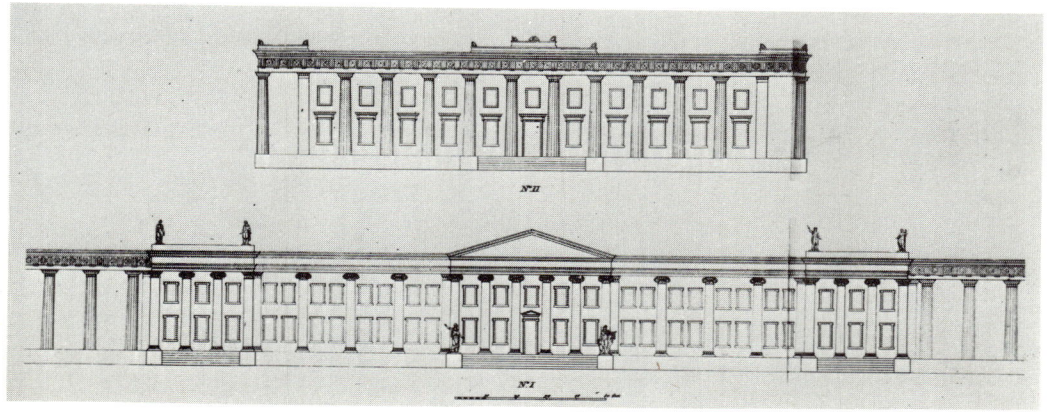

Kelsall, project for a University, elevations; from Phantasm.

age bent on learning. This university was to discourage the teaching of Latin, but to encourage science, including 'civil polity and language, a college of fine arts of agriculture and manufacture, of natural philosophy, of moral philosophy, and of mathematics'. The programme is therefore truly comprehensive. Kelsall believed in the significance of architecture, especially 'Italo-Grecian' elevations, to further his plans. He included 'Saxon' and 'Norman' courts – the latter term referring to Gothic. However, for the church he still adopted the 'Norman' style, based on Rheims, whilst his classicism is austere and simple, without detailed borrowings, similar, for example, to Soane's designs for the Chelsea Infirmary or Dulwich. Kelsall's ideas foreshadow the foundation of University College, but his architectural plans are rather more imaginative than those devised by William Wilkins for the latter purpose.[21]

An important factor in new developments is found in the field of adult education. The seeds had been sown in the Conservatoire des Arts et Métiers in Paris, founded in 1794.[22] This institution developed particularly under the influence of the Baron Charles Dupin, who instituted lectures there in 1819. The Conservatoire, still housed in the ancient monastery of St Martin des Champs, preserved the church. Originally it was no more than an exhibition hall for industrial models, to which lecture halls and class rooms were added.

In England, London and Manchester both lay claim to the earliest examples of a Mechanics Institute, the former built by McWilliam in 1825. The London building, no more than a big Georgian house, possessed an outstanding lecture theatre with surrounding galleries, which was used for practical demonstrations, as well as theoretical lectures. (Its roof required restoration as early as 1827.) The building in Manchester, of two storeys, showed a strong classical influence, and was a more dignified and imposing structure, especially erected for this purpose. Many problems beset these ventures. Lecture halls to seat about a thousand were to be provided in the larger centres such as the London Mechanics Institute. This lecture theatre, incorporated in what was originally a private house, possessed a gallery.[23]

Small museums were sometimes regarded as part of the educational provision, a function additional to, although different from, that of the ancient *cabinets*.[24]

Finance for Mechanics Institutes was either provided by wealthy patrons, or had to be raised by individual contributions from the workers, as students. In the former case, problems of freedom of expression arose, in the latter difficulties were found in the inability of the poorer sections of the community to raise the necessary funds. In both instances reality was seen as falling far short of the ideal, and this led to the dissolution of, or radical change in, the running of the Institutes.[25]

Similar to the arrangements in the Mechanics Institutes was the provision for separate education in prisons, such as in the Wandsworth House of Correction, where the prisoners, as an extension of John Howard's precepts, were educated in isolation.

Interest in education inevitably generated a concern with the development of libraries. The Bibliothèque Nationale, the ancient Royal Library, goes back to the 14th century, the period of King Charles V, and was originally housed in the Louvre. It moved to parts of the present site in the 18th century.

London Mechanics Institute, 1825; from London Mechanics Register.

Wandsworth House of Correction. Archives of the Greater London Council.

ADULT SCHOOL IN THE CHAPEL, ON THE SEPARATE SYSTEM, AT THE SURREY HOUSE OF CORRECTION, WANDSWORTH.

The buildings were, however, too small for the rich collections of books there and Boullée was in the forefront of endeavours to enlarge the library. The new *Salle de travail* was built by H. Labrouste between 1854 and 1857. It is interesting to note that it shows little relationship to French neo-classical planning.[26]

The only book by Boullée which was published during his lifetime was his *Mémoires sur les moyens de procurer à la Bibliothèque du Roi les avantages que ce monument exige* of 1785. In his prophetic plea for the enlargement of the library, then housed in the Palais Mazarin (his third attempt in advocating a new Bibliothèque Royale), he suggested covering the open rectangular forecourt. At a later stage, he proposed that three new identical wings should be added to enclose an inner quadrangular space. The books were to be displayed on four open tiers, and handed down swiftly, 'as quick as sound', by attendants assigned to these tiers. That the concept of this library was by no means Utopian, but on the contrary both easy and cheap to build, was emphasized in Boullée's *Essai*. Here he suggested a timber roof as the least costly arrangement, but admitted that a vault was also a structural possibility. It was only when, at a later stage, he developed designs for a National Palace, incorporating the library, that his plans became more ambitious. Here an inner dome similar to the one suggested for his Museum was to replace the central courtyard, and monumental avenues were planned as approaches.

Boullée's pupil J.-N.-L. Durand took up the theme in a plate of his *Précis*. He adapted Boullée's plan for the National Palace incorporating a central dome, but added radiating wings, as found in the hospital plans by Petit and Poyet. Furthermore he kept the *chemin de ronde* of the Halle aux Blés. Although

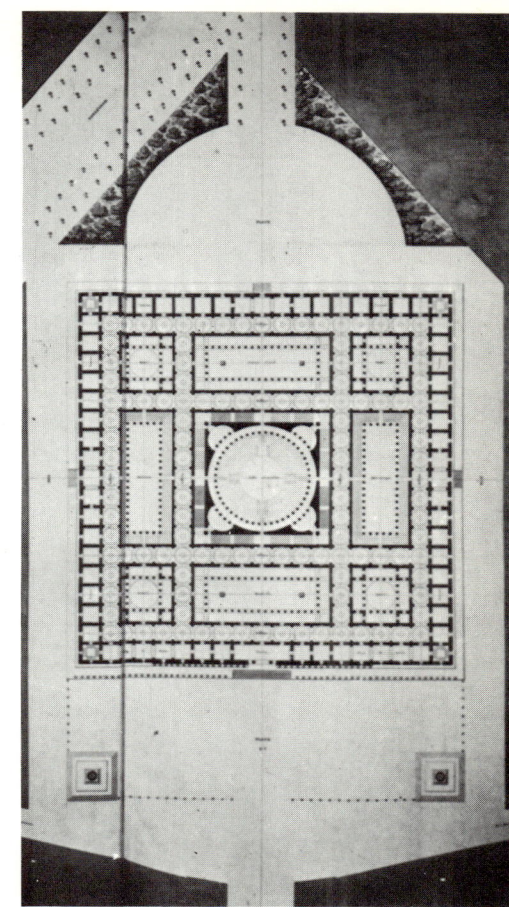

Boullée, project for a Royal Library, ground-plan. Cabinet des Estampes, Bibliothèque Nationale, Paris.

Left
Boullée, project for a Royal Library, section. Cabinet des Estampes, Bibliothèque Nationale, Paris.

these plans were not adopted for the Bibliothèque Nationale they aroused lasting interest.[27] This is reflected in a publication concerned with the building of a new Royal Library by the Baron Delessert, published in 1835. It was to be located near the Louvre, and structurally connected with it. Durand's radial division was maintained, and also the circular enclosure. Delessert's book came into the possession of the British Museum about 1840, according

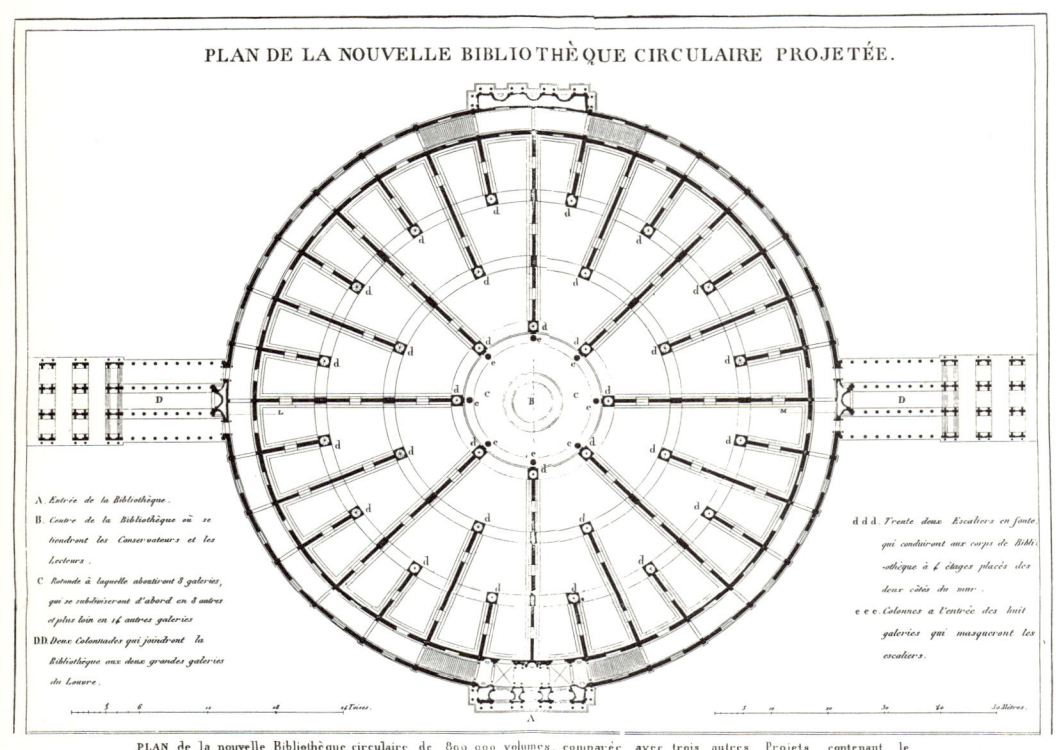

PLAN DE LA NOUVELLE BIBLIOTHÈQUE CIRCULAIRE PROJETÉE.

PLAN de la nouvelle Bibliothèque circulaire de 800,000 volumes, comparée avec trois autres Projets contenant le même nombre de Volumes.

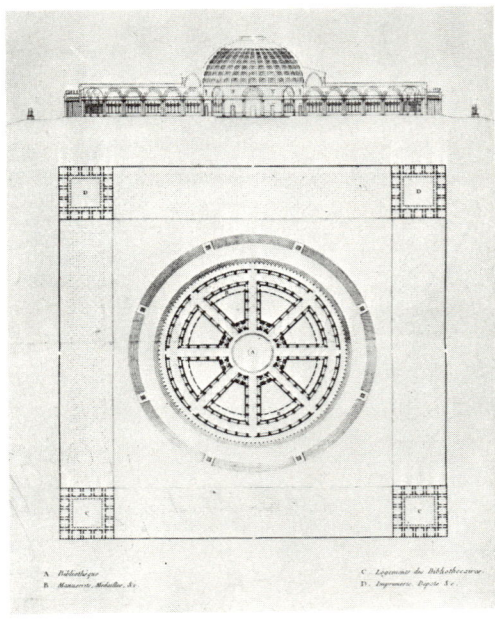

Durand, Library; from Précis.

Left
Delessert, project for a Royal Library, plan; from his Mémoire.

to its accession stamp, and could therefore have influenced Sidney Smirke's plan for the circular Reading Room, opened in 1857.[28] It is certain that Smirke was aware of Durand's publication, then one of the standard books in architectural education. The circular form had been used in earlier libraries, such as the Radcliffe Library in Oxford and the Ducal Library in Wolfenbüttel. The most significant precursor of the British Museum Reading Room in Britain is found at the Register House in Edinburgh, mainly constructed by Robert Adam between 1774–92.[29] None of these examples show a marked similarity to the British Museum Reading Room, however, especially as the radial divisions of space are absent.

The history of the present British Museum is briefly as follows: the first museum was established at Montague House, from 1759 onwards. Robert Smirke erected the present Museum and Library, in the form of four wings surrounding an open quadrangle, between 1823 and 1847. Thomas Watts discussed the use of the open space in an article in the *Mechanics Magazine* of 1837, without, however, suggesting any specific shape. Twelve years later William Hosking favoured a circular gallery for sculpture on the site. It was only after the acquisition of Delessert's treatise that Panizzi, the Keeper of Printed Books, produced a sketch for a new Reading Room in 1852. This sketch, first published by John Winter Jones in 1859, shows the circle within the quadrangle and radiating lines pointing to the centre.[30]

The radiating pattern was used by Durand and Delessert, although the latter dispensed with the quadrangular court found in Durand's library. Sidney Smirke, the architect of the Reading Room, was clearly indebted to the French neo-classical tradition and brought it, as it were, to a monumental conclusion. A model of the Reading Room, which was restored in the Victoria and Albert Museum and is preserved in the British Museum, gives a clear indication of the lavish decoration intended, which was to be the work of Alfred Stevens. Frescoes and sculpture were to enhance the structure, thus diminishing its architectural effect. Fortunately, perhaps, these decorations were omitted for reasons of economy.

A remarkable aspect of the conception of the British Museum is the combination of the Reading Room with the Exhibition galleries in one building. Although this arrangement is now wrongly regarded as obsolete by some, it represents not only an expression of the cultural synthesis which was the chief aim of the Enlightenment, but seems also to anticipate new tendencies in administration in favour of integrating libraries and art centres.[31]

The main development of museums took place too late to fall within the

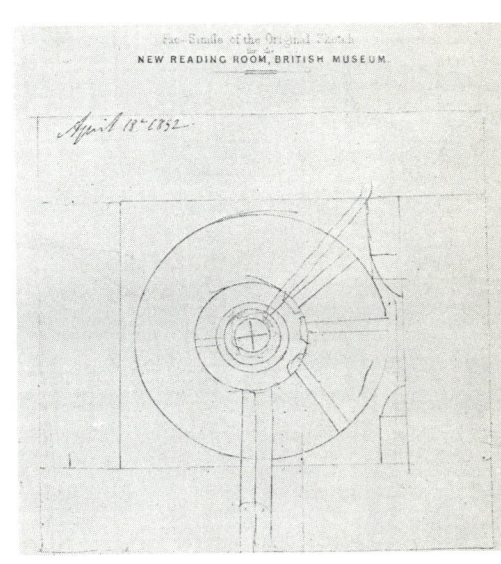

Panizzi, sketch for the British Museum Reading Room; from John Winter Jones, List of Books, *etc.*

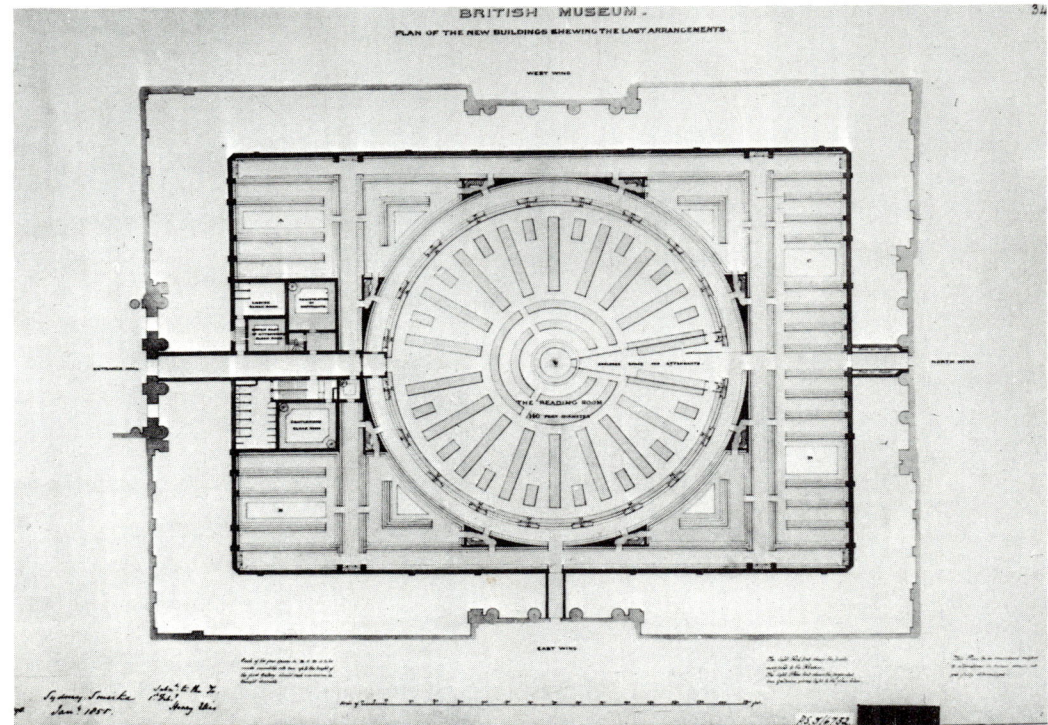

S. Smirke, ground-plan of British Museum, 1855. Map Room, British Museum, London.

Model of British Museum Reading Room. Photograph by kind permission of Mr Terence Hodgkinson of the Victoria and Albert Museum, London.

G. Dance the Younger, Boydell's Shakespeare Gallery, façade. Sir John Soane's Museum, London.

scope of this study. But their educational importance was realized during the Enlightenment. Boullée had envisaged a Museum as an expression of public gratitude: a large building, surmounted by a central dome, with startling effects of lighting. Durand's *Précis* followed this example in his prototype for a museum.

In London, the Shakespeare Gallery, Pall Mall, was intended for the exhibition of a series of paintings illustrating Shakespeare's plays. The building was erected in 1789 by George Dance the Younger for Alderman Boydell and served an educational as well as an æsthetic purpose. Sir John Soane's picture gallery in Dulwich, incorporating a mausoleum for Sir Francis Bourgeois, which was built in 1812, shows a similar synthesis of art and commemoration.[32] Sculpture was also to serve an educational purpose, as seen in d'Angivilliers' plans for a gallery of great men, or the competition he sponsored for a memorial to the Brothers Montgolfier.[33] (See page 116.)

It is against this background that J. P. L. L. Houël's design for a public monument in spherical form must be considered. Here, architectural tradition and ideas gathered from the Montgolfier monuments are combined, with a globe of the earth seemingly floating on clouds. A drawing in the Cooper Union Museum represents the scheme, which shows a global map of the earth, surmounted by the French Republic in a chariot, drawn by four horses and guided by Liberty. An alternative and simpler version is found in a pencil drawing in the Cabinet des Estampes of the Bibliothèque Nationale, which shows the French Republic on horseback, again accompanied by Liberty.

Both versions of the project are mentioned in a rare and short pamphlet in the British Museum written by Houël, entitled *Projet d'un monument*

Boullée, Museum. Cabinet des Estampes, Bibliothèque Nationale, Paris.

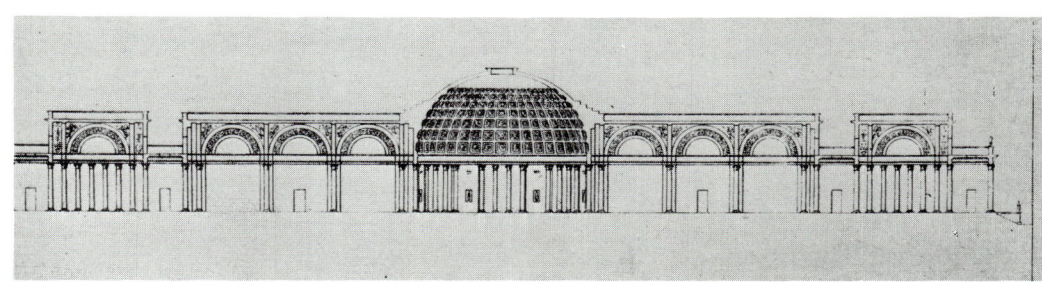

Durand, Museum; from Précis.

public, published in the year VIII of the Revolution. The monument represents, according to this text, a 'universal geography' Stars are mentioned, indicating the location of French Republican victories; furthermore the names of the victorious generals, including that of Napoleon Bonaparte, were to surmount these stars, thus combining didactic and ideological considerations. A *dessin* was to accompany the text, but whether this intention was ever fulfilled remains doubtful, as only one version was separately engraved, and financial stringency frequently made illustrations prohibitive. The pamphlet concludes with a poem, praising the globe as a symbol of equality and an

G. Dance the Younger, Boydell's Shakespeare Gallery, with adjoining houses, pencil drawing of 1796; from Architectural Review, *1917.*

Clodion, terracotta model for a Montgolfier Monument. Competition sponsored by d'Angivilliers; from Art Bulletin.

expression of the humanitarian aspirations of the age:

> *Un globe, en tous les tems, n'est égal qu'à lui-meme;*
> *C'est de l'égalité le plus parfait embleme.*[34]

This is an example of how educational purposes merged with concepts of Utopian and ideal planning, to be more fully analysed in the next chapter.

Houël, design for a Monument. Cabinet des Estampes, Bibliothèque Nationale, Paris.

1. F. Kimball in *Journal of the R.I.B.A.*, 35, 3rd series, 1927, pp. 679 ff., especially p. 680. *Designs of Inigo Jones*, 1727, II, pl. 52. The originals at the R.I.B.A. Burlington-Devonshire Collection. M. G. Jones: *The Charity Schools Movement*, London 1938.
2. On St-Cyr cf. P. Bourget and G. Cattaui: *Jules Hardouin-Mansart*, Paris 1960, p. 84.
3. R. Laulan: *L'Ecole Militaire à Paris*, Paris 1950, *passim*.
4. cf. on education in France, F. Ponteil: *Histoire de l'enseignement, 1789–1965*, Paris 1966, *passim*. R. Gal: *Histoire de l'éducation*, Paris 1966 (6th ed.).
5. On Fellenberg cf. C. Guggisberg: *Ph. E. von Fellenbergs Erziehungsstaat*, Bern 1953.

6. G. Compayré: *The History of Pedagogy*, London 1903, especially pp. 311 ff. and 390 ff.
7. *L'Architecture* I, pp. 206 ff., pls. 106–108 and *L'Architecture* II, pls. 290–291.
8. *Rochegude*, 420. *Hillairet*, II, p. 371 and *passim*.
9. Stieglitz II, op. cit., pp. 74 ff, I, pp. 447 ff.
10. *The Ideal City*, pp. 115 ff.
11. F. C. M. Fourier: *Le nouveau monde*, Paris 1829.
12. E. H. Pearce: *Annals of Christ's Hospital*, London 1901, especially pp. 84 ff. This is a chatty presentation, uninterested in matters architectural.
13. Elia (Ch. Lamb) *Essays: Christ's Hospital 5 and 30 Years Ago*, London 1823, pp. 27 ff.
14. *Notice historique sur J. R. Perronet*, Institut Royal de France, April 24, 1829. D. Gordon: *The House of History*, London 1932, p. 280. I. Tennen: *This England*, III, p. 249. *Handbook of the Lancastrian System*, 1831. B. Simon: *Studies in the History of Education*, London 1960.
15. Gourlier, Biet, Grillon, and Tardieu, op. cit.
16. J. Bentham: *Chrestomathia*, London 1815. *The Works of J. Bentham*, ed. J. Bowring: VIII, 1, pp. 1 ff. B. Simon, op. cit., pp. 79 ff.
17. Compayre, op. cit., *passim*.
18. A. J. Youngson: *The Making of Classical Edinburgh, 1750–1840*, Edinburgh 1966, pp. 123 ff.
19. *Prix*, pls. 57–59.
20. J. Gondoin: *Description des Ecoles de Chirurgie*, Paris 1780.
21. Ch. Kelsall: *Phantasm of an University*, London 1814. See *Journal of the R.I.B.A.*, 1933, frontispiece to January 14th. D. Watkins: *Thomas Hope 1769-1831 and the Neo-Classical Idea*, London 1968, passim.
22. Ponteil, op. cit., p. 215, and *passim*.
23. Th. Kelly: *G. Birkbeck, Pioneer of Adult Education*, London 1951.
24. A. Wittlin: *The Museum*, etc., London 1949, pp. 4 ff.
25. M. Tylecote: *The Mechanics Institutes of Lancashire and Yorkshire before 1851*, Manchester 1957, p. 119, and *passim*.
26. *Boullée*, especially p. 113, and *passim*. A. K. Esdaile: *National Libraries of the World*, London 1934. Labrouste is best known for the famous *salle de travail* of the Bibliothèque Ste Geneviève in Paris of 1850.
27. Durand in *Précis* suggests that, in small towns, museums and libraries could be combined. Neither the Radcliffe Camera in Oxford nor the original Bibliotheka Augusta in Wolfenbüttel can be regarded as prototypes. See S. Lang: *Architectural Review*, 105, 1949, pp. 183 ff., and O. Karpa: *Wolfenbüttel*, Deutscher Kunstverlag, 1951, p. 18.
28. Baron B. J. P. Delessert: *Mémoire sur la Bibliothèque Royale*, etc., Paris 1835.
29. Youngson, op. cit., p. 66.
30. A. K. Esdaile: *The British Museum Library*, London 1946, pp. 177 ff. E. Miller: *Prince of Librarians, Panizzi*, London 1967. J. W. Jones: *A List of the Books of Reference*, etc., 2nd ed, London 1859, pp. 209 ff. N. Pevsner in *Architectural Review*, 113, 1953, pp. 179 ff. and in *Journal of the R.I.B.A.*, 3rd series, LIX, 1951–2, pp. 89 ff. Also *Studies in Art, Architecture and Design*, London 1968, I, pp. 175 ff.
31. H. Selling in *Architectural Review*, 141, 1967, pp. 103 ff.
32. A. Stratton in *Architectural Review*, 41, 1917, pp. 49 ff. For an interior view with top lighting characteristic of George Dance, see *Microcosm*, I, pl. 13. The Shakespeare Gallery had become The British Institution. *Colvin*, pp. 557 ff., with good bibliography, to which D. Stroud: *The Architecture of Sir John Soane*, London 1961, should be added.
33. F. H. Dowley in *Art Bulletin*, 39, 1957, pp. 259 ff., and Rosenau in the same *Bulletin*, 50, 1968, pp. 65 ff.
34. [J. P. L.] Houël: *Projet d'un monument public*, year VIII of the Revolutionary calendar.

6
Utopian and Ideal Visions

At first sight it may seem astonishing that the study of social purpose in architecture should lead on to a discussion of Utopian and ideal visions. The foregoing chapters suggest, however, that the benevolence and social concern of the period under consideration led to an architectural programme based on deeply felt moral values. These were regarded as universal, thus showing affinity with Utopian and idealistic thinking. It was recognized that such visions are not only of value in themselves, but can also inspire participation in public life; in this manner the visionary element fostered revolutionary change, as is most clearly seen in France. By contrast, in our own more technologically minded civilization, thought and resources are being concentrated on the possible rather than the visionary. Models, when used, demonstrate this fact in a pragmatic manner.

Ideas on the nature of Utopias or Nowhere vary and no precise meaning of the term seems to emerge.[1] Nevertheless, it is possible to establish a descriptive usage, which suggests the evocation of a geographically remote place and of a distant period in time. It is stipulated that in Nowhere societies possessing high moral standards are found. However, as any thinker is bound to be circumscribed by his own society as well as by personal factors, the authors of Utopias are singularly deficient in transcending their respective environments. They do no more than establish a blue-print of their own predilections, as Nowhere is, in fact, their country of origin improved by social reform. It is for this reason that the significance of Utopias appears primarily in the historical field. They seem out-of-date after a relatively short lapse of time, and fail to an astonishing degree to bring about radical political and social change.

The French Utopians from Morelly and Babeuf to Fourier dealt with reactions to, and delivery from, certain abuses in the wake of political and industrial change. By comparison, Robert Owen remained severely practical, not so much as a Utopian, but as an advocate of feasible reform.[2] The solutions suggested in France emphasized tidiness and uniformity, characteristics deplored by Marie Louise Berneri.[3] What they share in spite of differences is the burning desire to promote change. In a society based on class structure in which the poor lived in squalor, Morelly had thought of planned cities, Babeuf of idealized villages, Fourier of palatial comprehensive designs on a monumental scale. Ledoux's Chaux III remained mainly architectural in conception and made no attempt to express a comprehensive view of society. It can therefore hardly be classed as a Utopia. Its arrangement of neo-classical buildings, set around an elliptical core and opening into the countryside, was a forerunner of the garden city, developed in England about seventy years ago by Ebenezer Howard.[4]

See illustration on page 15

Obviously, no rigid division between Utopias and ideal visions is possible, although in individual cases the tendency towards one or the other appears dominant. Ideal visions are even more difficult to define than Utopias. They share with the latter concern for a better life, but do not express a desire to impose it, or to make converts. However, they evoke images of serenity, which may be copied or adapted. Values are appreciated for their own sake, without serving any external interest or influence.[5] Art is inspired by this attitude in the late 18th century, corresponding closely to Kant's approach to

the beautiful in his *Kritik der Urteilskraft* of 1790. Classical models, frequently adapted, enhance the underlying sense of value by contrasting timeless monumentality with the trivial occupations of their own period.

William Blake the poet and John Martin the painter both testify to the power of Utopian vision. More significant in an architectural context, however, is a series of three drawings by John Flaxman (1755–1826), now in the Art Museum of Princeton University. All three show a stepped triumphal arch, of semicircular form, probably intended for Greenwich Park.[6] Their date, about 1799, can be determined by reference to *A Letter to the Committee for Raising the Naval Pillar or Monument*, etc., to commemorate the 'Genius of the Empire'. In this pamphlet, the sculptor discarded the possibility of building an obelisk, because he considered this form to be too slender, also that of a triumphal arch, as this did not allow for enough space to display sculpture adequately from a distance. He therefore decided on the erection of a giant statue, the model for which still exists in the Sir John Soane's Museum, London.[7] Flaxman also mentioned that it was George Dance the Younger, the architect, who suggested the summit of Greenwich Hill as the location for this work. The unusual structure, a semi-circular stepped arch, is quite isolated in Flaxman's *oeuvre*. In one of the drawings it appears with the column almost as an illustration for this *Letter*. The arch is quite in keeping with Dance's architectural style, and it is therefore reasonable to suggest that he was the originator of the scheme which the sculptor eventually dismissed.

The motif of the stepped semi-circular triumphal arch was resuscitated by John Martin in 1820 in two drawings now in the Print Room at the British Museum. This arrangement is unique in Martin's work: his architectural vision is far more fantastic, as exemplified in the 'Deluge'. Not only were Flaxman and Martin contemporaries and both living in London, but the former became a Royal Academician in 1800, while the latter exhibited at the Royal Academy from 1811, so there was ample opportunity for encounters. Martin must have seen Flaxman's drawings, as he was undoubtedly influenced by them. He changed the garden setting for the arch, substituting a view of Park Crescent, opposite Regent's Park.[8]

Left
Flaxman, design for Greenwich Park. Yale University Collection.

Right
Martin, project for a National Monument. Print Room, British Museum, London.

An alternative type of design for a memorial is found in W. Wood's pamphlet, previously mentioned. Here it is the pyramid which provides the main feature, flanked by lions. This arrangement suggests that it was the architectural form, enhanced by sculpture, rather than the isolated motif, which was regarded as æsthetically satisfying in England.

But the most important motif in architecture during the period under discussion is the globe. The Monument to Newton by Boullée has impressed a great number of art historians and critics in recent years. His style has been more fully understood, and the meaning of the Monument more fully appreciated. Its design is intended as a tribute to Newton's genius, rather than an endeavour to commemorate him as a person.[9] By a reduction of form to its essence, Boullée achieves an expression of immensity, order and greatness. A similar attitude is expressed by David Gilly in his unexecuted project for a Monument to Frederick the Great of Prussia, planned between 1787 and 1797.[10] The design has as its main feature a Grecian Temple, showing no discernible relationship either with the King or his career. It is a tribute to an invisible and non-existent hero, an ideal architectural vision of a sculptural quality.

Further reference must however be made to Boullée's Cenotaph for Newton,

See illustration on page 48

Right, above
Boullée, Newton Memorial by night. Cabinet des Estampes, Bibliothèque Nationale, Paris.

Right, below
Gilly, Monument for Frederick II; from Oncken's Gilly. Schinkelmuseum, Berlin.

Boullée, Newton Memorial by day. Cabinet des Estampes, Bibliothèque Nationale, Paris.

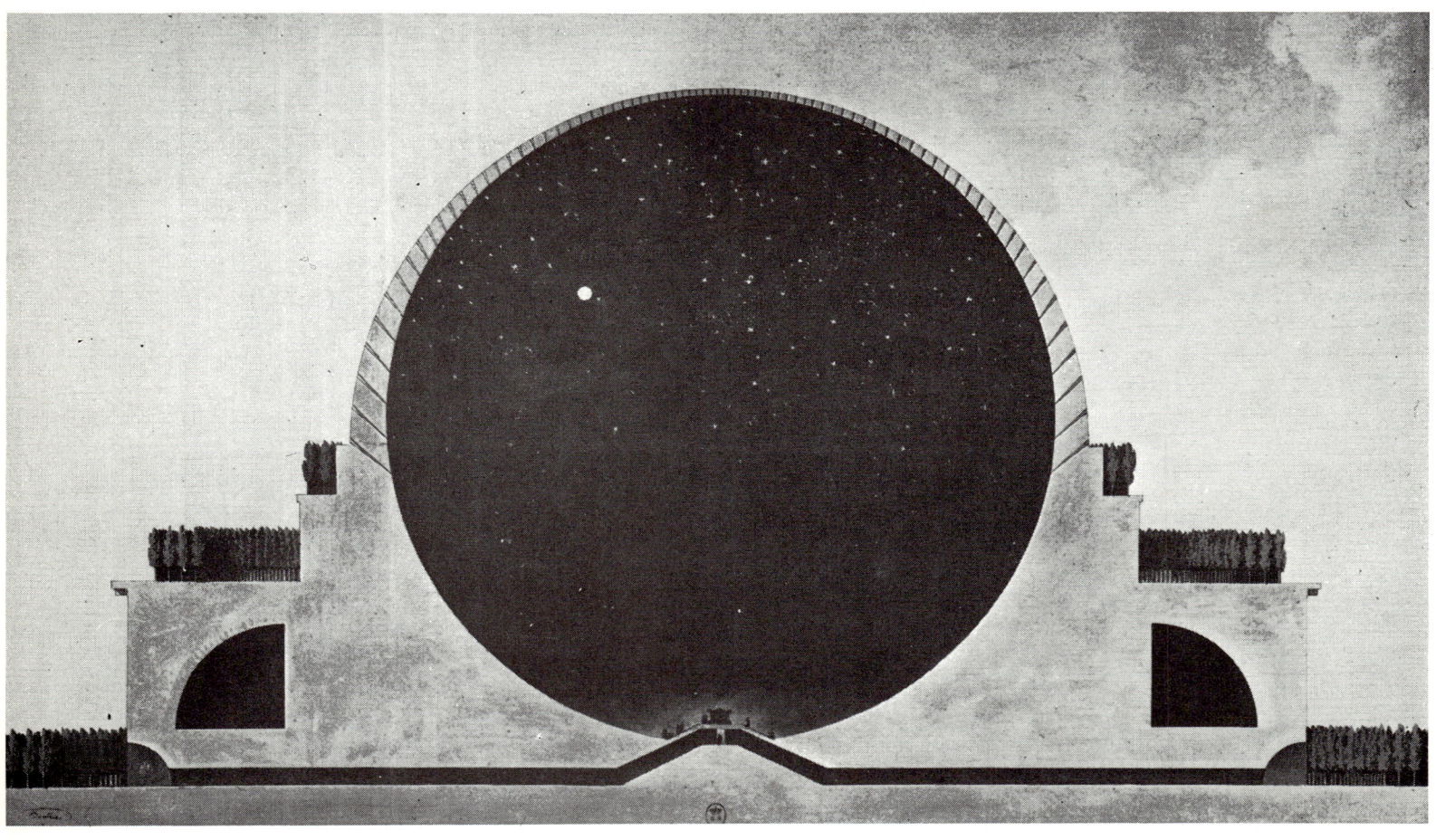

as a more detailed discussion illuminates not only his individual contribution, but also throws light on the role of the classical tradition in architecture. Boullée appears to have had no direct knowledge of the literary side of this tradition. His source in most cases seems to have been the *Encyclopédie*, in which a fount of knowledge was conveniently accessible.

The articles 'Cyprès' and 'Monument' are particularly revealing. In the former it is stated that the Tomb of Augustus had the shape of a hillock covered by cypress trees. Boullée suggested three circles of trees, as seen in Du Pérac's restoration of 1575. By having the globe as the main feature, Boullée produced an adaptation, but by no means a copy of the Roman tradition. Durand in the *Recueil* was no doubt influenced by Boullée's design, adding a classical façade and changing the globe to a cone, thus reverting to the older prototype. A similar arrangement is seen in Palmstedt's *Mausoleum Augusti*.[11]

Durand, Survey of Cenotaphs; from Recueil.

Philibert de l'Orme, ground-plan for a Convent; from Novvelles Inventions.

Boullée represents the Newton Memorial in daylight, illuminated by slits in the dome which simulate the star-lit sky. He shows the contrasting arrangement during the night, when an armillary sphere is to be illuminated by interior sun rays. In both designs the visionary element is considerable, as buildings of this nature could neither be erected nor lit in the late 18th century. But this did not cool the architect's ardour: he seems to have found great enjoyment in his work for its own sake, regardless of its implementation.

It has been shown that the designs for cenotaphs by Flaxman, Boullée and Gilly give no clear reference to a particular subject: they are representations of abstract ideas, rather than memorials to human beings. This attitude can be well expressed by the old Gothic term *Mal*, corresponding to a structure without a specific meaning; by the addition of a prefix, the word *Mal* can have its function specified, as in *Schandmal* or *Ehrenmal* – a monument to shame or glory.[12]

During the French Renaissance the circular form was often used, as in Philibert de L'Orme's plan commissioned by Henry II for the Convent of the Benedictines of Montmartre, following the destruction of the Convent by fire in 1559. The dormitory with cells was intended for the second storey, whilst the ground-floor was assigned to the service quarters; the circular domed building, with a central open light or alternatively a lantern, is consciously based on the Pantheon, according to the architect: '*Car elle (l'oeuuvre) eust representé à ceux de Paris un globe terrestre ou celeste, qui eust esté tresbeau, et encores plus admirable, si par curiosité on y eust marqué les heures de iour, par l'ombre du Soleil, ou quelque Geographie que l'on eust peu discerner sur la couuverture*'.[13] The cosmic interpretation of the globe is expressed, in the word '*Geographie*'. This can be understood to mean a map of either the earth or the sky.

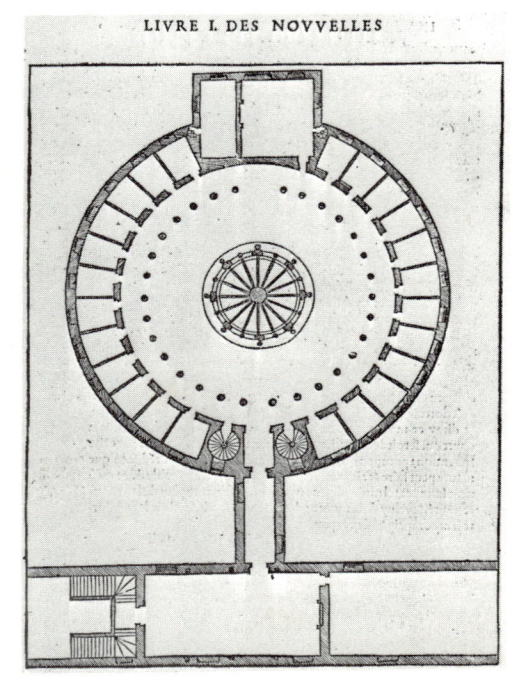

The treatment of the Universe as subject matter is based on the astronomical and astrological thought of the Renaissance, expressed, for example, in the domes of the Old Sacristy of San Lorenzo and the Pazzi Chapel in Florence.[14] These ideas still persisted in the map on the exterior of the dome of the Temple by Bélanger for Voltaire in the gardens of Beaumarchais in Paris; they are also seen in the designs for the Temple Décadaire by Durand, and the Cenotaph to Newton by Gay.[15]

Particularly interesting is the Temple of Immortality by Sobre, published in *Annales du Musée* (3), in which the visual image of a full globe is achieved by placing a hemisphere on the ground, surrounded by water. Lequeu, who is frequently mentioned with Boullée and Ledoux, is far more derivative. This can be seen in his design for a monument to Sainte Légalité among others, which is an attempt to express abstraction by coupling it with medieval concepts of sanctity: a typical instance of his approach. Boullée's and Ledoux's contribution to ideal planning has already been mentioned. Suffice it to say here that Ledoux's approach is more educational than visionary, and that his Pacifère, House of Union, and other such projects express abstract thought,

Bélanger, Memorial for Voltaire (detail). Musée Carnavalet, Paris.

Sobre, Temple of Immortality; from Annales du Musée.

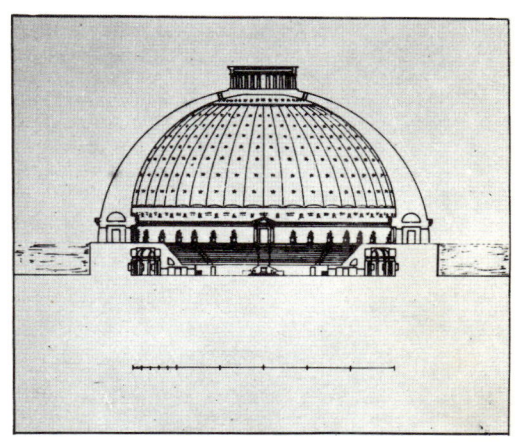

Lequeu, Temple de Justice. Cabinet des Estampes, Bibliothèque Nationale, Paris.

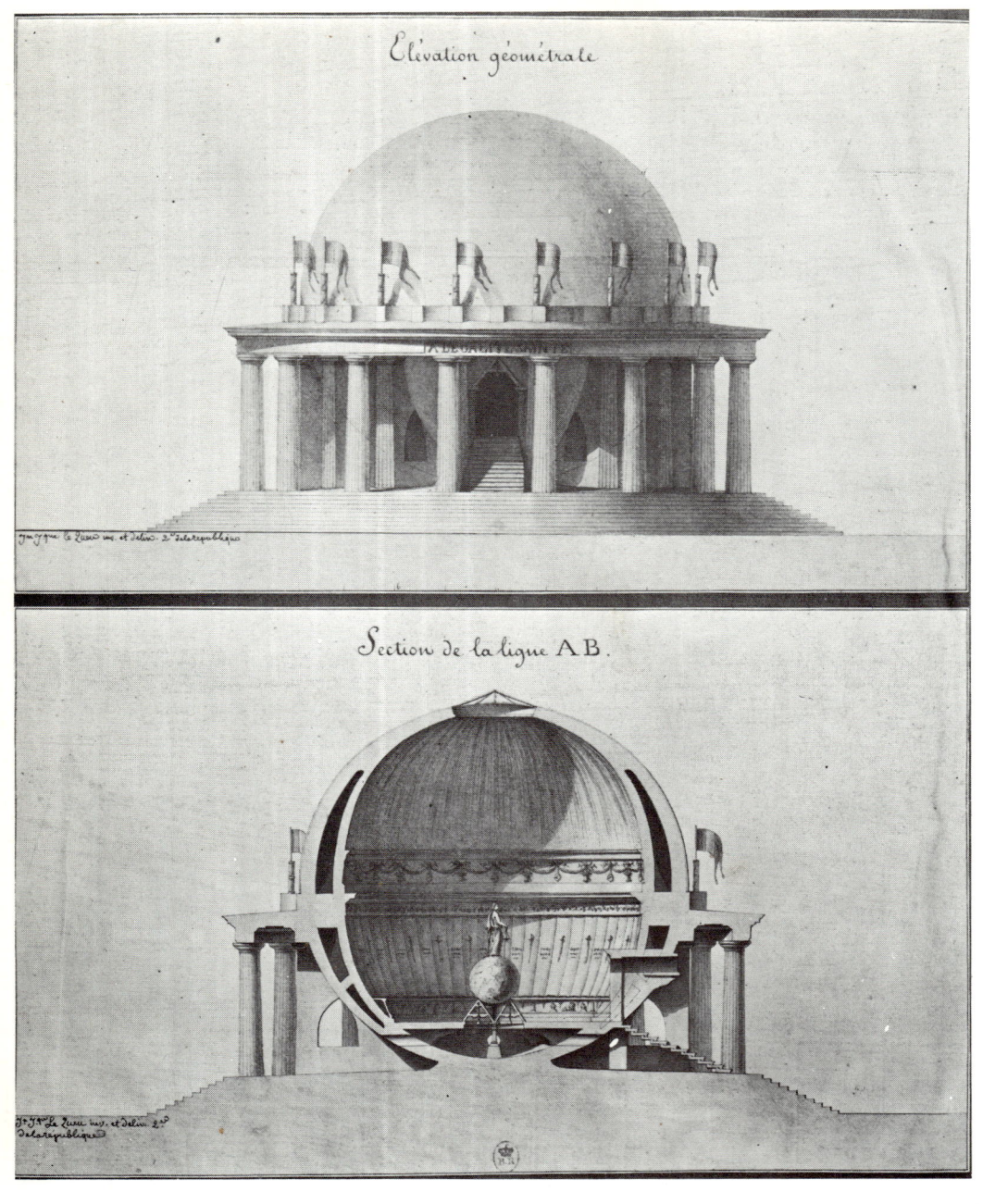

Élévation géométrale

Section de la ligne A B.

tending towards practical improvements. How far were these visionary projects connected with a social purpose? The gap appeared wide, but was not un-traversable. When Vaudoyer designed a house for a Cosmopolitan in 1785, he bridged the realm of the visionary and the practical with a neat piece of planning including a spiral staircase.[16] The educational value of the Public Monument by Houël has been discussed earlier.

In contrast to this type of monument, William Kent's design for the Newton Memorial, executed in 1731, is again primarily sculptural, as is typical for

Right
Vaudoyer, House of a Cosmopolitan, elevation and section; from Annales du Musée.

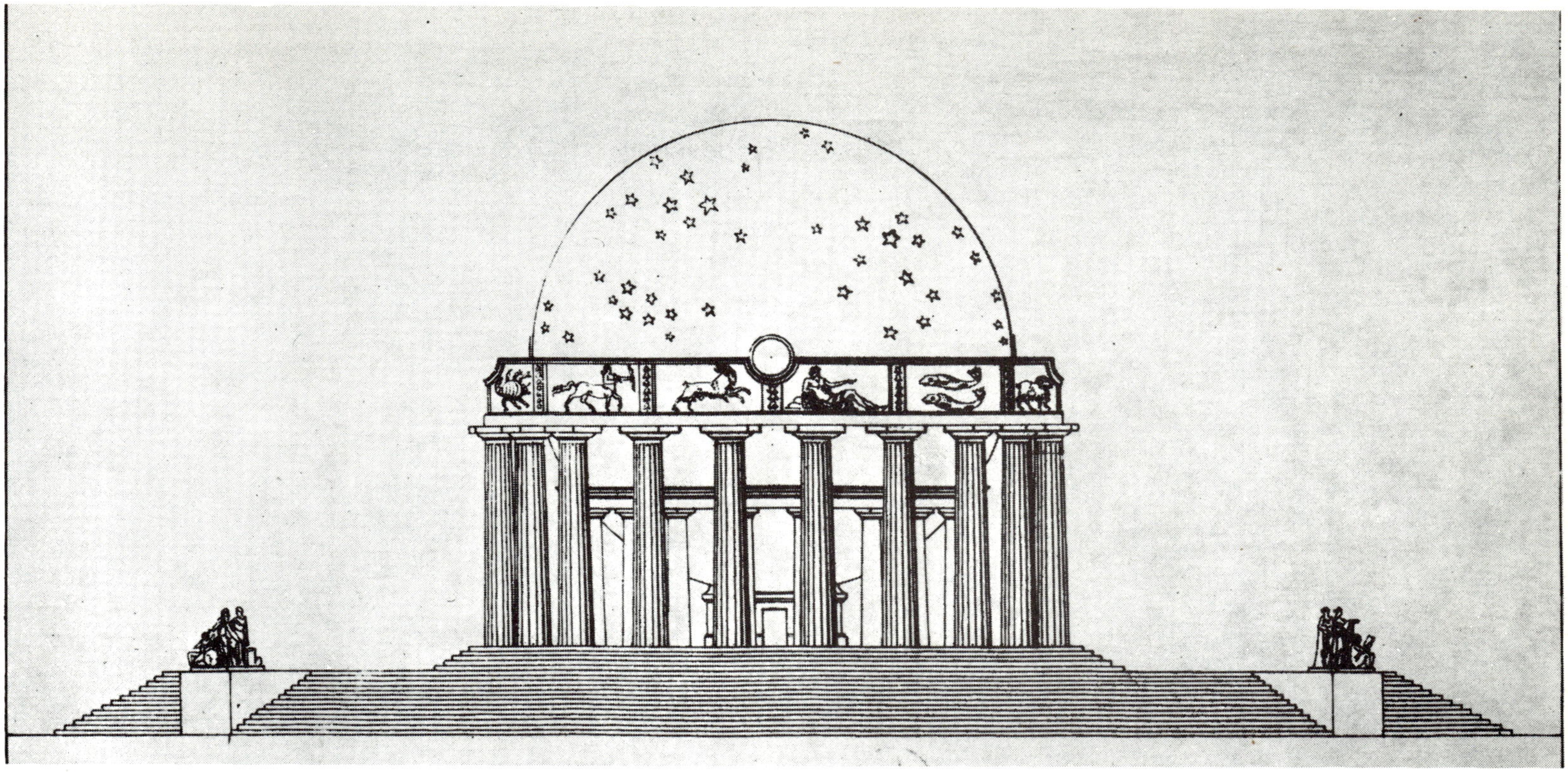

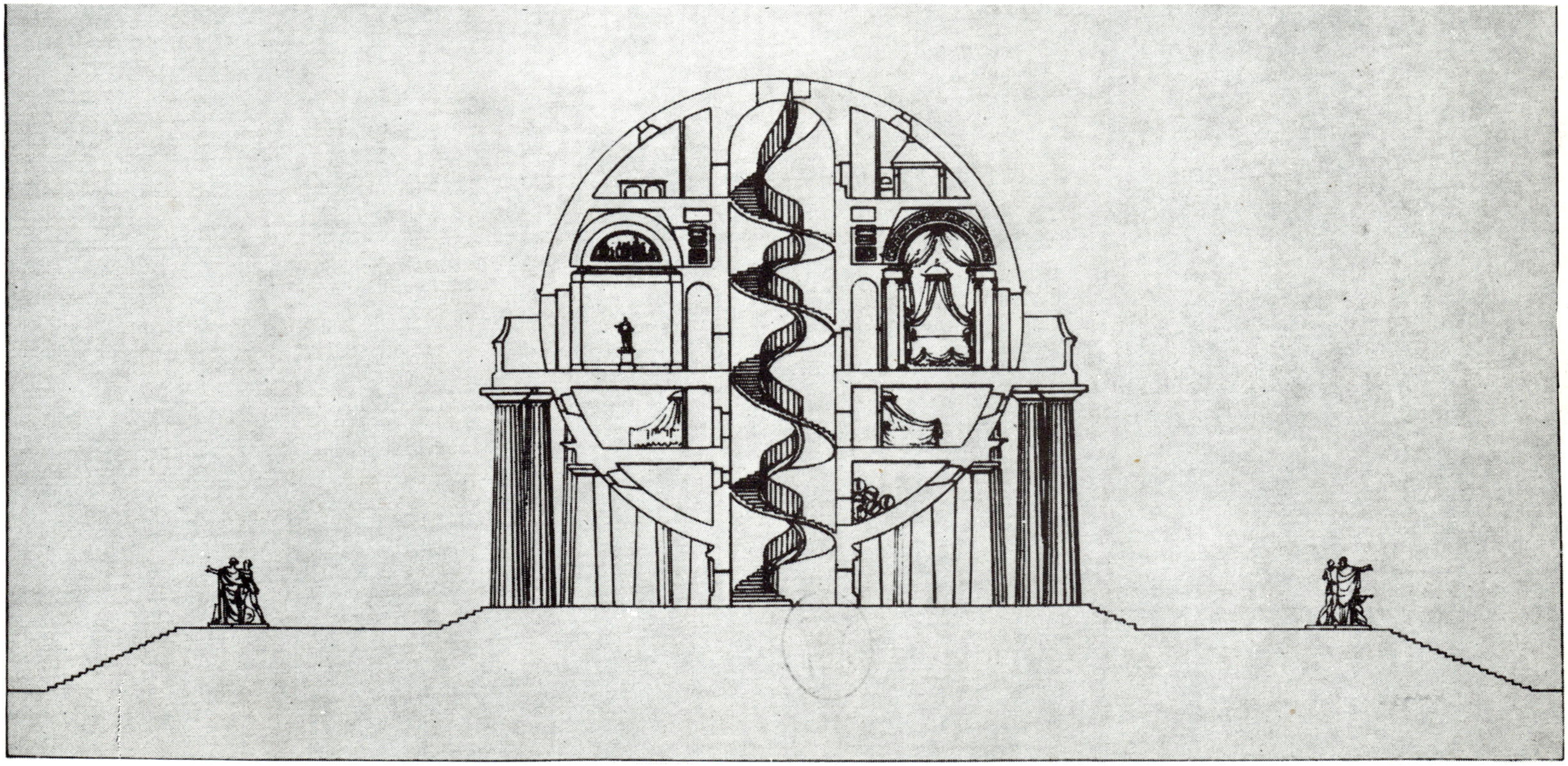

Kent and Rysbrack, Monument to Newton, Westminster Abbey. The Warburg Institute.

Goldicutt, Project for a Nelson Memorial in Trafalgar Square; from The Competition, *etc.*

England. Rysbrack's statue of Newton is surmounted by a globe, as a symbol of scientific achievement.[17] The architect's inscription:

Gul. Kent Pict:
et Archit: invenit

is clearly visible on the accompanying pile of four books.

A design of 1839 submitted by John Goldicutt for a Nelson Monument in Trafalgar Square brings the neo-classical tradition to a close as far as this aspect is concerned. A globe is used as a base for the statue of the hero. It is surrounded by heavy neo-baroque additional structures which are, no doubt, intended to express the greatness of the hero, but only result in a meaningless profusion of forms. This project, which was rejected, shows the distintegration of the neo-classical style and its replacement by historicism in architecture. Although Goldicutt admitted the influence on his work of Roman coins, there can be no doubt that French models also had a part to play, based presumably on the ubiquitous *Prix* designs.[18]

Obviously Utopian and ideal visions are only tenuously connected with any particular site. Nevertheless, it is interesting to observe how the two capitals, Paris and London, acted as magnets and inspired their respective inhabitants. Paris, the centre of French life, became the focus of planning. Even if this is not explicitly stated, it is the capital which appears as a challenge. Plans for London were localized more clearly within the existing townscape or landscape. The Physick Garden of Chelsea is an outstanding example of the blending of the picturesque with research. The freehold was given by Sir Hans Sloane, the founder of the British Museum. The gardens combined the collections of scientific specimens with an appreciation of beauty; especially famous were the two cedars, then unusual in England and notable because of

Clapham Common, as laid out by Christopher Baldwin; from Lysons, The Environs.

I

their great size and singular shape. The creation of an 'exotic' environment in Clapham Common by Christopher Baldwin testifies to the same taste.[19]

The French equivalent can be seen in Vien's design for a Memorial to the sailor Lapeyrouse, who disappeared in Oceania in 1788. Here the wild landscape forms a strong contrast to the cultivated scenery prevalent in much of English design.[20] It is possible to see English gardens primarily as Romantic follies. But should the Elysian Fields not be taken more seriously, as part of an ideal vision, superimposed on and organizing the forces of nature? Pope's statement 'Mahomet imagined Elysiums, but Kent created many' should be considered seriously.[21]

There is, however, another side to English vision. Some of Joseph Michael Gandy's designs foreshadow John Martin's in their emphasis on the bizarre, as, for example, 'Merlin's Cave' or his dreamlike 'Imperial Palace', both at the Royal Institute of British Architects. More subtle are two 'Grecian' landscapes, kept at the same Institute. One of these shows a column in the foreground, of which the lower part is separated from the higher by a cloud; the other, perhaps even more compelling as a landscape, again shows a column, a Temple and a group of buildings. Particularly arresting also is another fine drawing, tinted in delicate colours, which shows 'A New Senate House'. This was exhibited at the Royal Academy in 1835, according to the catalogue of the R.I.B.A's Prints and Drawings Department. Above the palatial structure, Westminster Abbey and Westminster Hall appear elevated in whitish and grey clouds. (These do not look like a fire, as erroneously suggested in the catalogue.)[22] This may date roughly from between 1822 and 1826 when Soane, Gandy's master, was engaged on work for the Houses of Parliament. The

Vien, Monument to Lapeyrouse; from Prix.

Left
J. M. Gandy, a New Senate House. Royal Institute of British Architects, London.

J. M. Gandy, Column in Grecian Landscape. Royal Institute of British Architects, London.

drawing brings to mind an entirely different 'elevation', that of the cemetery of Chaux, represented by the earth among other planets. This engraving, the work of Bovinet, could easily have been seen by Gandy, as Ledoux's book on *Architecture* formed part of Soane's library.

Gandy also published two books on rural architecture, in which he seems to be more French than the French in designing a village of eight concentric clusters of eight cottages. However, it is doubtful whether, as Sir John Summerson suggests in his perceptive study, Gandy is quite in the class of Piranesi or for that matter, Boullée.[23] However, if comparisons have to be made, it is Sir John Soane who comes to mind, whose inventive spirit may be regarded as a contrast and counterpart to Boullée's. Here is the perfect contrast between a disappointed Utopian and a serene visionary. This is clear from the biographies of the two architects: Boullée, unambitious and a devoted teacher, projected his personality through his designs, while Soane, in spite of honours and fame, still felt frustrated in his ambitions. His statement, 'In every Architectural Composition, the style of the *Exterior* determines the character of the *Interior Decorations*' is a denial of the functional element in buildings,[24] and it certainly does not apply to his own house in Lincoln's Inn Fields, where a simple and austere façade hides a rich interior. Numerous mirrors give a sense of expanding space, transcending the limitations of the site. This also gives an indication of Soane's personality, perhaps implying a

Ledoux, 'elevation' of the Cemetery for Chaux; from L'Architecture.

See illustrations on page 46 and page 140, above.

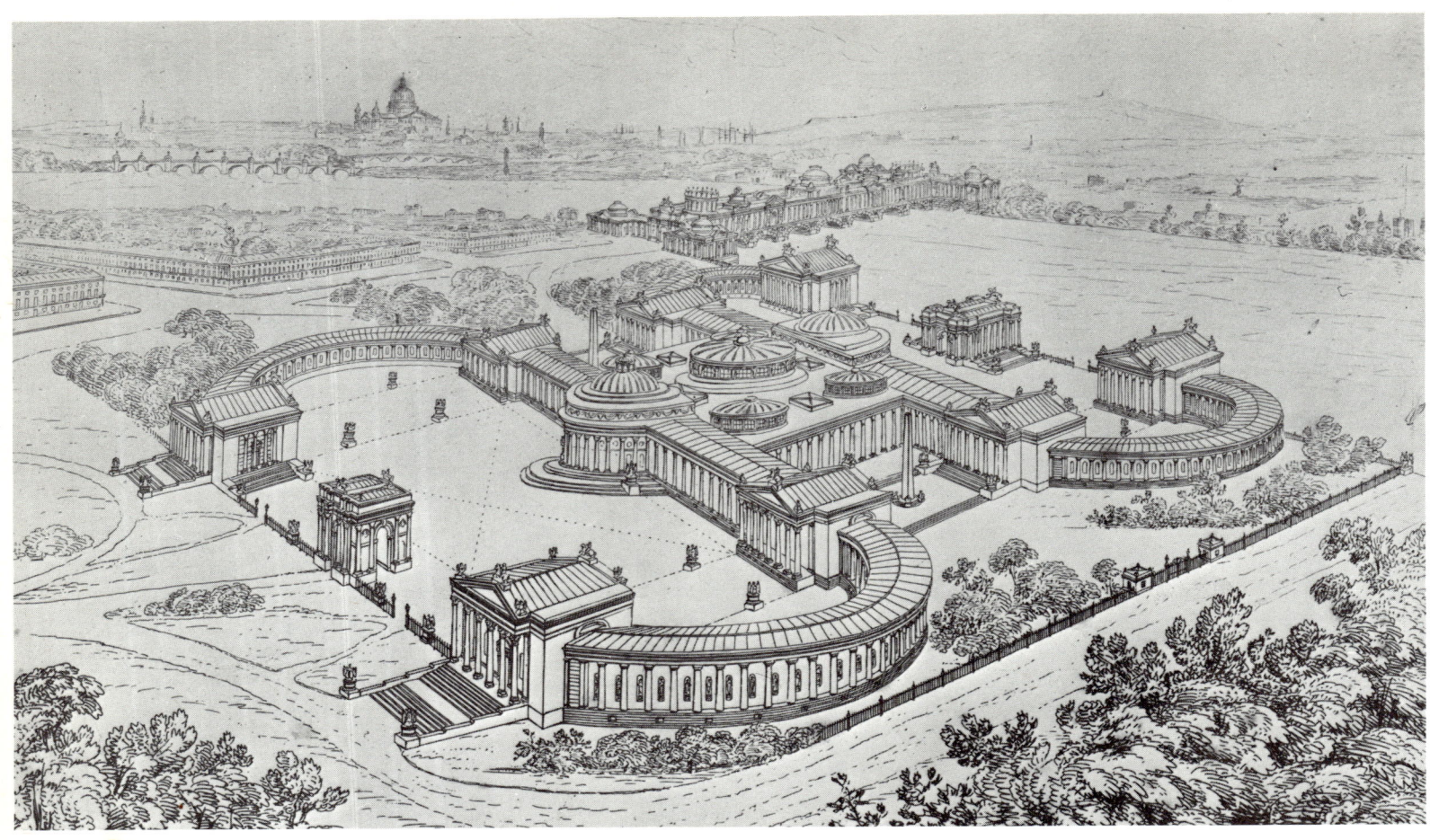

Sir John Soane, design for a Senate House; from Designs for Public Improvements, *etc. Royal Institute of British Architects, London.*

desire for personal aggrandisement.

The same criteria apply to Soane's major contributions to planning. Although his designs for the Bank of England and other schemes were realized and made him famous, many others were only partially executed, such as the new Law Courts and Houses of Parliament. There can be no doubt that any rejection caused an acute sense of frustration in Soane. This may be one reason why he lovingly referred back to older plans, for example when he published as late as 1828 designs for a Senate House and two Royal Palaces; one of these, dated 1779, he wanted to use on Constitution Hill, the other of 1822, was connected with the House of Lords. These schemes reveal a classicism inspired by Roman models. Views of the Thames and important London buildings were added to the original designs for publication and show a marked difference in style. They were intended to acclimatize Rome in London, as it were, and add an almost surrealist touch to the compositions. Whether this juxtaposition was originally Soane's or Gandy's idea is uncertain, but the evidence favours the latter, as fantastic and nostalgic forms are characteristic of his work.

Perhaps the most revealing passages as far as Soane's personality is concerned are found in his opinions of fellow architects.[25] Here his bitterness is

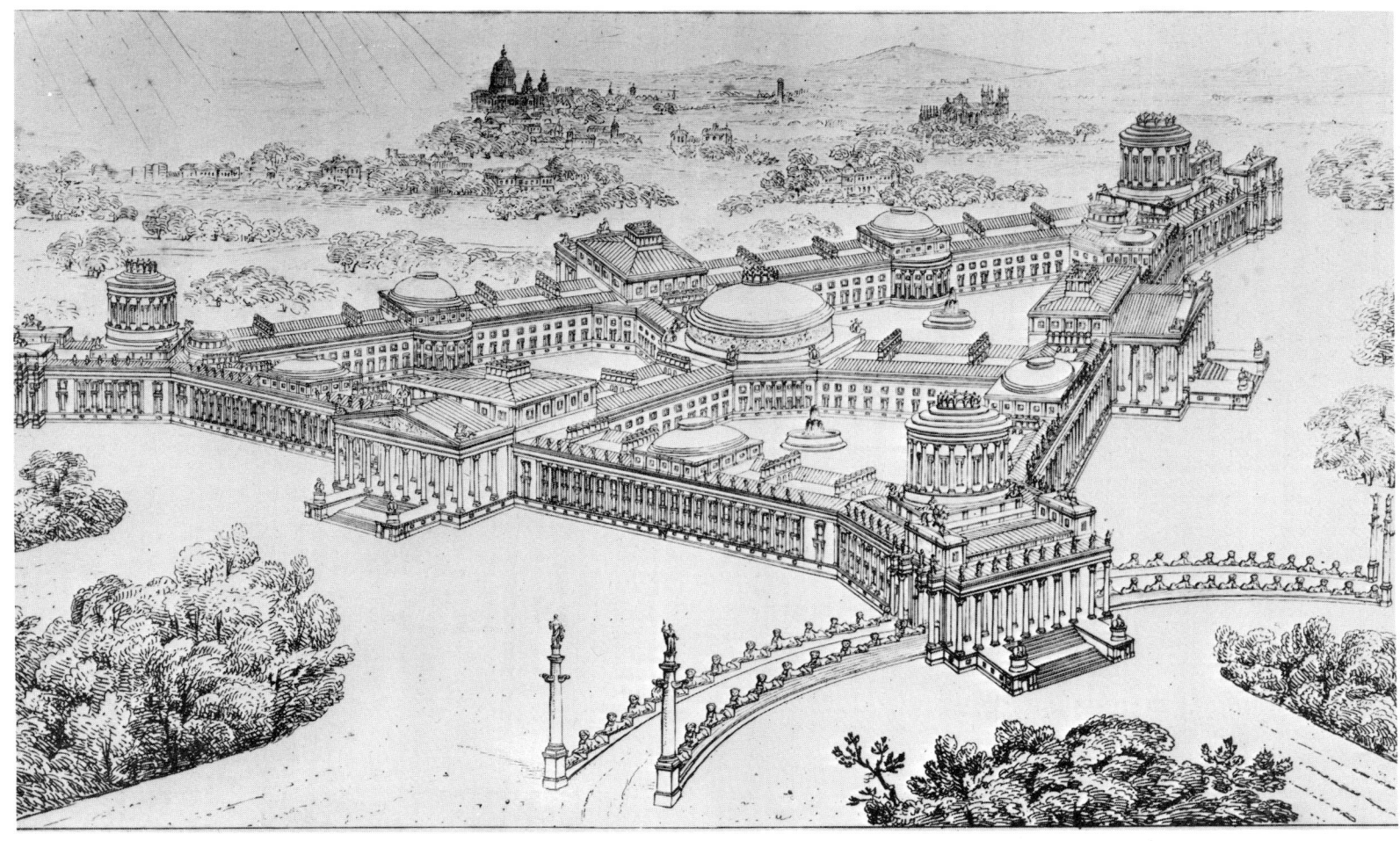

Sir John Soane, design for a Royal Palace;
from Designs for Public Improvements, etc.
Royal Institute of British Architects, London.

undisguised. He assesses soberly, but critically, various types, and his sarcastic comments throw light on the abuses of the age. Here a neurotic element is present, which leads him to overstress failings and difficulties. Soane divides architects into five categories.[26]

I. *The Heaven Born Architect*. He is inventive and goes in for a mixture of styles, sponsored by a Lady Patroness, taking the place of a goddess. The result is 'moon shine', architecture without control.

II. *The Chinese Architect*, in this period regarded as old-fashioned, and replaced by what Soane is pleased to call the 'Adametric', no doubt referring to the work of the brothers Adam.

III. *The Middle Ages Architect*. He is not the medieval architect, but one who has reached middle age. He admires the Invalides and the Carousel in Paris, but is blind to the values of the column of the Place Vendôme, which Soane feels should serve as a model for a monument to the legitimate monarch.

IV. *The Dilettanti Architect*. He is in essence a patron, who may recognize merit and show original invention. It is his task to further the renewal of architecture.

V. *The Classical Architect*. He deplores the degraded state of art, and is in fact, by implication, of Soane's own generation. The influence of France is seen here in the expressed desire to replace the plaster found outside houses by façades built in solid stone for 'grand hotels'.

This chapter suggests how closely Utopian and ideal visions are interlinked, while not becoming identical. They gave a spiritual dimension to a period in which the importance of function in a material sense was recognized. The conjunction of utilitarian and idealizing tendencies is typical of the period of Enlightenment, and thus contributes to its distinctive character.

1. K. Mannheim: *Ideology and Utopia*, numerous editions. M. L. Berneri: *Journey through Utopia*, London 1950. M. Buber: *Paths in Utopia*, London 1949.
2. J. Harrison: *Robert Owen and the Owenites in Britain*, London 1969.
3. Berneri, op. cit., p. 5. R. Zeitler, *Klassizismus und Utopia*, Stockholm 1954.
4. *The Ideal City*, pp. 142 ff.
5. This can be seen as an interpretation of Platonism as far as the arts are concerned. cf. Zeitler, op. cit. Also P. F. Fisher: *The Valley of Vision, Blake as Prophet and Revolutionary*, Toronto 1961.
6. M. Campbell in *Record of the Art Museum, Princeton University*, XVII, 1958, pp. 65 ff. R. Rosenblum: *Transformations in late 18th Century Art*, Princeton University Press, 1967. cf. also A. Dufour: *Letter to the . . . Committee for Raising the Naval Pillar*, etc., London 1800; a reply to Flaxman's *Letter*.
7. Campbell, op. cit., pp. 66 ff. I wish to thank Mr J. Physik for his advice on Flaxman drawings.
8. W. G. Constable: *John Flaxman, 1755–1826*, London 1927. Th. Balston: *John Martin, 1785–1854*, London 1947.
9. cf. E. Kaufmann: *Three Revolutionary Architects: Boullée, Ledoux and Léqueu*, Philadelphia 1952; also *Boullée*. Lately J.-M. Pérouse de Montclos: *Boullée*, Paris 1968. M. Vogt: *Boullée's Newton Denkmal, Sakralbau und Kugelidee*, Basle and Stuttgart 1969. Also K. Lankheit: *Der Tempel der Vernunft*, Basle and Stuttgart 1968.
10. A. Oncken: *Friedrich Gilly*, Berlin 1935. A. Rietdorf: *Gilly*, Berlin 1943.
11. Th. Ashby, ed.: *Topographical Study in Rome, in 1581*, London 1916. See also A. C. E. Setterwall: *Eric Palmstedt*, Stockholm 1945. On the classical tradition, cf. J. B. F. Lajard in *Mémoires de l'Institut de France, Académie des Inscriptions et Belles Lettres*, XX, 2, 1854.
12. J. and W. Grimm: *Deutsches Wörterbuch*, ed. M. Heyne. *Mal, signum*, Gothic *mêl*.
13. *Novvelles inventions povr bien bastir et a petits fraiz*, I, Paris 1561, pp. 32 ff. On the architect in general, Sir Anthony Blunt: *Philibert de l'Orme*, London 1958.
14. A. Warburg: *Gesammelte Schriften*, Leipzig–Berlin 1932, pp. 169 ff., and 366 f.
15. For a brief summary of the material, cf. Kaufmann, *passim. The Ideal City*, p. 85.
16. H. M. Fletcher in the *Journal of the R.I.B.A.* 42, 1935, pp. 774 ff. This is based on Landon's *Annales du Musée*, 2, An X, 1802, pp. 123 ff. and 3, An X, 1802, pp. 103 ff.
17. M. I. Webb: *Michael Rysbrack*, London 1934, pp. 82 ff.
18. J. Goldicutt: *The Competition for the Nelson Monument Critically Examined*, London 1841.
19. G. Taylor: *Old London Gardens*, London 1953, pp. 129 ff. D. Lysons: *The Environs of London* I, London 1792, pp. 159 ff., and II, 1795, pp. 166 ff.
20. *Prix*, pls. 64 and 65.
21. O. Siren: *China and the Gardens of Europe*, London 1950, pp. 15 ff. H. F. Clark: *Journal of the Warburg and Courtauld Institutes*, 1943, pp. 164 ff.
22. cf. J. M. Crook: *The Greek revival*, London 1968, p. 14, pl. 9.
23. J. Summerson: *Heavenly Mansions*, London 1949, pp. 111 ff.
24. Soane, op. cit., p. 8.
25. See Soane, op. cit., *passim*. The list of contents as opposed to the text and caption suggests the date 1778 for the Senate House.
26. Soane, op. cit., pp. 49 ff.

7
Concluding Notes on Form and Function

The relationship between form and function is a basic problem of æsthetic theory.[1] Max Dessoir, the German æsthetician, suggested as early as 1906 that the appeal of a work of art cannot be entirely explained by æsthetic considerations.[2] For this reason he advocated *Kunstwissenschaft*, applying the term to a functional theory of the arts. If this approach is true in general, it is even more relevant to architecture, in which the purpose of a building is of predominant importance.

Despite Leith's narrow interpretation of function in the 18th century as allied to and based on propaganda, a widening of the meaning of the term is now required. This has to take into account the complexity and variety of the subject matter involved, and the psychological associations connected with it. Such an attitude, basic to the understanding of late 18th century architecture, has an increasing appeal today, when the younger generation are particularly aware of social priorities, and interested in their implementation. However, contemporary analytic æsthetics offers little guidance in understanding the past, for it deals mainly with subjective reactions and categorizations, while being on the whole strangely silent about architecture.[3]

By contrast, the 18th century was deeply concerned with architecture. This concern inspired Burke's ideas on the sublime; even more revealing are the appropriate comments in Kant's *Critique of Judgement*, first published in German in 1790. His statement that 'The beautiful is the symbol of the morally good' (par. 59) epitomizes the prevalent thought of the period. The differentiation made by Kant between 'free' or 'vagrant' and 'adherent' or 'attached' beauty, stresses the purposeful element in much of architectural appreciation. (Par. 16 of the *Critique of Judgement*: *Pulchritudo vaga* as against *pulchritudo adhaerens*.) It is significant that Kant introduced Latin words here to clarify his meaning, the German language at the time still lacking the precision required.

The Utopian and idealizing tendencies of late 18th century art and architecture formed a parallel to and were an inspiration for the philosophy briefly discussed here. Furthermore, the associations they evoked were of a symbolic nature, correlated with those found in religious art. In both cases they tended towards the sublime rather than the beautiful, transcending any clearly definable utilitarian purpose.[4] The quest for perfection characterized the late 18th century, when a high level of execution coupled with the avoidance of trivial subject matter in art was demanded. Function and form were seen as coexistent in artistic unity, and the social value of function was thus believed to lead to distinction of form.

Architects during this period were conscious of the basic elements in structure: the circle, the globe, the square and the cube. The triangle, and especially the pyramid, are also in evidence. In the past, these geometrical shapes were seen as possessing a symbolic meaning, based on their inherent simplicity and completeness. Even when this original meaning was largely forgotten, notions of the ancient significance lingered on and enhanced their underlying universal appeal.[5]

The architect's imagination was also fertilized by a study of environment, which was then changed to express pure form. This is seen in the pyramidal

Boullée, project for a National Library, after 1789. Cabinet des Estampes, Bibliothèque Nationale, Paris.

Ledoux, ordnance factory; from L'Architecture.

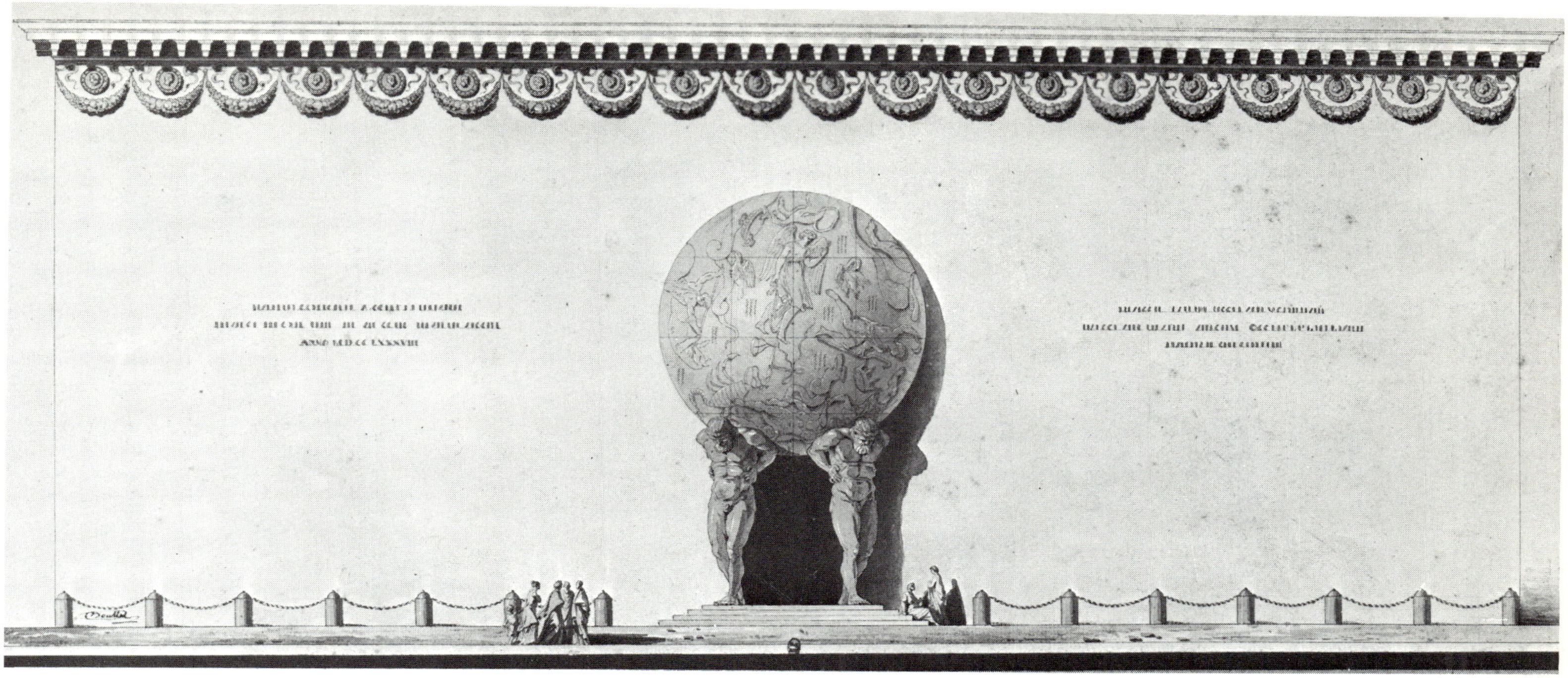

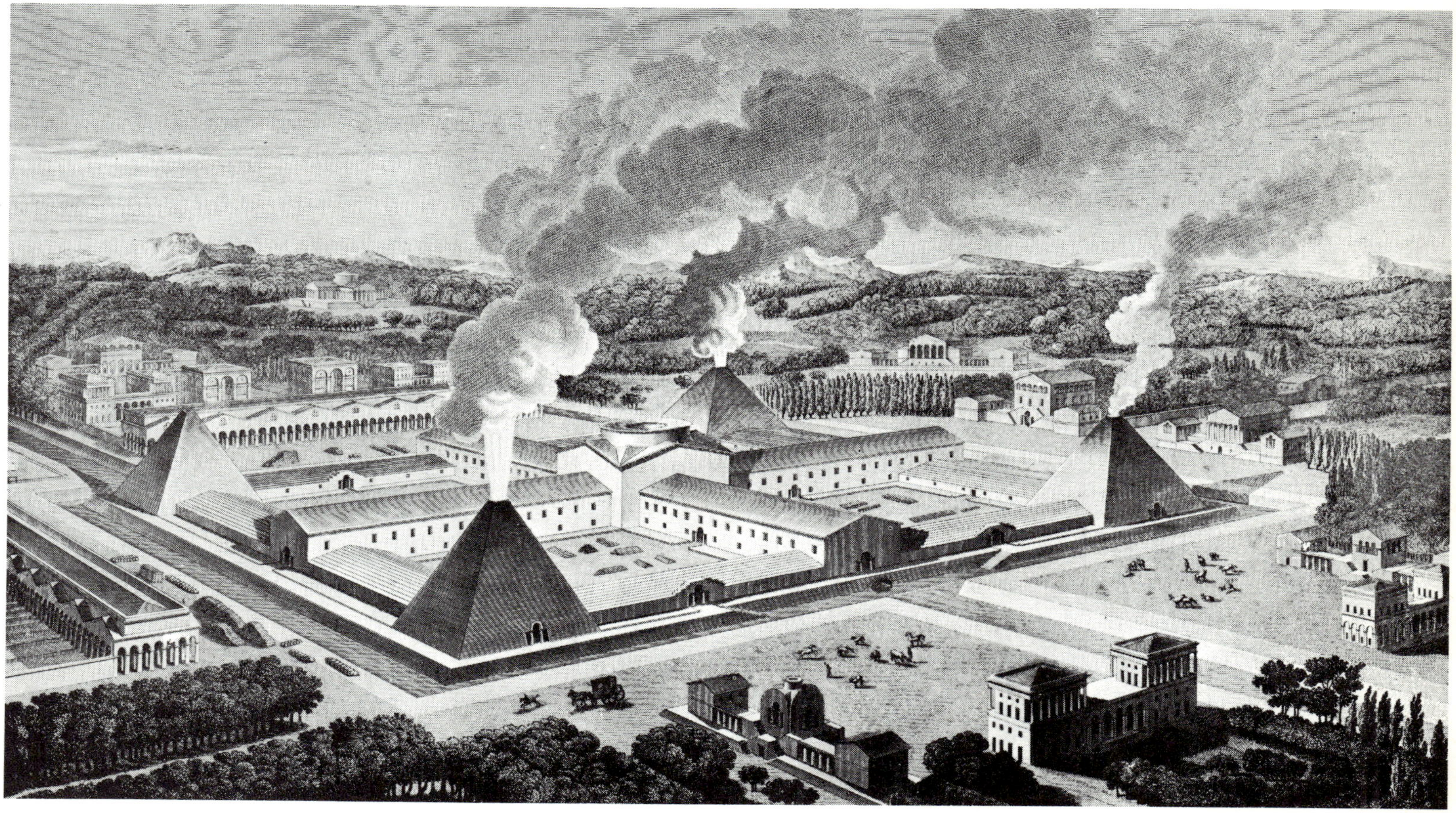

Boullée, Cenotaph. Cabinet des Estampes Bibliothèque Nationale, Paris.

shape of Ledoux's ordnance factory, which may be compared with the cones of the tile kilns of London and other places. Such simple outlines stimulated artistic fantasy, and it is worth examining one of Boullées cenotaphs from this angle. Its interior is based on the Pantheon, the exterior on Babylonian reminiscences. Nevertheless, it is worth remembering that cones were used in industrial chimneys, and that the source of architectural inspiration may be rather more complex than hitherto suggested. Altogether incongruous is the popular motif of the pyramid in works such as Middleton's design for a church, showing how the form had become acclimatized, as it were, to alien surroundings.[6]

It is remarkable that engineers and architects of our own time, such as Nervi and Doxiadis, are still imbued with the Mediterranean tradition, and base their designs on simple geometric forms. Nervi applied these ideas to individual structures. Some of Doxiadis' dynamically expanding town designs show an open pattern, in the shape of a parabola, within which circles and squares are inscribed; thus the enclosed simple forms appear as a contrast within the overall arrangement. Once Doxiadis' parabola obtains a large size, however, it inflates the scale of the subunits, which become unwieldy.

C. T. Middleton, Chapel; *from* The Architect and Builder's Miscellany.

Left, above
The Tyle Kilns, Bagnigge Wells, between 1775 and 1828. Archives of the Greater London Council.

Presumably at this point new sets are required, leading eventually to groupings of parabolas. Nervi's æsthetics remain rather vague, the beautiful inevitably following function, a concept also found in J. M. Richards' appreciation of industrial architecture.[7]

In contrast to Doxiadis' expanding designs, the previously mentioned schemes for a village by J. M. Gandy, dated 1805, consist of eight clusters of concentric cottages, each cluster repeated to form a circle of eight. This arrangement is also found in an alternative drawing, showing only one of the clusters of eight cottages. Indeed, the enclosed shapes of the neo-classical period and the open forms of Doxiadis represent not only opposing attitudes, but demonstrate also the common fascination of geometric patterns.

In the late 18th century, the significance of large scale was recognized in architectural theory and practice. This led to monumentality, which was not only demanded by vast architectural programmes, but also fostered by æsthetic considerations inherent in the concept of the sublime. Thus the collective element in planning had direct repercussions on formal values. The age was opposed to Romanticism, defined as an attitude based on powerful and subjective feeling. Its emphasis was on a collective and social consciousness, a concern with mankind rather than the individual. In this quest classicism provided powerful models, which were not copied but freely adapted to new functions and objectives.[8]

These factors may account for some of the reasons which have led to a growing interest in neo-classicism at the present time. Indeed, in recent years this style, with its sparse and austere forms, as seen in Gropius' and Mies van der Rohe's work, has been revived in European art. However, the artistic hollowness of much of Fascist and Nazi art and architecture, for example, demonstrates that the revival of neo-classical models, without insight into humane values, produces a travesty of the style, rather than a creative adaptation.[9]

The current rediscovery of neo-classicism is not an isolated or uncommon event. Renaissance or revival are historical concepts,[10] particularly applicable to European evolution. In other societies continuity seems more characteristic than change, possibly because the economic base underwent fewer transformations. By contrast, in Europe economic change was pronounced, and concurrently ideologies changed, although these had their own momentum. The transition from conventional religiosity to theism for example had spiritual roots, and so has the emphasis placed on religious values by some contemporary thinkers.[11]

It is not only the process of revival which seems characteristic of Europe. Even more remarkable is the way in which older forms persisted, and how the break between different periods was not altogether complete. One can think of the medieval world surviving during the Renaissance, and in the arts one can speak of a neo-Gothic, almost as much as of a neo-classical style. Even political revolutions have their traditions in Europe, and the unity of European culture persists through many vicissitudes. It is because of this that revivals are possible. Had there been complete discontinuity, they would naturally have been impossible.

European revivals took two different forms. In some cases individual works were rediscovered, as was the case of the Laocoön in the Renaissance. However, even these individual discoveries raise larger issues, when, as is usual, a style is revived in its entirety. This does not occur only for formal reasons, but because the forms promote associative responses. It is perhaps most clearly seen in A. W. N. Pugin's *Contrasts*, where Gothic is based on and stimulates a religious mood. On the other hand, France, from the Renaissance onwards, fostered classical revivals, and neo-classicism there forms a link in an historical chain. Descartes' interest in architecture and planning, found in his *Meditationes*, especially in his seventh set of objections, is characteristic.

It is in this context that architects as well as artists find their place. They seem to belong to three main categories. The greatest minds were eager to use older models to enrich their individual inspiration, while they were simultaneously transforming and transcending them. Outstanding examples of this type of historical adaptation can be seen in the designs for Boullée's Cenotaph for Newton or in Sir John Soane's Houses of Parliament. By comparison, the lesser practitioners were more consolidators than originators, and for this reason they are the propagators of styles. When they use antique models they adapt to them to a greater extent, archaeology thus sometimes taking the place of vision or transformation. Their positive contribution should not be underrated, however, as they represent high qualitative standards. The classical and Gothic revivals as prevalent styles were created by them.

The third group, those who copy rather than invent, have value from an historical or sociological rather than an æsthetic point of view. In periods of classicism they follow the prescribed patterns; when abstract tendencies predominate, they will favour abstraction. Their field is mainly that of the applied arts.

The richness of the late 18th century tradition from an artistic point of

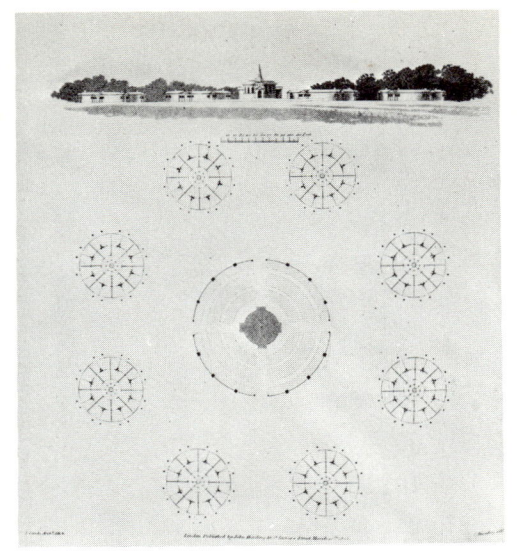

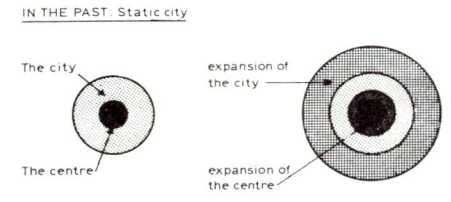

IN THE PAST: Static city

The city

The centre

expansion of the city

expansion of the centre

The concentric expansion strangles the centre which struggles with other functions

IN THE FUTURE: Dynapolis

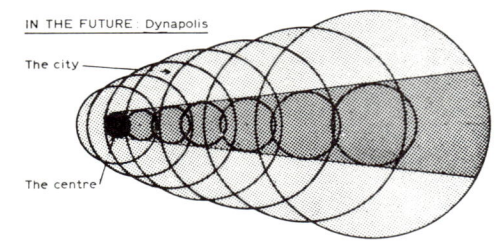

The city

The centre

J. M. Gandy, cluster of Cottage units; from Designs for Cottages.

Doxiadis, Dynapolis; from Architecture in Transition. *By kind permission of the Hutchinson Publishing Group Ltd.*

view is based on these three aspects in conjunction, ranging from the craftsman's skill to the inspired revelations of the creative work. No break existed between these two aspects of art, because a middle group acted as interpreters and links, thus bridging the qualitative gap. Architecture expressed social values which were not imposed but freely accepted.[12]

The doctrine of benevolence and compassion so characteristic of the period must inevitably have led to a positive influence on architecture. Robert Adam had commented on the sterility of private patronage, and some concern was voiced by Sobry, who advocated the rights of families of a socially inferior status. The doctrine is seen in the programme for the *Prix* designs and in the setting of the statue for John Howard, planned by George Dance. It is particularly apparent in the collaboration between architects and doctors in hospital building. The liberating effect of secular thought was felt, side by side with an almost religious belief in humane values, making for a balanced view of life.

See illustration on page 44

Economic and political issues differed from those of our own period. However, like today, their impact was strong and often brutal and certain of the problems of distribution of power and wealth have remained with us. The greatest contrast is found perhaps in the prevalent pessimism and disillusionment, when seen against the background of the belief in human unity and perfectibility, so characteristic of the Enlightenment. In the recent past there has been a tendency towards specialization and separation, but tentative efforts are now being made to recapture some of the lost beliefs. It is in this context that the study of the late 18th century could be particularly significant with regard to formal discipline and social involvement.

1. cf. V. J. Scully Jr. in *Reflections on Art*, ed. S. Langer, New York, Oxford, 1961, pp. 342 ff., on meaning in architecture.
2. M. Dessoir: *Aesthetik und Allgemeine Kunstwissenschaft*, Stuttgart 1906.
3. An excellent survey of contemporary problems is found in *Aesthetics in the Modern Work*, ed. H. Osborne, London 1968. See Chap. I, note 7.
4. B. Bosanquet: *Three Lectures on Aesthetics*, London 1915. On the Critique of Aesthetic Judgement, cf. R. K. Elliott in *The British Journal of Aesthetics*, VIII, 3, 1968, pp. 244 ff.
5. S. Heckscher in *Jahrbuch der Hamburger Kunstsammlungen*, VII, 1962, pp. 35 ff. This deals with Goethe's garden monument in the form of a globe, surmounting a cube, and its antecedents.
6. Ch. Middleton: *The Architect and Builder's Miscellany or Pocket Library*, London 1799. An interesting example of cone-shaped chimneys was also found in the famous works of Le Creusot.
7. U. Kultermann: *New Architecture in the World*, London 1966. P. L. Nervi: *Aesthetics and Technology in Building*, Cambridge, Mass. 1966. J. M. Richards: *The Functional Tradition in English Industrial Buildings*, London 1958. C. Doxiadis: *Architecture in Transition*, London 1963.
8. S. Giedion: *Spätbarocker und Romantischer Klassizismus*, Munich 1922. Crook, op. cit., p. 5.
9. On the special problems of Nazi architecture and neo-classicism see J. B. Weber in *Architectural Association Quarterly*, I, 2, 1969, p. 49 and passim.
10. E. Panofsky: *Renaissance and Renascences in Western Art*, Stockholm 1960.
11. cf. P. Teilhard de Chardin: *L'Avenir de l'homme*, Paris 1962.
12. On 'axiology' cf. M. Juzl in *Zeitschrift für Kunstgeschichte und Allgemeine Kunstwissenschaft*, XIV 2, 1969, pp. 188 ff.

Select Bibliography

(To prevent this bibliography from growing too unwieldy, readers are referred to the notes at the ends of chapters, in which numerous other works are cited.)

ACKERMANN, R.   *The Microcosm of London*, London 1808, etc.

BAUCHAL, Ch.   *Nouveau Dictionnaire biographique et critique des architectes français*, Paris 1887 (still useful).

BRAILSFORD, H. N.   *The Levellers and the English Revolution*, ed. Ch. Hill, London 1961.

FOCILLON, H.   *G. B. Piranesi*, Paris 1918.

HARRISON, W.   *A New and Universal History, Description and Survey of the Cities of London and Westminster*, London 1775, also 1776 and 1777.

KAUFMANN, E.   *Architecture in the Age of Reason*, Harvard University Press, 1955.

KENT, W.   *An Encyclopædia of London*, numerous editions.

KLOPFER, P.   *Von Palladio bis Schinkel. Eine Charakteristik der Baukunst des Klassizismus*, Eszlingen 1911.

LEFEBURE, G.   *Etudes sur la Révolution Française*, Paris 1963, 2nd ed.

LEMONNIER, M.   *Procès-Verbaux de l'Académie Royale d'Architecture*, Paris, 1911–29.

MUMFORD, L.   *The City in History*, London 1961.

ONCKEN, A.   *Friedrich Gilly*, Berlin 1935.

PEVSNER, N.   *The Buildings of England, London*, I; 2nd ed. 1962, Penguin Books.

POETE, M.   *Paris, Son évolution créatrice*, Paris 1938.

TALMON, J. L.   *The Origins of Totalitarian Democracy*, London 1952.

THIEME, U., and BECKER, F.   *Allgemeines Lexikon der Bildenden Künstler*, Leipzig 1907, etc.

WATKIN, D.   *Thomas Hope and the Neo-Classical Idea*, London 1968.

ZEITLER, R.   *Klassizismus und Utopia*, etc., Stockholm 1954.

INDEX

Page numbers in *italic* indicate illustrations

279